*Images of Fear*

### 1997

1. Michael R. Pitts. *Western Movies*
2. William C. Cline. *In the Nick of Time*
3. Bill Warren. *Keep Watching the Skies!*
4. Mark McGee. *Roger Corman*
5. R. M. Hayes. *Trick Cinematography*
6. David J. Hogan. *Dark Romance*
7. Spencer Selby. *Dark City: The Film Noir*
8. David K. Frasier. *Russ Meyer—The Life and Films*
9. Ted Holland. *B Western Actors Encyclopedia*
10. Franklin Jarlett. *Robert Ryan*

### 1998

11. Ted Okuda *with* Edward Watz. *The Columbia Comedy Shorts*
12. R. M. Hayes. *3-D Movies*
13. Steve Archer. *Willis O'Brien: Special Effects Genius*
14. Richard West. *Television Westerns*

### 1999

15. Jon Tuska. *The Vanishing Legion: A History of Mascot Pictures*
16. Ted Okuda. *The Monogram Checklist*
17. Roy Kinnard. *Horror in Silent Films*
18. Richard D. McGhee. *John Wayne: Actor, Artist, Hero*
19. William Darby *and* Jack Du Bois. *American Film Music*
20. Martin Tropp. *Images of Fear*
21. Tom Weaver. *Return of the B Science Fiction and Horror Heroes*
22. Tom Weaver. *Poverty Row HORRORS!*
23. Ona L. Hill. *Raymond Burr*

# Images of Fear

*How Horror Stories
Helped Shape Modern Culture
(1818–1918)*

*by* Martin Tropp

McFarland & Company, Inc., Publishers
*Jefferson, North Carolina, and London*

*The present work is a reprint of the library bound edition of* Images of Fear: How Horror Stories Helped Shape Modern Culture (1818–1918), *first published in 1990. McFarland Classics is an imprint of McFarland & Company, Inc., Publishers, Jefferson, North Carolina, who also published the original edition.*

Library of Congress Cataloguing-in-Publication Data

Tropp, Martin.
　　Images of fear : how horror stories helped shape modern culture, 1818–1918 / by Martin Tropp.
　　p.　cm.
　　Includes bibliographical references and index.
　　ISBN 0-7864-0754-9 (paperback : 50# alkaline paper) ∞
　　1. Horror tales, English—History and criticism.　2. English fiction—19th century—History and criticism.　3. English fiction—20th century—History and criticism.　4. Gothic revival (Literature)—Great Britain.　5. Civilization, Modern—19th century. 6. Civilization, Modern—20th century.　7. Fear in literature. 8. Fear.　I. Title.
　　PR830.T3T76　1999　　　823'.0873809—dc20　　　　89-43633 CIP

British Library Cataloguing-in-Publication data are available

©1990 Martin Tropp. All rights reserved

**Cover image:** ©1999 Photodisc

"Bombardment," by Richard Aldington (page xiv), is ©Catherine Guillaume and is used by permission.

*No part of this book may be reproduced or transmitted in any form or by any means, electronic or mechanical, including photocopying or recording, or by any information storage and retrieval system, without permission in writing from the publisher.*

Manufactured in the United States of America

*McFarland & Company, Inc., Publishers*
*Box 611, Jefferson, North Carolina 28640*
*www.mcfarlandpub.com*

Again, to my family,
and especially
my daughter Rachel

# Contents

*Preface* ix
*Acknowledgments* xiii

Introduction: The Argument of This Book 1

### Part One: The Art of Fear (1818–1830)

1 Hooked on Horror: Reading and the Gothic Revival 12
2 Monsters and Machines 28

### Part Two: Reading the Landscape (1851–60)

3 The City Imagined 44
4 Beneath the Crystal Palace 67

### Part Three: Myths and Mysteries (1886–97)

5 The Proximity of the Past 90
6 Dr. Jekyll & Jack the Ripper: The Power of the Will 110
7 *Dracula* and the Liberation of Women (I) 133
8 *Dracula* and the Liberation of Women (II) 157

### Part Four: Shaping the Darkness (1900–18)

9 The Fantasy of Reality 172
10 The Transformation of the Dead 195

*Bibliography* 221
*Index* 231

# Preface

> What happens to the idea of a democratic culture . . . if the increasingly powerful and self assured literary academy, barely challenged by critics outside its walls, remains aloof from the larger culture, remains content to live and work within its own space?
> — Irving Howe

Writing this book was a risky venture when I began, some five years ago, and it remains risky as the book finally sees the light of publication. This is not because I write about horror stories, although the subject has at times resulted in two extremes of unreliability: abstruse academic excursions into textual and psychological analysis or popular pastiches of inaccurate commentary on fiction and films. The difficulty stems from the dimensions of this study, which determined the nature of my research, and the intended audience, which I kept in mind throughout the long process of writing and revision.

In 1976, I published *Mary Shelley's Monster: The Story of Frankenstein*, which attempted to reach the "common reader" with an exploration of the reasons for the popularity of a modern myth, traced from the 1818 novel through the twentieth century films. Though the topics ranged from galvanism to Freudianism, and I discussed creators of the myth from Mary Shelley to Mel Brooks, the single story itself limited the scope somewhat. In this book, I examine how a series of images of "horror" in fiction interacted with an emerging modern culture over a century, shaping attitudes towards such aspects of life as new technology, urban crime, and gender relationships — culminating in the recasting of life and death on the Western Front of World War I in the mold of the horror story.

Thus, the scope is enormous. At the same time as I wish to tread selectively on this vast terrain, I hope to avoid limiting my audience to those already familiar with the latest critical theory or the complexities of Victorian culture. In short, I tried (in advance) to heed the admonition Irving Howe gave in the June 12, 1989, issue of the *New Republic*: "Critics might learn once more to speak to the common reader, as if he still matters, as if she will soon respond; and to speak in English, a language that for some time served criticism well" (31).

I assume my reader, like myself, wants to see how popular literature and mass culture intersected, and how the conjunction helped determine (and still accounts for) the popularity of the literature and the way we see the world around us. One way to do that is to seek "universals" in fiction: the shape of the narrative, psychological patterns, linguistic tensions. Though a bit of all that works its way into my book, I have chosen to focus on how these texts emerged from and reshaped their time. There are, certainly, other reasons for their power and other critical works that examine those reasons. The bibliography and references direct readers towards those studies. In the text, I trace a process that took a hundred years and encompassed bits and pieces of many aspects of literary analysis and cultural history—namely, the movement of the images of fear from distant fantasies to contemporary realities.

In the course of my research, I have examined many works which explore in greater depth information essential to my overall theme or which look at the same information from different perspectives. For example, after finishing a draft of the manuscript, I examined *"Dr. Jekyll and Mr. Hyde" After One Hundred Years*, a collection of criticism published in 1988. Many of these essays take some issues I mention—from the book as detective fiction to the influence of *Frankenstein*—much further than I do. But the purpose there is to elucidate the novel itself, primarily for an audience of academics. I have a different purpose and another audience.

Similarly, two other recent books, *Fasting Girls* by Joan Brumberg and *Idols of Perversity* by Bram Dijkstra, examine an image found in *Dracula* that I look at—the Victorian ideal of beauty as a pallid woman wasting away, what Dijkstra calls the "consumptive sublime." Much of the information in those two books (and a third recent study, *Myths of Sexuality* by Lynda Nead) overlaps. But the context differs; Brumberg is interested in the history of anorexia nervosa, Dijkstra in the iconography of the image in Victorian art at the turn of the century, while Nead sees types of women (such as the prostitute) linked to concepts such as disease. All of them deal with the fact, as Nead says, that "the respectable woman was represented in terms of physical frailty" (30). But each author chose a different way to connect that fact to a larger structure of meaning. For my purposes, the iconography of the woman at her most beautiful when she is between life and death elucidates *Dracula*, which takes that cultural stereotype to a horror story conclusion, destroys it, and replaces it with another. The other contexts and content, though valid and fascinating to read, are not within the scope of my study.

Thus, this book is original in the way it examines the intersection of literature and culture, using a narrative structure that attributes the continuing wide appeal of certain horror stories to the less well known facts of a century of cultural history. Placing these modern myths into a pattern of development that links literature and life, fantasy and fact, imagination and experience, helps us better understand how one side of the equation illuminates the other. The intent here is to account for the power of popular fiction in its historical context, as well as to show that such an account can reach a popular audience.

Although books have been written about astronomy, history, biology, psychology, and other academic subjects for a wider group than specialists in these fields, somehow studies of literature have meant (at least recently) academic literary criticism, a genre that excludes a vast number of literate readers. Not only are such books written by and for professors, lately they tend to narrow themselves even further. Fiction is at times examined apart from the culture that spawned it and the readers that made it popular; it often is discussed in opaque jargon or seen through the clouded lens of the latest theory, sometimes reflecting the cleverness of the critic rather than illuminating the meaning of the literature ostensibly under discussion.

There may be a place for examining *Frankenstein* in such a way that the reverse alphabetical order of the names of the Monster's victims has significance (as one critic argues). But there is also a place for examining why the Monster, as an image of man as machine, machine as man, has helped shape our response to the dangers of technology for over 150 years. Both approaches, like the audiences for both, can coexist—can sometimes even overlap. What is still needed, and what I have kept in mind as I have enjoyed researching and writing this book, is to speak to the common reader in our common language. I hope to convey in the following pages not only the results of my research, but also my respect for the perspicacity of the popular audience that gave stories like *Frankenstein, Dracula* or *Dr. Jekyll and Mr. Hyde* enduring life.

# Acknowledgments

I would like to acknowledge the help of both people and institutions. First of all, I deeply appreciate the aid of the Babson Board of Research and its chairman Professor Edward Handler who made researching this book possible, and my wife Sandy, who helped immeasurably during its composition, editing everything (including this sentence) with care, encouragement, and good humor. I am also grateful to all those responsible for making the following libraries available to provide me not only with resource material, but also with many pleasant hours of research:

In the United States: Harvard University Libraries, Boston University Library, Wellesley College Library, Babson College Library, Newton City Library, Boston Public Library

In the United Kingdom: Library of the British Museum, British Museum Newspaper Library, London Library, University of London Library, Victoria and Albert Museum, Imperial War Museum, Camden Libraries, Library of the Science Museum

## THE PAINS OF SLEEP

...But yester-night I prayed aloud
In anguish and in agony,
Up-starting from the fiendish crowd
Of shapes and thoughts that tortured me:
A lurid light, a trampling throng,
Sense of intolerable wrong,
And whom I scorned, those only strong!
Thirst of revenge, the powerless will
Still baffled and yet burning still!
Desire with loathing strangely mixed
On wild and hateful objects fixed.
Fantastic passions! maddening brawl!
And shame and terror over all!
Deeds to be hid which were not hid,
Which all confused I could not know
Whether I suffered, or I did:
For all seemed guilt, remorse or woe,
My own or others' still the same
Life stifling fear, soul-stifling shame...

*Samuel T. Coleridge (1803)*


## BOMBARDMENT

Four days the earth was rent and torn
By bursting steel,
The houses fell about us;
Three nights we dared not sleep,
Sweating, and listening for the imminent crash
Which meant our death.

The fourth night every man,
Nerve-tortured, racked to exhaustion,
Slept, muttering and twitching,
While the shells crashed overhead.

The fifth day there came a hush;
We left our holes
And looked above the wreckage of the earth
To where the white clouds moved in silent lines
Across the untroubled blue.

*Richard Aldington (1919)*

# Introduction: The Argument of This Book

> Scientific and poetic or imaginative accounts of the world are not distinguishable in their origins. They start in parallel, but diverge from one another at some stage. We all tell stories, but the stories differ in the purposes we expect them to fulfill and the kinds of evaluations to which they are exposed.
> —Peter Medawar

> Popular fiction responds to the shared dreams and hidden fears of its audience.
> —Leslie Fiedler

This is a book about the relationship of popular literature to life. Specifically, it examines how images of fear in some famous works of Victorian fiction helped give form and meaning to the frightening events that have come to mark modern culture. Literary criticism usually can't find an audience outside the ranks of college professors and other specialists. But this isn't a book of literary criticism. And, despite the fact that much of it is about horror stories, it isn't only for lovers of vampire movies, though both academics and aficionados of the tale of terror are welcome. Instead, the following pages focus on how and why a few very special stories have helped determine the way we see the world around us.

After their first appearance in nineteenth century England, three quickly became classic tales of terror, the modern equivalent of myths: Mary Shelley's *Frankenstein*, Robert Louis Stevenson's *Dr. Jekyll and Mr. Hyde*, and Bram Stoker's *Dracula*. The other two—Jane Austen's *Northanger Abbey* and Charles Dickens' *Bleak House*—haven't the same myth creating power (though they are still widely read), yet help show the subtle ways two great novelists imprinted the dark design of horror on the fabric of reality.

All five became part of the popular consciousness between 1818 and 1918, a century that brought Western society from the first decades of the

Industrial Revolution to the cataclysmic disaster of the First World War. Along the way, accepted gender and class relationships, belief in progress and perfectibility, and faith in the unchanging nature of Nature itself were replaced by widespread insecurity, disillusionment, and fear of the future—the hallmarks of the twentieth century. Horror fiction and real terror coincided, and the same audience read and reacted to both.

In order to understand why horror stories continue to have such a hold over our imagination and perceptions, we also will be exploring diverse aspects of culture—architecture from medieval castles to glass palaces, evidence of man's barbarity from Jack the Ripper to the Battle of the Somme, scientific theories from Charles Darwin's to Havelock Ellis', popular movements from the first modern stirrings of women's liberation to the last gasps of nostalgia for the vanished order of the Middle Ages. Throughout, the focus will be on their fictive quality—the ways they came to be seen by an audience steeped in popular literature.

As the biologist Peter Medawar has pointed out, we cannot make sense of the world around us without some structure which gives it meaning—there is no such thing as pure observation. To understand new phenomena, we must place them within an imaginative pattern that later can be modified or discarded if it does not conform to further observation. For instance, in the nineteenth century, the scientific study of our geological and biological past was marked by the painful process of abandoning the Bible as a conceptual framework when it could no longer account for the great age of the earth and the gradual evolution of life. It was replaced with a model that gave the impetus for change, not to cataclysmic, purposeful acts by an all powerful creator, but to the countless minuscule effects of unseen forces over vast stretches of time—the erosion of wind and water, the adaptions wrought by natural selection, even the landscaping power of earthworms. That new model influenced more than geology, biology, or religion; it became the pattern into which change was fit, a new way of seeing how change affects our lives.

The other transformations of that time were just as destructive of the patterns of belief that had served for centuries. They also needed to be fit into models that made sense of both the events themselves and the feelings they engendered in all those who had to live with them. And, as we shall see, the pattern that continued to be imposed on those frightening realities often came from the tale of terror, slowly transformed from an imaginative fantasy to a way of encountering the world.

The term "horror" itself denotes both fantasy and reality. In fiction, it designates one kind of vicarious experience, existing in another realm, dealing with supernatural events and unbelievable characters, that readers approach with the expectation of an escape from the realities of daily experience. At the same time, the darkest of inescapable truths—natural disasters, human suffering, and organized depravity—bear the same label. Imagination and experience, fiction and fact, are linked by language. The horrors of pulp literature and the horrors of war, the most frivolous and the most cataclysmic of human creations, are each signified by the same word.

This curious connection was brought out at the turn of the nineteenth century by Jane Austen in *Northanger Abbey* when her heroine, Catherine Morland, a devotee of Gothic novels, announces that "something very shocking indeed will soon come out of London.... I have only heard it is more horrible than anything we have met with yet" (90). Her listeners don't realize she is speaking of the manufactured terrors of the latest Gothic tale, and imagine instead that she is predicting a replay of the French Revolution, with "a mob of three thousand men assembling in St. George's Fields, the Bank attacked, the Tower threatened, the streets of London flowing with blood" (91). (Of course, Jane Austen's readers are also privy to this conversation and well aware of the third meaning in her words; if the novel Catherine Morland awaits is anything like the bulk of popular Gothic fiction, it will indeed be terrible, awful, horrible—which then, as now, were synonyms for what's simply bad writing.)

Though the confusion of meaning within Austen's novel is part of the comedy, it also suggests the way we'll be looking at horror stories themselves. Catherine Morland's audience heard another meaning in her words because, at the time, many feared the recent Reign of Terror in France would be repeated on British soil; a series of riots in 1780 had caused ten times the property damage to London as was done to Paris during the French Revolution (Briggs 178). Catherine Morland alluded to the synthetic horrors of the hackneyed plots of popular fiction; her listeners heard in those words a real disaster that imagination had already shaped in the popular consciousness. She hoped for a few hours' quiet diversion; her audience pictured the possibility of the wholesale destruction of a way of life, the end of England as it had been known for centuries.

Jane Austen plays upon the difficulties of communication, the distinction between what "I mean" and what "the word means" that has become a cornerstone of much recent thinking about language and literature; she also confronts directly what was, from the start of the Gothic movement, one source of its power over its readers. The "horror" in Gothic fiction continued to contain this contradiction. While ostensibly the means to an innocent escape, it aroused in its Victorian audience fears that lurked beneath the surface, fears connected with the ongoing upheaval of a culture discarding a way of life that had been unchanged for centuries and, amid the social, industrial, and scientific revolutions of the nineteenth century, making a modern world. Conversely, those who wrote about the real horrors of the period often used the language, imagery, and structure of the supernatural tale of terror, evoking in their audience reactions conditioned by popular fiction. Thus, the ambiguous meaning of horror that Jane Austen used for comic effect is at the very center of its power.

Nor is that the only ambiguity. Whether fantastic or factual, horror stories attract their audience by frightening it, two seemingly contradictory impulses. Tobias Smollett, whose novel *Ferdinand Count Fathom* (1753), was one of the earliest Gothic tales, defined fear as "the most violent and interesting of all the passions." In reading horror fiction, we still seek to make a violent emotion interesting and safely remote, within the refuge of a book which we can close at any time. We also find refuge in the unreality of the imagery and the predictability of the plots, the very unlikeliness which, when we are having a nightmare, we can never recognize. The superiority of the readers of *Northanger Abbey*, who laugh at the characters' misunderstanding of the horror Catherine describes, is the attitude of readers of all horror fiction. While vicariously participating in the confusion and fears of others, the audience is always aware that the "horrible" events the characters encounter (often conveyed in horrible writing) are also unlikely.

As one reader among many, rather than as an individual suffering a nightmare, we can be reassured by the unseen audience of other readers. It is fear without isolation, with an instant escape, with familiar objects around us, with our rational faculties intact. As a collective experience (made immediate in our century when film enabled us literally to be alone together in the darkness) the popularity of the horror story transformed private nightmares into communal events.

In the process, it gave shape to fear; as E. H. Gombrich points out, Freud believed that "only those unconscious ideas that can be adjusted to the reality of formal structures become communicable." Freud, Gombrich argues, "insisted on that degree of adjustment to reality that alone turns a dream into a work of art" (36). Thus, horror stories are not nightmares transcribed, but fears recast into safe and communicable forms—a concrete, related, yet separate reality. In the act of fixing the shifting and subjective terrors of the subconscious into words on paper, the writer of the tale of terror created something quite different from the dream that was often its inspiration; he moved, in other words, from the privacy of the self to the shared conventions of communication, using language to wed nightmare to culture.

In reading of the actual horrors of our world or watching films that document the darkest corners of reality, our motives and responses may be quite different from when we encounter the fantasy of the horror story, though the curiously contradictory power that draws and repels us is similar. Thus, though we hope to be surprised and terrified by the invented horrors of popular fiction and film, and though we may be profoundly shocked by the actual horrors of history, we want to be reassured by them as well. For both, our place as audience insulates us; they complete their meaning after they are completed, when we are free to close the book or leave the theater and retreat into safety.

Horror stories, when they work, construct a fictional edifice of fear and deconstruct it simultaneously, dissipating terror in the act of creating it. And real horrors are filtered through the expectations of readers trained in responding to popular fiction, familiar with a set of images, a language, and pattern of development. Horror fiction gives the reader the tools to "read" experiences that would otherwise, like nightmares, be incommunicable. In that way, the inexpressible and private becomes understandable and communal, shared and safe.

This book looks at the interplay between the two meanings of horror in the century leading up to the First World War—how a vast new readership, trained through reading horror fiction, learned to read the horrors of the world around it in similar ways. Thus, you are about to follow, not a history of Gothic fiction, but an exploration of the way, over time, meaning and understanding changed as the world changed. Those works of horror fiction which have lasted (a minute fraction of a huge output) continue to speak to their audience because they echo fears that have remained with us. The novels themselves remain perennially popular. In addition, the stories and characters in those novels still are evolving, re-emerging in other books, plays, films, and popular culture—keeping pace with the continuing needs and evolving uncertainties in the audience that has kept them alive.

Their power comes from more than the tapping of the ancient and private sources of nightmare; they use those materials to connect individual lives with the group experience of culture. In the century we are considering, horror in fiction moved from a safe remoteness to a frightening immediacy, from subjective to objective reality. It bridged the gap between the two poems quoted at the start of this book—"The Pains of Sleep" (1803), Samuel T. Coleridge's confession of the tormenting emotions behind his own nightmare, and "Bombardment" (1919), Richard Aldington's account of the communal horror of his comrades trapped in the nightmare of war. In both, sleep evokes terror, though the intervening century has transformed the source of fear from the "maddening brawl" of secret passions to the "bursting steel" of artillery, from the private creations of an individual imagination to the common threat of a hostile reality, turning metaphors for the unconscious into narratives of experience. ·

Just as the stories we will look at are familiar, the events are familiar as well—chronicles of Victorian poverty and crime, the Great Exhibition at mid century, the horrors of the First World War. At those moments, when the fears given form through fiction came up against the real horrors of day to day experience, imaginative fiction helped shape the response. For Coleridge, the nightmare reveals "deeds to be hid which were not hid"; similarly, the horror story transforms the elements of nightmare to explore the dark side of society and hint at its collective secrets. Finally, by the end of the First World War, history itself had become a tale of terror, a nightmare from which we in the Twentieth Century are all still trying to awaken. World War I made clear that the pattern of fear in the popular fiction of the previous century had not been an escape from the outside world, but a way of seeing deeper into it, as well as revealing the shape of things to come.

This book, then, speaks to anyone who wishes to know why certain stories have continued simultaneously to attract and repel us for over a hundred years, how the metaphor of horror slowly evolved from a frivolous escape to a model for an inescapable reality. For that reason, I have avoided arcane critical language or extensive scholarly apparatus. At the same time, the text builds upon (and credits) the work of many other people. It is possible, precisely because these stories are so familiar, for a study of the sources of their power to be accessible to a wide audience—to anyone interested in how modern myths like *Frankenstein, Dracula* or *Dr. Jekyll and Mr. Hyde* came to be, and why they remain so popular.

I persist in believing that any aspect of literature or culture can be discussed intelligently without jargon, that it does no injustice to either subject or readers to use familiar diction, a clear style, and a strong narrative drive. There is a fascinating story to be told here, encompassing frightening events and great achievements, imagined characters who became almost real and real people who lived through almost unimaginable horror. It starts with the bizarre dreams of a few upper-class eccentrics and the harmless pastime of a small literate class; it ends in the collective nightmare of an entire generation.

Hayden White has written of the difficulty of making sense of human culture, that "the data always resist the coherency of the image which we are trying to fashion of them" (1). Just as horror stories imposed a limiting fictional pattern on frightening experiences to make them coherent, this book of necessity reduces the complexities of social change to a narrative that leaves much out. For example, for the sake of coherence I have scrupulously avoided the temptation to break chronology and draw comparisons with contemporary life. However, to make clear the aspects of a vanished time that remain with us (and avoid tedious plot summary or obscure commentary), I have confined the discussion almost totally to fiction and nonfiction still in print and popular. Even when I examine World War I memoirs, though I use some archival material, most references are drawn from the more familiar published sources such as the memoirs of the soldier poets Siegfried Sassoon and Robert Graves or the beautifully written diary of Edwin Campion Vaughan, *Some Desperate Glory,* reprinted in the United States in 1988. Thus, any reader of this book can find much of the writing it discusses in any good bookstore.

The stories examined in this book are not only still read—some have become the center of minor industries, sources of films, plays, further adventures, as well as artifacts of popular culture, familiar to nearly everyone. Like classical or Christian mythology, stories like *Frankenstein, Dracula* or *Dr. Jekyll and Mr. Hyde* thoroughly permeate our culture; you don't need to have read the novels to have felt their power. Chris Baldick has pointed out that all the familiar retellings, reworkings, and re-encounters with descendants of original tales such as *Frankenstein* are not merely corruptions of the myth—they *are* the myths. And if myths in general are, as J. A. Hadfield argues, the dreams of our race, then these myths have become our recurrent nightmares. As Claude Levi-Strauss has written, the constant retelling of such tales is part of their definition: "Mythical thought for its part is imprisoned in the events and experiences which it never tires of ordering and re-ordering in its search to find them a meaning."

The continual remodeling of popular myth is behind not only of the purpose and power of the horror tale, but also, as Bruno Bettelheim has shown us (in *The Uses of Enchantment*) one reason fairy tales have remained popular among generations of children. Bettelheim argues that fairy tales have also been shaped by their audience to reflect their wishes and fears. Certain patterns recur because the problems they echo are common to children—among them the fear of abandonment by parents, competition with siblings, the conflict between the allure of pleasures and the demands of growing up. Both horror stories and fairy tales give their audience a safe way to exorcise their fears by entering a parallel world, complete with language, imagery, and characters that have become both frightening and familiar, the embodiments of an unacknowledged "other" and old friends. On a conscious level, neither the audience for horror tales nor for fairy tales is aware of why such stories exert such a hold; meanwhile, below awareness, the work is done.

To understand the many ways fiction and reality found meaning together in the century before the First World War, I have focused each chapter of this book on a different small aspect of the story. For example, the reasons for the immense popularity of Gothic fiction at the start of the modern age can be seen through one book better than them all—Jane Austen's parody of the Gothic novel, *Northanger Abbey* (1814), which examines what happened when a vast new audience got hooked on horror stories.

*Frankenstein* has inspired a shelf full of analytical books and articles, not to mention the hundreds of film versions and sequels that trace at least the faint outline of Mary Shelley's tale of an overreaching scientist and his deadly creation. Rather than attempt to do justice to the complexity of this seminal story I look at one reason *Frankenstein* became immediately popular upon its publication in 1818, early in the Industrial Revolution. In part, *Frankenstein* and its Monster have remained with us since then because the new machinery and the factory system entwined technology in our daily lives, blurred the distinction between man and machine, and gave a new and fearful face to the future. Living through the feelings engendered by Mary Shelley's fictional creature still helps us to live with the dehumanizing and unstoppable machines all around us. When it first appeared, *Frankenstein* gave its audience a way to visualize an ambiguous relationship to the new technology, which was engendering both exhilaration at what ingenuity could accomplish and fear of what it might destroy. Mary Shelley's ambiguous creature, both appealing and appalling, gave those inchoate fears enduring life.

Much of this book is not about fiction at all, but reality read as fiction. Thus, the architecture of fantasy — the actual castles and labyrinths, dungeons and dark places of the denizens of horror tales — is compared to the Victorian city in actuality and the ideal city of the Great Exhibition of 1851. One of the newest movements in contemporary architecture sees the building as a text with narrative detail, a grammar of shape and texture, material and decoration, which means it can be read like a book. In mid-Victorian England, many such "texts" were constructed, embodying idealized visions of the past or wishful thinking about the future. But around and beneath them all was the landscape of urban slums and rural poverty, a more sinister architectural narrative read by the culture as a work of Gothic fiction. At mid century, Charles Dickens made that text explicit within the labyrinthian fictional structure of *Bleak House*.

Another frightening urban phenomenon — anonymous crime and the criminal as creator of a work of horror — was modeled in the fictional case of Dr. Jekyll through the contradictory meanings of the Gothic concept of the power of the will. Soon after, the pattern was applied to an actual series of murders committed by the anonymous and elusive person known as Jack the Ripper. At the time of *Dr. Jekyll and Mr. Hyde* and the Ripper murders, in the late 1800's, men and women faced new anxieties that threatened the cultural cult of Respectability. Men were troubled by Darwinian evidence of a brutish past and believed that throwbacks to the caveman lived among them, while women, no longer content to remain subordinate and propertyless, were caught between their traditional roles and aspirations for sexual and social equality. Those conflicts are also played out in *Dracula* (1897), a novel that gives us a model for the struggle between the sexes in a battle between an undying past and an uncertain future, fought within the bodies of two young women.

Finally, we will look at the years leading up to World War I and the experience of the generation that fought and died in a landscape of true horror. The day to day reality of life on the Western Front, in battles such as the Somme and Passchendaele, revealed the darkest visions of a century of horror stories to be not metaphor, but prophecy. Every soldier saw in the light of day the working out of the fantasies that had peopled the literature of fear. Those who came of age in the trenches found themselves in a common nightmare from which there was no escape.

And, as we shall see, their diaries and other accounts of the war try to make sense of a supremely senseless existence by using the language and imagery of the horror story. Sometimes consciously, often instinctively, young men lost in a Gothic landscape perceived it in the way they had come to view horror fiction—reading in the world around them a fantastic yet familiar universe of death brought to life, the pattern of the tale of terror.

The reality of the First World War made clear that the horror tales of the previous century had given form to human experience. What had been whispered in the darkness to a huge audience for over a hundred years was validated in the mud and blood of Flanders. From that soil blossomed the attitudes toward individual life and collective destiny that define modern thought. Such stories still speak to us. They have evolved as the reality of mass destruction and anonymous death has evolved, from the senseless battles of World War I through the targeting of civilians in the Second World War and the systematic murder of millions in the Holocaust, into the fear of nuclear annihilation that now lurks behind the everyday life of every human being. What horror stories gave the men of 1914, they still provide—a way to escape the fears of our century and, paradoxically, to face them.

The parallel development of the modern tale of terror and the modern world show us how literature and life create each other. As we shall see, the heritage of horror taught a society undergoing a frightening metamorphosis to face its fears, give them form, and, perhaps, to live with them in uneasy peace.

Part One
# The Art of Fear (1818–1830)

*Chapter One*
# Hooked on Horror: Reading and the Gothic Revival

> The moral and political character of the age or nation may be read by an attentive observer even in its lightest literature
> —Thomas Love Peacock

Jane Austen's *Northanger Abbey* (1818) has been described as both a devastating parody of the Gothic novel and the first novel of ordinary life, a reaction to the phenomenal popularity of horror stories that accompanied the explosion of literacy over the previous quarter century. Austen's comedy grows out of the implications of mass readership on the perception of reality—the confusion between ordinary life and Gothic imaginings, between actual and invented places, between creating the fictions that sustain social relationships and coming to believe in the fictions of others, between each of us as author and audience of our life's experiences. In fact, throughout her novel, the relationships within a triangle of more or less ordinary men and women—actors in their own lives—are intertwined with their places in the audience for the new popular fiction—the sentimental novel and the tale of terror. As a close look at *Northanger Abbey* and the Gothic craze that surrounded it makes clear, the act of reading gave a vast new audience a way both to escape the world and to find deeper meaning in it.

Catherine Morland, the young woman whom we follow from an unexceptional childhood as a clergyman's daughter in the obscure village of Fullerton to the fashionable resort of Bath, to the mysterious and ancient Northanger Abbey, and home again to marriage and maturity, is defined from the start by her contrast with the characters of popular fiction. "No one," the narrator tells us in the first line, ". . . would have supposed her to be born a heroine." (No one, that is, but Jane Austen.) She is what she isn't—neither accomplished, nor beautiful (her father once compliments her by calling her "almost pretty today"), nor destined for a special fate.

Like the audience for Gothic fiction (of which she is an avid member) her reading provides the framework for her imaginative life. But it also influences the way she sees the world around her. The false conjectures she makes about the people she meets and places she sees are shaped by the fantastic fiction she reads. When she visits the ancient abbey of the title, the ancestral home of the Tilney family, she expects every locked cabinet and fluttering curtain to conceal dark secrets. Instead, they harbor the mundane—laundry lists, folded blankets, and sometimes, nothing.

However, in *Northanger Abbey,* Jane Austen goes beyond making fun of the power of popular fiction to distort our view of reality. For, by the end of her novel, Catherine Morland has indeed become heroic, and the Gothic fiction she reads has indeed proven true, though in ways far more subtle than she first imagined. Her obsession with the literature of fear turns out to be less a retreat from ordinary life and more a way into it. Her propensity to read life as if it were a tale of terror becomes a strength, not a weakness, and a key to understanding the continuing hold horror stories had on the imagination of an entire culture for the next century, and beyond.

Catherine Morland's love of Gothic fiction makes clear her role as the representative of the ordinary reading public, since at the time Jane Austen created her experiences, the horror story was the most popular fiction in England.

The Gothic craze had begun in earnest one June night in 1764 when Horace Walpole, fourth Earl of Orford, Member of Parliament, and son of the Prime Minister of England, awoke

> from a dream, of which all I could recover was, that I had thought myself in an ancient castle ... and that on the uppermost bannister of a great staircase I saw a gigantic hand in armor. In the evening I sat down and began to write, without knowing in the least what I intended to say or relate [ix].

The content he recalls (supernatural events in a medieval setting), and his method of making it fiction ("automatic" writing that meant what flowed from his pen would be close to the unconscious sources of his nightmare) were the basis for the formula that led to the Christmas Eve publication of his phenomenally successful *The Castle of Otranto: A Gothic Story.* The other ingredients could have been taken off eighteenth century bookshelves: Daniel Defoe had told a ghost story in 1706 in the "True Relation of the Apparition of one Mrs. Veal," various realistic writers including Henry Fielding and Tobias Smollett had invoked the atmosphere of ruined castles, and a number of "graveyard poets" had given form to nightmare visions. Walpole's originality came in the way he put these elements together with his own private eccentricities and obsessions to create a compelling and infectious brew.

This recipe was reused with little variation in the countless Gothic tales churned out at breakneck speed to flood bookstalls and fill libraries for the next seventy years. The vast output (and the often inordinate length of many of these productions) was one byproduct of the method; it often amounted to cribbing shamelessly from previous books, inserting subplots that usually bore little or no relationship to the overall story, and writing quickly while rarely changing a word. (The technique worked for poetry as well—the "Spasmodics," some years later, also produced massive "spontaneous" tomes, some of which, like Philip James Bailey's *Festus* [1839], grew alarmingly with every new edition.)

It became possible for nearly anyone who was literate and familiar with the genre to add to it. Authors and audiences from all levels of society participated, meeting each other's needs by retelling the same stories over and over in slightly different guises. In *Northanger Abbey*, Catherine Morland lists seven such works, all of which actually existed: "*Castle of Wolfenbach, Clermont, Mysterious Warnings, Necromancer of the Black Forest, Midnight Bell, Orphan of the Rhine,* and *Horrid Mysteries.*" Her friend Isabella breathlessly asks ". . . but are they all horrid, are you sure they are all horrid?" (25) And indeed they are, in both senses of the term.

At first, those who wrote Gothic fiction had presumed a traditional British reading audience—leisured, small, largely upper class and well-to-do. For example, Mrs. Ann Radcliffe's *The Mysteries of Udolpho* (1794) (Catherine Morland's favorite) earned for its author the "then colossal sum of 500 pounds" and cost its readers a considerable one pound four shillings for the four hefty volumes (Punter 24–25). But a new audience and new methods of production and distribution soon meant that popular literature in the nineteenth century reached a significant portion of the populace. It has been estimated that the reading population of Britain increased from one and a half million in 1780 to between seven and eight million by 1830, a period that roughly coincides with the phenomenal popularity of the Gothic story (Quinlan 161).

For the vast majority of the newly literate, horror tales were the first imaginative fiction read, shaping attitudes not only to literature, but to the act of reading it as well.

Unable to afford books like those of Mrs. Radcliffe, these millions of new readers had to get their thrills through cheaper sources, in ways that blurred the traditional identification of a specific story with a particular book. A whole new industry arose to serve them by mass marketing the Gothic pattern. As a result, the major novels themselves reached their widest circulation only indirectly, filtered through new forms of fiction that preserved the skeleton of the plots while eviscerating the contents.

The sheer number of these works, their similarities, and their availability to all classes of the reading public impressed the main elements of the horror story upon the culture with a nearly indelible force. Individual tales with their own peculiarities were submerged under an ocean of imitations, each one a variation of the simple formula that chilled spines and sold books. The impact became collective, testimony to the mythic power in the few stories at the center of it all.

The most familiar of these was told and retold with few variations. It takes place in an ancient abbey or castle, liberally supplied with ghosts and gruesome sights, cursed by an ancient prophecy, and run by a tormented villain. To this sinister setting comes a young woman who ends up pursued by the villain with equally sinister plans; along the way, she is frightened by real or imagined brushes with the supernatural while lost in the intricate maze of passages, what Walpole called the "long labyrinth of darkness" underlying the castle. Somehow, amid a tangle of subplots, flashbacks, false turnings and dead ends, the heroine emerges unscathed. The curse hanging over the castle is fulfilled, the villain overthrown, and the poor but honest hero (who has been hanging about since the start) is revealed as the true heir to the gloomy pile of masonry that has housed them all.

In the same way that fairy tales were shaped by a juvenile audience that demanded the same few stories in thousands of guises, the somewhat older audience for horror fulfilled its needs by demanding literally thousands of versions of this same tale of terror. In the case of fairy tales, the process of creation by audience took centuries, through a largely oral tradition. For Gothic fiction, however, it happened much more quickly, spurred in large part by one man who wasn't a writer at all. He was William Lane, publisher and entrepreneur, the first to apply mass marketing techniques to the creation and distribution of literature.

From 1790 to 1820 Lane operated his Minerva Press, employing at least thirty men working full time on four presses to grind out thousands of Gothic titles. Until he came along, publishing had been a small scale enterprise. Lane quickly realized that the new, large literate public could have its reading hunger fed by cheap editions of tales of terror. He acquired grist for his mill in three ways. At a time when the going rate for a first work was between five and twenty pounds, he offered would-be hacks around thirty. First authors, often women, showed up at his office at 33 Leadenhall Street, London, with thrillers they had produced in their spare time; these he could obtain for small sums and the flattery of publication. Thus the audience became the authors. He also pirated American novels in great numbers, paying those authors nothing at all. It comes as no surprise, given his methods, that over half his books were published anonymously or under pseudonyms.*

---

*My information on William Lane comes from Dorothy Blakely, Minerva Press (1790–1820) and Montague Summers, A Gothic Bibliography.

Although *Northanger Abbey* never was a Minerva Press book, its curious publishing history coincides with the years William Lane was in his heyday and gives us some insight into the process. Begun around 1799 as *Susan*, it was sold to a publisher in 1803, yet didn't appear, for reasons the author herself could never determine. A revised version didn't reach print until a year after her death, in 1818, through the efforts of her brother. Thus, one of Jane Austen's first novels became the last to reach the bookstalls. Perhaps when she sold the novel (intended, like all of her books, to be published anonymously), it was taken as just another Gothic story by an unknown woman author that failed to adhere properly to the formula and was passed over for the many that did. In any case, the fifteen year hiatus between payment and publication for her parody of the tale of terror inadvertently became a testament to the haphazard nature of the business of producing such tales themselves.

Minerva books were the most unreadable ever produced, though they were read in great numbers (at least two of the books Catherine Morland mentions are William Lane productions). Full of typographical errors, printed on coarse yellowish or gray paper in miniscule type, they were constantly condemned in reviews for their overall shoddiness, their "wretched paper and imperfect letter . . . carelessly written and printed." Lane, of course, couldn't care less, since the economies of his method made his books affordable to a less affluent audience, who didn't seem to mind the condition of the vehicle as long as the horrors emerged unscathed.

Although his books were cheaper than novels had been, they were still out of reach of many readers. Before Lane, libraries were for the favored few, access was difficult, and permission to borrow rarely given. Lane solved this problem by organizing and supporting lending libraries; the subscriber, for a small periodic sum, could borrow one book to read, then exchange it for another. Lane himself owned the Minerva Library of his own titles, which numbered some fifteen thousand volumes by 1800. For obvious reasons, he also encouraged the founding of provincial libraries, extending the influence of Minerva fiction throughout the country while aiding in the growth of a great new spur to widespread literacy. In this activity Lane outdid himself, selling prospective founders entire libraries complete with instruction books, using the franchise plan so familiar to fast food addicts today. William Lane did, after all, feed and help determine the taste of his audience by supplying the literary equivalent of junk food.

The vast number of Minerva books were quickly written, quickly read, and quickly forgotten, as distinctive as individual Harlequin romances. They were formula literature, throwaway literature, hardly literature at all. The introduction to one has this injunction: "Critics . . . disregard this humble tale. The amusement of a few solitary hours cannot be worthy of your high attention." It's not clear if the "few hours" were those spent reading or writing the book, though the ambiguity makes clear how close author and audience were, and reminds us again of the ephemeral nature of both sides of the relationship.

For those without even the means to obtain Minerva books, or for those who lacked the patience to extract the terrors from hundreds of pages of text, the bluebook was a still cheaper and more efficient source of thrills. The ancestor of the Victorian "penny dreadful" and today's comic book or cheap paperback, the bluebook was so called because its four by seven inch pages (36 for a sixpence, 72 for a shilling) were stitched into a cover of flimsy blue paper. Although the advertisements promised tales "embellished with elegant engravings," the illustration was usually limited to a lurid frontispiece. The text was often cribbed from a longer novel, but with most of the horrors intact. The result was a plot that proceeded at breakneck speed with unexplained gaps. The record for abridgment was probably held by the nameless author of *Almagro and Claude*, who filled four left over sheets in a bluebook with a condensation of Lewis' novel *The Monk*—a story which in the original covers well over three hundred pages!

Bluebooks were written on almost every subject still found on drugstore shelves, from cookery (*The Family Cookery Book*), to the occult (*The Art of Fortune Telling*), to music (*The British Songster*), to advice to the lovelorn (*Female Policy Detected, or the Arts of a Designing Woman Laid Open*). Still, the most popular ones had titles such as *The Black Forest, or The Cavern of Horrors!*, *The Midnight Assassin*, *The Castle of Oravilla*, or *The Mysterious Stranger*. The titles became as interchangeable as the stories, which were simply the distilled essence of the Gothic formula; like American pornographic comic books of the 1930's, bluebooks supplied the thrills with a minimum of plot, without the complications of character development, and with the sole aim of arousing the audience.

The flimsy framework of bluebooks drew author and audience even closer, bound together by their familiarity with the Gothic situation. By filling in the blanks of the story, readers became collaborators in the act of creation, using what they had previously read to make sense of what would otherwise be a disconnected set of inexplicable scary situations. As the author of one typical bluebook recognizes on the title page, one sentence is enough to provide a blueprint for his readers to construct a narrative:

> *Lovel Castle, or the Rightful Heir Restored, a Gothic Tale:* Narrating how a Young Man, the Supposed Son of a Peasant, by a Train of unparalleled circumstances, not only Discovers who were his real Parents, but that they came to Untimely Deaths; with his Adventures in the Haunted Apartment, Discovery of the Fatal Closet, and Appearance of the Ghost of his Murdered Father; Relating, also, how the Murderer was Brought to Justice, with his Confession and the Restoration of the Injured Orphan to his Title and Estates

The vast majority of the Gothic output between 1800 and 1830 could be represented by this page. The anonymous author recognizes this, as he writes of "the haunted apartment" and "fatal closet" as locales well known to his readers (though he must also realize the "unparalleled circumstances" were paralleled *ad nauseum* in every bookstall). Though stories like these are the least interesting as literature, they tell us much about the great and obsessive nature of the Gothic hunger. Avid readers weren't seeking original plots and characters; they were eager to experience, again and again, the thrill of fear in the familiar architecture of the classic Gothic situation and its implausible resolution.

There have been many reasons given for the obsessive power of Gothic tales; one obvious source is the nightmare nature and sexual overtones of their dream symbolism. The classic Gothic pattern—of the young heroine pursued through murky corridors, subject to the threat of the villain's dark designs and the continual shocks of assorted frightening situations—is certainly the stuff of which dreams are made.

At the same time, the heroine, like her readers, consciously seeks out those terrors, wandering the gloomy passages of the labyrinth in the crumbling castle as the readers follow the almost indecipherable lines of print in their shoddily made books. Both are caught between the lure of their secret wishes and the dread of their fulfillment. This helps to explain why Gothic heroines (like Gothic readers) are always putting themselves in the most frightening situations, then expressing shock and revulsion at what they uncover. In one sense, then, the horror story is about the experience of the reader of such fiction—entering a strange new world, exploring its sinister "passages," more than half-expecting the horrors that lurk around the corner of nearly every page.

The tale of terror was perfectly suited to the desires of the newly literate, able to keep them turning the pages with stories that imbued reading itself with an almost supernatural power, the power of language to create an alternative reality. Like the invocation of ghosts and spectres in the Gothic castle, reading was the incantation that brought imagined beings alive. Merely anticipating the act of reading a mysterious manuscript she finds in her room keeps Catherine Morland awake most of her first night at Northanger Abbey.

At the same time as the Gothic story grounded its appeal in the dreamlike domain of the self and what was for many the new and adventurous act of reading, it also built upon a broader foundation—the landscape and architecture of an idealized medieval world. In *Northanger Abbey*, the impressionable Miss Morland is clearly most attracted to wild settings and ruined castles, in both literature and life. She bitterly regrets missing a trip to "Blaize Castle" and finds the prospect of staying at Northanger Abbey almost unbearably exciting, since she hopes that place will link her fictive world with reality. For the larger audience she represents, Gothic architecture became a similar magnet, drawing readers into the tale of terror, while at the same time connecting sinister imaginative settings with the actual landscape of England at the start of the nineteenth century.

## II.

Horace Walpole, the founder of the modern horror story, dreamed of the castle of Otranto while living in his modern reconstruction of just such a place, his home in Twickenham, Strawberry Hill. This was a romantic's idea of an ancient structure, newly built of plaster and lath, with wallpaper painted to resemble stone; Walpole wore out a number of fake battlements in his lifetime. Building and remodeling the castle was Walpole's lifelong passion. His castle became an emblem for the Gothic movement — constructed of modern materials to give a barely convincing illusion of age and permanence. Like the novel it inspired, Walpole's castle was a pastiche of mock medievalism made for modern consumption. Still, it looked medieval enough from a distance, and visitors were encouraged to keep their distance by a five acre maze of walks and gardens.

The mock medieval retreat of William Beckford, creator of the Oriental horror novel *Vathek,* was even more bizarre. It shared with Strawberry Hill an architectural evocation of a vanished past, but added a dangerous reminder of the grandiosity of its creator's fantasy: Fonthill Abbey boasted the highest spire in England, a 300 foot tall monstrosity that collapsed while Beckford was in London. He later said his only regret was not seeing the catastrophe, and he soon had it rebuilt. It was rumored that he planned to have it destroyed while he watched, but it didn't collapse again until after he had sold the building. Beckford's gardens at Fonthill were also on a grand scale, surrounded by a twelve mile long wall to keep intruders out. Anyone foolish enough to climb the fence confronted the pack of wild dogs Beckford let loose in the grounds every night. One uninvited afternoon visitor to Fonthill (the cousin of the painter W. P. Firth) was treated graciously by Beckford, then informed of the dogs that evening as he was ushered out the door. He spent the night in a tree.

Though few members of the reading public had the means to recreate feudal fiefdoms, some could indulge a taste for medieval settings. As early as 1748, Sanderson Miller designed a sham Gothic ruin for an aristocratic patron; for the next seventy years, carefully constructed "hermits' caves" and "ruined abbeys" complete with skeletons graced the gardens of the wealthy. Such stage sets were more than decorative motifs; they led to ruminations on the power of chaos to overthrow order, the hold the past retains upon the present, and the dust to which all of us must return. They made landscape into literature, while imposing the Gothic blueprint on the contemporary world.*

Whether created by man or part of the natural order, any dark and gloomy scenery, crumbling ruins, or moments of pain and privation were dubbed "sublime" if they aroused feelings of awe and terror. To the tastemakers of the day such as Edmund Burke, Dr. John Aiken, and Archibald Alison, the sublime was the highest aesthetic standard. For Burke, whose *Philosophical Enquiry into Our Ideas of the Sublime and the Beautiful* (1757) was popular throughout the period, "great though terrible scenes," like the Dublin flood he described in a letter written in 1745, were sublime because they "fill the mind with grand ideas, and turn the soul upon itself" (Monk 84).

John Aiken's influential essay, *On the Pleasure Derived from Objects of Terror* (1773) argues that "the more wild, fanciful and extraordinary are the circumstances of a scene of horror, the more pleasure we receive from it." The pleasure comes in our reaction, and Aiken (describing it in sexual terms) assumes that "we rather choose to suffer the smart pang of a violent emotion than the uneasy craving of an unsatisfied desire" (Skarda 12, 13). In his *Essays on the Nature and Principles of Taste* (1790), Archibald Alison even quotes a book called *Observations upon Modern Gardening* which includes a description of the perfect garden, complete with caverns, skeletons, and the site of a young woman's suicide. He concludes "it is surely unnecessary to remark how the sublimity of this extraordinary scene is increased by the circumstances of horror which are so finely connected with it" (17).

Thus fiction was created from the language of landscape, enabling the viewer to participate in an imaginative fantasy. Like bluebooks, the castles and gardens presented stage sets for shocking scenes and invited the audience to construct narratives around them. Belief in the sublime linked the intensely private, dreamlike pleasure of reading horror fiction with places that became texts to inspire terror.

Even after the craze for prefabricated ruins faded, architecture and landscape continued to be "read" as fiction, even if that was not its conscious design; for the next century, horror stories were conveyed through structures of stone and landscapes of death. An audience schooled in the sublime and familiar with Gothic narrative came to see their surroundings, from urban slums to Flanders fields, as a text to be read, as a tale of terror.

---

\* *The grandest fiefdom of all, a feudal plantation in Jamaica complete with slaves, was owned by Matthew Gregory Lewis, creator of the scandalous horror novel* The Monk. *Returning from the island in 1818, Lewis met the most Gothic of fates. When he died of yellow fever on May 14, he was buried at sea the same morning. For some reason, the weights on the coffin slipped off and the canvas cover blew up to form a sail. When last seen by the ships' terrified crew and passengers, the body of Matthew Gregory Lewis was silently sailing back towards Jamaica.*

Jane Austen's Gothic centerpiece, Northanger Abbey, with its modern home, gardens, and offices abutting the remnants of an ancient and decayed structure, stands, like Strawberry Hill and Fonthill, in the worlds of both Gothic medieval fantasy and ordinary modern life. To Catherine Morland it becomes an imaginative and sublime construct and an historical reality, architectural confirmation that the imaginative possibilities of Gothic fiction and the shadowy corners of the contemporary world can literally occupy the same space. She turns her visit into an act of creation, transforming Northanger Abbey into the Gothic castle she wishes it to be.

The narrative she imposes upon the scene makes her host, the mercurial General Tilney, a Gothic villain responsible for the untimely death of his wife. When, in a supremely embarrassing moment, she reveals her suspicions to his son, Henry, and simultaneously realizes how absurd they are, "the visions of romance were over," and the abbey descends into ordinariness. It collapses as an imaginative construct, as unstable as Beckford's actual tower at Fonthill or Walpole's fictional castle of Otranto, which disintegrates at the end of his novel when the curse that hangs over it is finally fulfilled. Every reader of Gothic fiction, when he closes his book and returns to the safe and mundane world around him, feels something of the same sense of collapse, a combination of deflation and release—the end of a dream, a nocturnal pleasure satiated.

Catherine Morland's mortification appears at first to confirm the comic consequences of an overindulgence in Gothic fiction, the foolishness of confusing sublime fantasies for reality and the supernatural for the ordinary. Her false conjectures—about the secrets hidden in the abbey, the nature of its owner, the danger she perceives herself to face—all can be read as a satiric attack on the Gothic movement itself as frivolous and unconnected to the real business of life. At the end of the novel, Catherine has returned home with her visions of heroism and Gothic adventure shattered, but her view of reality clearer and more mature. Read this way, *Northanger Abbey* seems opposed to horror stories as proper preparation for life, confirming Catherine's concern throughout the novel that her reading tastes are something to be ashamed of when in polite company.

But the son, Henry Tilney, who closes the Gothic novel Catherine has created in her imagination, is an unabashed fan of such works himself. From the start, he is the moral center of the novel, teaching her to distinguish social fiction and fact, teaching her how to live. And what he teaches her is diametrically opposed to this surface impression; for he shows Catherine Morland and us that Gothic fiction, like fiction itself, is not a diversion from ordinary life, but a way to see into its deep structure. Catherine's propensity to read her life as if it were a Gothic novel proves, in the end, to be both a defect of perception and an insight into experience.

Early in their relationship, Henry announces, "I consider a country dance as an emblem of marriage. Fidelity and complaisance are the principal duties of both, and those men who do not choose to dance or marry themselves, have no business with the partners or wives of their neighbours" (58). Catherine argues that "they are such different things," but Henry goes on to draw a long list of similarities, tongue in cheek to be sure, but making the point that the artificial structure of the dance is a model and preparation for the partnership of marriage. Throughout the book (and indeed from his entrance), Henry has pointed out the artificiality of social structures, their fictional quality. But he also continually argues that learning to read them prepares one for life.

When Catherine Morland first meets him, in the Pump Rooms at Bath, he announces his need to ask a number of standard social questions, making clear at the onset that he knows they are required dialogue for the "fictional" setting they share. Then he asks his questions ("Have you been long in Bath, Madam?" "Have you been to theatre" etc.) also making clear that his reaction to her answers is equally artificial ("But some emotion must appear to be raised by your reply, and surprise is more easily assumed, and not less reasonable than any other").

Thus, Henry mocks the similarity of social introductions to bad novels, laughing at their predictability as well as their distance from real feeling. But at the same time he exposes his discourse as fiction, it works to introduce him to Catherine, elicit information, form a social bond. In fact, because he shares with her his knowledge that they are acting, they paradoxically become even more genuinely linked. Thus, he doesn't reject the fictions of society; they work very well, provided we read them *as* fiction.

Throughout the novel, fictional structures contrast with the ordinary lives of the characters, just as the dance apes the social dance of the triangle of friends seeking partners for life. When Catherine takes a carriage ride against her will, it is compared to the midnight abduction of a Gothic heroine, while her ostensible friends (and insufferable boors) the Thorpes continually see themselves as hero and heroine in a fiction they call their life. What this all suggests is that fictional models — from dances and social conversation to Gothic and sentimental novels — both take us from the ordinary world and prepare us for it. Catherine's education consists in learning not that fiction and life are unconnected, but that knowing how to read experience through fiction and the "fictions of experience," can teach her to be author of her own life.

The lessons are learned slowly and painfully (at one point Henry argues that the words "to torment" and "to instruct" are synonyms) because the nature of such fictions is to masquerade as something else. Whether a country dance or a letter from a false friend, the truth is found beyond the surface, revealed by the technique of careful reading. Thus, early in the novel,

Henry is able to see the social choreography behind a country dance and interpret it for Catherine; by the end, Catherine herself can see beyond the self serving words of Isabella Thorpe, reading the true meaning beneath them, responding to that and not to the fictional surface ("She must think me an idiot, or could not have written so").

And the most fantastic escapes of all—the fictional excursions into the supernatural and medieval world of the tale of terror—in the end, probe deepest at the terrifying core of ordinary life. If the dance contains the structure of marriage, and the fictions of false friendship mask the reality of competition and selfishness, then Gothic imagery conceals the darkest truths about family and society behind the most frivolous and frightening fantasies.

Consider Catherine's misperceptions about Northanger Abbey and its patriarch, Henry's father, General Tilney. She believes he has murdered his wife or imprisoned her in a secret wing of the building. It's hardly an original thought, since every master of a Gothic castle (from Manfred in *The Castle of Otranto* onward) is tormented by a similar family secret. Manfred, the patriarch of a rather troubled family, rejoices in the death of his son, renounces his wife, and murders his daughter as he single-mindedly tries to force a marriage with Isabella, his dead son's bride to be. The archetypical Gothic situation unfolds—the obsessed male pursuing the persecuted maiden through a maze of secret passages and subterranean chambers in a crumbling castle. Catherine Morland similarly follows the labyrinth of passages through Northanger Abbey, seeking the room where Mrs. Tilney was last seen, hoping to find evidence of her murder orthat she is still alive and a prisoner. Instead she keeps encountering the General, who seems intent on stopping her explorations.

Catherine's Gothic fantasy of the Tilney family, like the other fictions of the novel, is both absurd and illuminating. For what the Gothic household illustrates in wild excess is the nature of the contemporary family structure. On one level, tales like *The Castle of Otranto* play out family conflicts at a time when the family was dominated by the authoritarian figure of the patriarch—a model that reflected the structure of British society. In "The Paterfamilias of the Victorian Governing Classes" (in Wohl 59–81), David Roberts points out that the father in such households was usually remote, almost always the unquestioned sovereign, often benevolent to his heirs but sometimes cruel or brutal. His home was a microcosm of the state, his family subject to his whims. The source of the father's power was his control over inheritance—also the motivating force in the plot of *The Castle of Otranto* and many of its imitations.

When Walpole writes of the "House of Otranto" he means both the physical and the family structure; the first obviously stands for the second. The fight over the right to the castle between the aging nobleman, the false tenant, and the young, apparently low born hero who is the true heir thus becomes a thinly veiled portrayal of the age old fight between generations. For women, who, like Catherine Morland, were the bulk of the audience for such fiction, the excesses of the Gothic family were a romantic escape from the burdens of nineteenth century family life and, read more deeply, echoed its worst secrets. The women of horror fiction—pursued by unwanted suitors, or confined in their rooms by imperious husbands—were not so different from their modern readers. On the dream level at which Gothic fiction drew its power, both sets of women shared the same fears.

The gulf between Gothic family secrets and nineteenth century family life may seem at first blush too wide to be plausible—we may at first respond, as Catherine Morland did about Henry Tilney's equation of marriage and the dance, that "they are such different things that they cannot be compared together." But Jane Austen shows us the connection in the person of General Tilney himself, master of Northanger Abbey. Although Catherine's conjecture that he is a full fledged Gothic villain proves ridiculous, he does turn out to be a contemporary equivalent. Tilney's wife is not hidden away in a secret room—she is dead and buried—yet she remains "alive" in the family, a secret wellspring of his dark moods and capricious cruelty.

From the beginning, Captain Tilney is given to fits of brooding over her death and moments of dangerous instability. When the family is delayed in leaving Bath, he almost loses control when he threatens to pitch Catherine's writing desk out of the window of the coach—implying, perhaps, that he fears her power to transform her experience into words. And, whenever he enters the room, Catherine notices that his children are silent and seemingly terrified of him.

His strangest obsession is with time. Catherine is warned from the start that "the strictest punctuality to the family hours would be expected at Northanger" (132), and later, after Henry's sister expresses her fear at being late for dinner, they all witness General Tilney lose control, "having on the very instant of their entering, pulled the bell with violence, ordered 'Dinner to be on table *directly!*'" (134). Like the would-be heirs of the Gothic novel, General Tilney's two sons seem not only in fear of him and relieved when he is out of the room, but also always aware that his approval is needed to determine their future. General Tilney's anger at the passage of time suggests that he is cursed like villains of Gothic romances, constantly reminded of the eventual transfer of family power to a new generation, obsessed with the need to control the movements of his household like a well oiled watch.

Thus, in the end, the patriarchal family in Northanger Abbey, headed in military fashion by a General haunted by the memory of his wife, who keeps his subjects in fear and is himself fearful of the passage of time, is not so different from the ghost ridden households in the tale of terror. At the basis of both is the undying power of the past, a fight over control of the present, and the awareness that generational change is a "prophecy" that will inevitably determine the future. Catherine Morland's overblown fantasies were, at their worst, misreadings of the truth. Seeking a mysterious manuscript in the dark corners of her room, she found only a laundry list and was keenly disappointed; instead of a Gothic mystery, she uncovered the conflicts of an ordinary family. The final irony of *Northanger Abbey* is that terror really could be read in those mundane objects and trivial events, the unspoken secrets of family life.

General Tilney may not have imprisoned his wife in a hidden wing of the abbey, but he was jailer to his children nonetheless. They cannot marry without his consent and cannot be comfortable in his presence. And he has his own dark mysteries. We never learn exactly why he spends his nights in solitary brooding or what fuels his constant anger and impatience. In the end, he performs an act of seemingly inexplicable cruelty, suddenly turning Catherine out of his home with no warning because he has learned that her family is of a lower class than he had supposed. Catherine, the representative of the new middle class reading public, enters the aristocratic domain in her reading and in her life, and discovers how in both, generational and class tensions are the secret sources of fear.

Thus Gothic tales, like Jane Austen's parody of the Gothic, reflect tensions beyond the family, within the larger realms of society. Sir Walter Scott pointed out that the characters in Gothic fiction take on the features of their class and, in fact, become more representative of their class than individuals (Scott 110). The early nineteenth century was marked by an obsessive preoccupation with preserving one's family name and social station. A rapidly growing middle class developed new sources of wealth, many aristocratic families experienced hard times, and massive migration brought about by the Industrial Revolution destroyed age old social patterns. Class was no longer easily defined or synonymous with wealth. As a result, much effort was spent to maintain the fiction of artificial class distinctions, to define a narrow social circle, to restrict oneself to a kind of incestuous inbreeding in marriage and other social relationships, to remain safe but sterile.

General Tilney's anger and rudeness were, then, the result of the threat he saw in Catherine to the position of his family as well as his own private demons. Like Walpole's fictional House of Otranto, his castle was also in danger of collapse. When Morland first abandoned her fantasies about Northanger Abbey, it became "no more to her now than any other house," a judgment that comes to have its own ironic truth. By the end of the book, when General Tilney has thrown her out and tried to prevent her marriage to his son, she has learned the real meaning of her experience and begins "to feel that in suspecting General Tilney of either murdering or shutting up his wife, she had scarcely sinned against his character, or magnified his cruelty." In the comic world of Jane Austen's Gothic parody, we find a sober reality; she shows us that Gothic images are themselves a parody of everyday life, an exaggeration that shows us its inner truth.

For the next century, the aesthetic of the horror story continued to mingle fictional settings and real fears, the ideal and the actual, architecture and landscape created in the imagination and echoed in the outside world. Lovers of the Gothic like Walpole functioned in the world of their contemporaries (Walpole himself was one of the most prolific letter writers of the century), yet lived (actually or vicariously) in a reconstructed medieval world of the imagination. But in its nostalgia for a past that never was, the Gothic tale enabled its readers to deal with a future that was equally uncertain and fraught with terror. Women, who suffered the most from this stifling social system, had another reason to become the most avid readers and prolific creators of the subversive joys of Gothic fiction and among its most prolific creators. They read and wrote such stories for escape, but the pattern of that escape hinted at unfulfilled needs as well as guilty pleasures.

The sublime landscape of Gothic literature, rife with ruins, castles, vast landscapes and subject to violent storms, is in tune with the labyrinthian nature of the decaying interiors, inhabited by characters subject to equally unsettling storms of passion. Every castle conceals a network of dark tunnels, secret passages, and locked doors — architectural models of confusion and chaos, of secrets imperfectly hid and a past difficult to escape, places where the mind, free from the constraints of reason, can use imagination to shape the darkest fears.

The story told most often, of the peasant who claims rightful ownership of the castle and finally establishes his true nobility, is a model that gave form to widespread anxieties on all levels. It reflects not only generational tensions in the patriarchal family and the class tensions in a changing society, but also draws its power from the cataclysmic political events in France in the decades surrounding the Revolution.

The same Edmund Burke who wrote of the transforming terror of the sublime was violently upset by the Terror unleashed across the Channel; his *Reflections on the Revolution in France* (1790) provoked many books and pamphlets throughout the period, which kept the fear of an English Revolution at the forefront of public consciousness. As Chris Baldick has pointed out (18–19), it's significant that Burke uses imagery from Gothic literature to shape his response to the Revolution. Thus, he sees what happened in France as "parricide"—the overthrow of a patriarchal society by ungrateful children—and, in a famous image, echoes the end of the *Castle of Otranto* when he writes that "out of the tomb of the murdered monarchy in France has arisen a vast, tremendous, unformed spectre" (*Works*, vi. 88).

What's interesting here is that the reference in that line is to the moment in *Otranto* when the "father," Manfred, is overthrown by a "peasant," Theodore, who discovers his right to the castle through the intercession of a spectre, "dilated to an immense magnitude" that rises over the ruins of castle. In other words, in violently attacking the Revolution, Burke uses a Gothic image that implicitly supports the overthrow of patriarchal power and implies that true nobility resides in the peasantry. (The same is true when the image is echoed again in 1847, in the first line of Marx and Engels' *Communist Manifesto,* when they invoke the spectre of Communism haunting Europe.)

Thus, Gothic imagery reflected political fears in two ways. For much of the nineteenth century, Chartist and other popular movements struggled to gain power for the new, literate, and disenfranchised industrial class. Those people, like Austen's Catherine Morland or Walpole's Theodore, sought not only to enter the castle and learn its secrets, but to claim a share of the inheritance. Simultaneously, the patriarchs of English society, were, like the fictional fathers Manfred and General Tilney, fearful of what time would do to their power, and saw in the French Revolution the worst of all spectral visions—the crumbling of the castle itself.

In myriad forms, horror in fiction continued to evolve over the next century, told and retold to its readers and reshaped by them, cloaking in fantasy the secret fears of its audience. By participating in the act of creation—vicariously living through the terrors of the characters, connecting disconnected threads of plot, depending upon past reading to make sense of new variations—millions of the newly literate joined the traditional audience in learning, like Catherine Morland, to view life through the lens of literature.

All those stories that reached a mass audience helped continue the collaboration of author and audience that marked the evolution of the tale of terror. Horror tales in their many forms continued to reflect fears of personal, familial, and social instability by creating places and situations with the safe remoteness of fantasy and the frightening intimacy of nightmare. Collectively, they enabled their readers to see their world as a landscape with, in Edmund Wilson's words, "horizons beyond rationality and institutionally approved emotions." Readers of horror stories, believers in the sublime, learned to read experience with the same tools and to find the same terrors. Gothic fiction and ordinary life—the two themes of *Northanger Abbey*—became one. Together, they expressed what Sigmund Freud at the start of our century called the uncanny: "that class of the terrifying which leads back to something long known to us and once very familiar."

*Chapter Two*
# Monsters and Machines

> If the time should ever come when what is now called science, thus familiarised to me, shall be ready to put on, as it were, a form of flesh and blood, the Poet will lend his divine spirit to aid the transfiguration, and will welcome the Being thus produced, as a dear and genuine inmate of the household of man.
> —William Wordsworth

In the labyrinth of possibilities opened up by the Gothic novel, most authors went down well worn paths. Some, such as William Beckford, who merged the Oriental and Gothic traditions in *Vathek*, pursued directions that proved to be blind alleys. But a few followed a new way that led from medieval fantasy to contemporary reality, adopting the powerful subtext and appeal of Gothic fiction to the emerging terrors of daily life.

An informal ghost story competition devised to fill the empty hours of a rainy summer in 1816 led to two of the most enduring outgrowths of the traditional Gothic tale of terror. In the Villa Diodati near Lake Geneva, Percy and Mary Shelley, her half sister Claire Clairmont, and their friends Dr. John Polidori and Lord Byron passed their time reading some unexceptional horror stories from a book called *Fantasmagoriana*, translated from the German to French by J. B. Eyries. Mary Shelley recollected fifteen years later that Byron then proposed, "We will each write a ghost story."

The competition that followed eventually produced only two completed works, neither of them by the two famous poets. Dr. Polidori's, published as *The Vampyre: A Tale* in 1819, used Byron himself as the model for the evil Lord Ruthven, who in turn served as a model for all the fictional and cinematic vampires that followed. Seventy five years later, his most famous descendant, Count Dracula, became, as we shall see, the embodiment of a whole range of late Victorian fears and greatly eclipsed his ancestor. Polidori's story, the first vampire tale in English, was thus influential, though not itself long lived or particularly memorable.

The same cannot be said for the most enduring result of that informal contest, Mary Shelley's *Frankenstein* (1818), which was an instant success when published, repeated its success when put out in a revised version in 1831, and has remained immensely popular ever since. Though the story of its composition may have had all the elements of a Minerva Press potboiler—the first time woman author was only eighteen years old, her intent was to write yet another Gothic tale, and it was first published anonymously—the story itself certainly was not. It has continued to be treated with respect as a complex parable encompassing such themes as the relationship of women to their children, the power of subconscious drives to take on their own life, and the nature of reality itself. In the twentieth century, *Frankenstein* has spawned not only a myth in its own name, but has been credited with parenting the genre of science fiction.

The reason Mary Shelley was able to take the Gothic novel down this new and fruitful path is hinted at in one other subject that she recalls Byron and Shelley discussing that "wet, ungenial summer," on the evening she had the dream that led to *Frankenstein:*

> Many and long were the conversations between Lord Byron and Shelley, to which I was a devout but nearly silent listener. During one of these, various philosophical doctrines were discussed, among others the nature of the principle of life, and whether there was any probability of its ever being discovered [8].

Mary Shelley had been a "devout but nearly silent listener" all her life. As the daughter of the novelist and philosopher William Godwin, she had been exposed to the intellectual and literary cross currents of the day, once hiding behind a sofa to listen to Coleridge recite his new poem "The Rime of the Ancient Mariner." Although we don't know what other subjects she overheard discussed that summer, it's clear that, as she says in her introduction to the 1831 edition, "invention ... does not consist in creating out of void, but out of chaos; the materials must, in the first place, be afforded" (8).

The search for those materials has ranged far, encompassing the writings of her philosopher father William Godwin and feminist mother Mary Wollstonecraft, John Milton's depiction of Satan and Adam in *Paradise Lost,* as well as what seemed to many to be a monstrous body politic given life in the French Revolution. There is also no doubt that Mary Shelley's life and inner conflicts contributed to the genesis of the Monster.

Our focus here, however, is on the Gothic novel linked to the contemporary belief that science and technology would soon be able to imitate life. Those two elements—one a tradition of popular literature rooted in a shadowy past, the other a half-formed vision of the future—became at this particular time in history, when fused in the Frankenstein story, a way of seeing the world that proved irresistibly compelling. Thus a modern myth was born, one that continued to grow and evolve as the industrialized feudalism of the nineteenth century changed the face of England.

It's important to point out, as Chris Baldick does in his book *In Frankenstein's Shadow*, that many of the "science fiction" aspects of Mary Shelley's novel were offshoots of the later myth, not the novel, which seems to deal with the creation of life, not machinery. However, even in the novel itself, the Monster is a product of technology strictly defined as applied science. When Victor Frankenstein learns the secret of "reanimating lifeless matter," instead of just reviving a corpse, he quickly sets up a one man factory in an attic room in the city of Ingolstadt. There he manufactures a unique product, a Monster who marries the horrors of Gothic ghosts and spectres to the goal of the Industrial Revolution — science used to imitate and replace man.

The creation scene is appropriately lit for a Gothic tale "by the glimmer of a half-extinguished light" (57), while the weather is conventionally wet and dismal. And one of Frankenstein's first encounters with his creation is a variation of the "discovery scene," "the horror behind the curtain," made popular by the Gothic novels of Ann Radcliffe — while he is in a state between sleep and wakefulness, the veil around his bed is lifted to reveal the apparition of the Monster, its hideous form lit by the "dim and yellow light of the moon." This scene, the most famous in the novel, comes at the start of Chapter Five, though Mary Shelley tells us that she wrote it first, inspired, like so many Gothic authors, by a dream — though in this case she calls it a "waking dream." Thus she conceived the novel in the same state as her fictional creator was when he gave life to the Monster.

Much of the rest of the novel replays the concerns of the Gothic story. The gradual decimation of Frankenstein's family over the course of the novel is straight out of the tradition, as is Victor Frankenstein himself, a tortured Gothic protagonist if there ever was one. And the writing is in many places (alas) not much better than many "horrid" works. Although the form of the novel and its psychological subtext are complex and fascinating, what is really new, of course, is the Monster, as well as the setting, which has moved from an idealized and shadowy past to a geographically precise present.

The Monster, endowed by its creator with an otherworldly ugliness no one can look at without a shudder, and an ability to materialize and vanish with astonishing ease, clearly evolved from the supernatural apparitions of horror stories. (At times its creator even calls the Monster a "dreaded spectre," seeing it when no one else present does.) More often, the Monster recalls the horrid creatures in the Gothic novels of Mrs. Ann Radcliffe such as *Mysteries of Udolpho* (1794) or *The Italian* (1797). There, too, the apparitions are the products of a (cruder) technological process, waxworks dummies or other constructions designed to fool those foolish enough to draw aside the veils that conceal them. By banishing the supernatural and providing explanations (no matter how far fetched) for her horrors, Mrs.

Radcliffe brought her stories one step closer to the realm of *Frankenstein*—the domain of monsters manufactured in a contemporary and secular world, not a place where visitors from another, spiritual dimension control the fate of the living.

The Monster in *Frankenstein* is constructed like a machine, made from interchangeable organic parts; it is able to learn to speak and read French, teach itself history and philosophy, and argue that it is fully human and deserves to treated as such. This may at first suggest that Mary Shelley's concerns were not with technological change, since the machinery of the Industrial Revolution was notably deficient in these abilities. However, despite its human origins and accomplishments, the Monster is closely connected to machines as mythologized in the early nineteenth century. For, from the beginnings of modern technology, and especially at the time *Frankenstein* emerged, the equation of the new machines and human beings was powerful, persuasive, and everywhere.

At this time, the rural landscape of England was radically transformed by technology into a country of new cities and new factories, places where people and machines worked together as one. As they rebuilt England and reshaped the world, technology was praised by many as imbuing man with a Godlike power to replace human beings with tireless substitutes. For others, the condition of workers in these modern citadels of industry raised new and disturbing questions about the future of man in a world of machines.

As far back as 1670, the Minutes of the Royal Society record an attempt to imitate life with machinery. Robert Hooke, on February 3, produced a "contrivance of his to try whether a mechanical muscle could be made by art, performing without labour the same office which a natural muscle doth in animals" (Jennings 15). A century later, in 1774, Henri Jacquet-Droz exhibited clockwork figures that Mary Shelley may have seen (they were exhibited throughout Europe and still reside in a museum in Switzerland). One, called the "Draughtsman," could make four different hand drawings. A few years later, Giovanni Aldini and others used electric shock to create momentary movement in the corpses of frogs and executed criminals by inducing muscle spasms.

What unites these experiments (the last mentioned were the source of Shelley and Byron's discussions of the possibility of creating life) was the way technology was conceived at the time *Frankenstein* was created—not only as a way to imitate and replace human power, but as proof that human life was essentially mechanical. For influential philosophers such as Claude Helvetius, people were no more than intricate machines powered by the force that powers the Monster—the galvanic "spark of life." Many were convinced that it was only a matter of time before the dead could actually be reanimated. Given the results when Frankenstein succeeds, it's probable that Mary Shelley agreed with what Coleridge later said about such experiments, that they give "an image of life . . . an image only; it is life in death" (Jennings 181).

Whether technology was welcomed or feared, the metaphor of the machine as man, man as machine kept reappearing. On November 29, 1814, *The Times* proudly announced its first issue printed by what it called "a system of machinery almost organic . . . [which] far exceeds all human powers in rapidity and dispatch." A device to draw, stretch, and twist yarn was described as "a machine . . . with the thought, feeling and tact of the experienced workman," dubbed by its operatives "the Iron Man" (Jennings 192). Andrew Ure, in 1835, echoed the subtitle of *Frankenstein* ("The Modern Prometheus") when he wrote that "the Iron man, as the operatives fitly call it, sprung out of the hands of our modern Prometheus at the bidding of Minerva" (Baldick 123). Some of these new textile machines could even "read" cards that determined the weaving patterns, a crude programming that at the time was equated to human intelligence and engendered absolute amazement.

But a critic of the system, James Phillips Kay, turned the metaphor around:

> Whilst the engine runs the people must work — men, women, and children are yoked together with iron and steam. The animal machine — breakable in the best case, subject to a thousand sources of suffering — is chained fast to the iron machine, which knows no suffering and no weariness [Jennings 185].

Nor was he the only observer to do so. The poet Robert Southy, after visiting Robert Owen's factories at New Lanark in 1819, commented on the same equation: "I never regarded man as machine; I never believed him to be merely a material being; I never for one moment could listen to the nonsense of Helvitius, nor suppose, as Owen does, that men may be cast in a mould (like the other parts of his mill)" (Jennings 157). Still, that goal became the basis of the Industrial Revolution itself, which has been defined as "the substitution of machines — rapid, regular, precise, tireless — for human skill and effort" (Landes 41).

People who had once worked at home and at their own pace in skilled and relatively high paid crafts such as weaving became what were called "hands" since that's all they now were, organic components in the vast machine of the factory, doing mindless work for long hours at miserable pay. And the factories multiplied at an astounding rate. In the first thirty years of the century, the number of power looms, for example, grew from 2400 to well over 100,000 (Landes 86). Coleridge, watching the forging of an anchor at the iron works in Portsmouth in 1804, called the men who worked from four in the morning to nine at night "pitiable slaves" who "become old men in the prime of manhood" (Jennings 122). As the historian David Landes has observed, "The factory was a new kind of prison; the clock a new kind of jailor" (43).

In prisons themselves, actually transforming a man into an organic cog in a huge machine became the most dreaded form of punishment. In 1817, a "gentleman of science" by the name of Cubitt invented the treadmill, first used in Brixton Prison. Shifts of twenty four men served as the source of power for a huge wooden wheel linked by a complex set of gears to a large windmill. The purposeless effort required was so tiring that shifts soon had to be limited to fifteen minutes to avoid total physical collapse. Working in enforced silence, men became the motive force for what its inventor called an "industrial machine" and the inmates called "grinding the wind" (Mayhew and Binney 288). Attempts were made to use Cubitt's invention to perform useful work, but it couldn't be done. Instead, his machine made of interchangeable living parts, like Victor Frankenstein's similar Monster ("invented" the following year), was a useless piece of technological ingenuity which resulted only in increasing the sum total of human misery. And, like Mary Shelley's fictional creation, it was a horrifying analog for the factory system itself.

The Monster's creator, too, is linked to the dehumanizing effects of the Industrial Revolution. Victor Frankenstein, tirelessly working night and day in what he calls "my workshop of filthy creation" sees himself as a factory worker transformed from craftsman to slave: "I appeared rather like one doomed by slavery to toil in the mines, or any other unwholesome trade, than an artist occupied by his favorite employment" (56). A physical wreck, he becomes estranged from his family, whom he never sees. In retrospect, he decides that the worst effect on himself of his ultimately purposeless labors on himself was to "interfere with the tranquility of his domestic affections" (56), to destroy his feeling for both his fellow man and nature while he locked himself away in a factory of his own devising. This same danger was foreseen in the rise of the factory system as early as 1801, when William Wordsworth predicted a "calamitous effect" of "the rapid decay of the domestic affections among the lower orders of society," caused in large part by "the spreading of manufactures through every part of the country" (Jennings 114).

Thus, Monster making took the industrial system to its implied end—turning machines into men and men into organic parts in the greater machine of the factory. That Mary Shelley would adapt the medievalism of the Gothic novel to convey this modern vision is not too surprising, since many of these new castles of industry had their own feudal and paternalistic quality not lost on contemporary observers. Matthew Boulton's huge factory near Birmingham, surrounded by workers' cottages, was a world in itself that resembled the castle seat of a new fiefdom, while the workers at

Richard Arkwright's factories were actually expected to hymn his praises at the start of every shift:

> Come let us all here join in one,
> And thank him for all favours done;
> Let's thank him for all favours still,
> Which he hath done beside the mill [Briggs 64]

Arkwright was both inventor and industrialist, designing both a water frame for cotton spinning and some of the earliest factories in which to use it. Victor Frankenstein, too, both invented and applied his invention, expecting adulation in return. His only stated purpose for the Monster is that "a new species would bless me as its creator and source" (54)—a purposeless goal that finally threatens to replace, not merely human effort, but humanity itself. The process of Monster making in *Frankenstein* thus plays out, in Gothic exaggeration, the fear that the new science and its technological products served some old and questionable motives.

Frankenstein's grandiose dreams and their gruesome results point out the gulf between idealistic fantasy and technological possibility. The "astonishing . . . power" of the secret of life comes to him in an instant, and instantly he resolves to use it. But it is the work of many months to "prepare a frame," as he calls it, to employ this power. Yet, though a "work of inconceivable difficulty and labor" he has no doubt he will succeed, bolstered in his confidence by "the improvement which takes place every day in science and mechanics" (53). From the start, however, he has to make technological compromises: "as the minuteness of the parts formed a great hindrance to my speed, I resolved, contrary to my first intention, to make the being of a gigantic stature" (54).

He also wishes it to be beautiful, though the results disgust anyone who comes near. Its hideousness seems to be the result of its visible internal mechanical structure, the "yellow skin [that] scarcely covered the work of muscles and arteries beneath" (57). Created by its maker to be what he calls a new Adam, the Monster itself finally recognizes that it is a mechanistic reincarnation of Satan. Its repulsiveness (and consequently the rejection that makes it dangerous) is thus directly related not only to the blasphemy of its creator's dream, but to the limits technology forces in the "frame" that brings his dream to life.

Interestingly enough, the first steam engines to appear in England were also of gigantic stature and for similar reasons, "because the mechanical construction of those days necessitated it" (Dickenson 91). It took James Watt seven years to build a smaller version of his steam engine. For the fifty years before that, modern technology meant huge, clumsy mechanical monsters dotting the landscape, powering the weaving machines (also called "frames") and dominating what William Blake, in his poem "Jerusalem" (1808) called the "dark Satanic mills" in the new factory towns. Around them was the ugliness of the growing industrial landscape, the urban slums or what was called the Black Country, a place where foul smelling smoke shut out the sun, and all around was evidence of human misery—a scene as repellent and unnatural as the hideous face of the Monster, the face of the new technology.

Mary Shelley thus gave the world a striking image through which to visualize the fears engendered by the Industrial Revolution. The materials from which it was constructed—Gothic medievalism, the equation of man and machine, and the power of both to dominate and change the landscape—had been part of the response to the new technology long before *Frankenstein.* In 1803, Dorothy Wordsworth, in a striking passage in her *Recollections of a Tour of Scotland,* remarked on a huge machine she, Wordsworth and Coleridge, had seen. Her description uses the same combination of medievalism and modernity as in *Frankenstein*—the factory as a castle with a mechanical giant come to life:

> Our road turned to the right, and we saw . . . a tall upright building of grey stone, with several men standing upon the roof, as if they were looking out over the battlements. It stood beyond the village, upon higher ground, as if presiding over it—a kind of enchanter's castle, which it might have been, a place which Don Quixote would have gloried in. When we drew nearer we saw, coming out of the side of the building, a large machine or lever, in appearance like a great forge-hammer.... It heaved upwards once in half a minute with a slow motion, and seemed to rest to take breath at the bottom . . . it was impossible not to invest the machine with some faculty of intellect; it seemed to have made the first step from brute matter to life and purpose, showing its progress by great power [Jennings 121].

Although this observation could not have influenced Mary Shelley directly (it wasn't published until 1874), clearly she created her Monster from metaphorical components familiar to her readers. The artistic chemistry of that otherwise "ungenial" summer of 1816 enabled her to infuse those tired materials with a spark of new and enduring life, at a time when fascination with industrialization had become tempered with fear. Throughout *Frankenstein,* readers' sympathies are divided between the noble but megalomanical Victor Frankenstein and the pathetic but pathologically destructive Monster, between the questionable dreams of technology and the ambiguous nature of its products. Contemporary feelings about the future of industry were also divided between pride in what ingenuity could achieve and fear of what it might mean for humanity, between a vision of workers as dehumanized parts of an industrial machine and potential revolutionaries bent upon destruction.

That Mary Shelley, the "silent observer" at the center of the Romantic movement, created a model for popular fears of the factory system in her horror story of man and Monster is in concert with what the Romantic poets around her were writing on the subject. William Wordsworth repeatedly examined the implications of industrialization, moving from the admiration expressed in his tour of Scotland in 1803 and his Preface to the Second Edition of *Lyrical Ballads* (1800), (quoted at the start of this chapter, and comparing, again, the new science with the creation of life). By 1814, in the eighth and ninth books of his epic poem *The Excursion*, Wordsworth explicitly described and condemned the evils of the Industrial Revolution. Five years later, the poet Robert Southey concluded that factories "turned men into little more than slaves" and predicted "the destruction of all character . . . the power of human society, and the grace, would both be annihilated" (Jennings 157). And, as we have seen, Coleridge wrote of the factory system as destructive of human values. Mary Shelley was no doubt aware of such widespread and growing concerns; they may well have been discussed the summer that *Frankenstein* was born, since Lord Byron also had a passionate interest in the effects of the new technology upon the lives of the lower classes.

In his first speech to the House of Lords in 1812, Byron had entered a debate upon a Bill designed to make breaking textile frames punishable by death. Although these machines had been around for a long time, the attempt to destroy them, the Luddite Movement (named after an early machine-wrecker, Ned Ludd), was more recent. The first outbreak began Nottingham in 1811 and lasted until 1816; in the spring of 1825 it came to Lancashire, with a thousand power looms destroyed in one week; around 1830 another wave of destruction broke out, this time directed at threshing machines. The workers who participated, known as "Frame-breakers," were protesting not only the loss of work the machines brought but also the impoverishment of those who tended them and the arrogance of the new mill owners. Both movements were near rebellions, accompanied by food riots, widespread crime and violence; the response was armed force and Draconian punishments such as that proposed in the Frame Work Bill.

Byron argued strongly in favor of the rights of the workers, declaring that "these men never destroyed their looms till they [the men] were become useless" (Hansard 968) and that the machines "superseded the necessity of employing a number of workmen, who were left in consequence to starve" (967). He based his opinions on first hand experience, reporting that

> . . . during the short time I recently spent in Nottinghamshire, not twelve hours elapsed without some fresh act of violence; and on the day I left the county I was informed that forty frames had been broken the previous evening [966].

The most significant part of his speech to *Frankenstein* came when Byron predicted what would happen if the proposed law was adopted. He saw a future of unending industrial strife, with men pitted against machines and the law taking the side of the owners, and asked the government a series of rhetorical questions that defined his fears:

> How will you carry the Bill into effect? Can you commit a whole county to its own prisons? Will you erect a gibbet in every field and hang up men like scarecrows? or will you proceed by decimation? place the country under martial law? depopulate and lay waste all around you? . . . Are these the remedies for a starving and desperate populace? [971]

These concerns remained current throughout the time Mary Shelley worked on *Frankenstein* and beyond. Byron composed a song to the Luddites in a letter to Thomas Moore written in December of 1816, while industrial disorders and the threat of bloody repression were realized in the Peterloo massacre of 1819, when a cavalry detachment charged a crowd of unarmed workers, inflicting hundreds of casualties. Shelley himself wrote the poem *The Mask of Anarchy* (1819) to condemn the massacre.

In *Frankenstein,* when the creature's monstrous frame appears among people, they react like Frame-breakers and try to destroy it. In revenge, it indulges its wish to "tear up the trees, spread havoc and destruction" (136), at one point replaying the effects of industrialization in one night by turning a rustic cottage and garden into a Black Country of smoke and desolation. It finally asks Frankenstein to build it a mate, promising they will go off into the wilds of South America and avoid human contact. But his maker, after some indecision, refuses, because he has already witnessed the natural hatred between man and the man-machine he has created.

Frankenstein, like Byron, examines what man's ingenuity might cost him in the future; he decides that to create a Mate would mean "a race of devils would be propagated on the earth, who might make the very existence of the species of man precarious and full of terror. Had I a right, for my own benefit, to inflict this curse upon everlasting generations?" (165) Thus the Gothic curse reemerges, tied to the contemporary fear Byron expressed that technology will be its modern embodiment, that the natural antagonism of man to machine must mean the destruction of one or the other.

All this links *Frankenstein* to another, larger concern of the Gothic novel—the threat to society of revolution. At the Peterloo massacre, the overreaction of the authorities was provoked by the overtones of what had happened in France only a few decades before. The workers, 60,000 strong, marched for suffrage while carrying banners emblazoned with such provocative slogans as "Unity and Strength" and "Liberty and Fraternity"—

The most significant part of his speech to *Frankenstein* came when Byron predicted what would happen if the proposed law was adopted. He saw a future of unending industrial strife, with men pitted against machines and the law taking the side of the owners, and asked the government a series of rhetorical questions that defined his fears:

> How will you carry the Bill into effect? Can you commit a whole county to its own prisons? Will you erect a gibbet in every field and hang up men like scarecrows? or will you proceed by decimation? place the country under martial law? depopulate and lay waste all around you? . . . Are these the remedies for a starving and desperate populace? [971]

These concerns remained current throughout the time Mary Shelley worked on *Frankenstein* and beyond. Byron composed a song to the Luddites in a letter to Thomas Moore written in December of 1816, while industrial disorders and the threat of bloody repression were realized in the Peterloo massacre of 1819, when a cavalry detachment charged a crowd of unarmed workers, inflicting hundreds of casualties. Shelley himself wrote the poem *The Mask of Anarchy* (1819) to condemn the massacre.

In *Frankenstein,* when the creature's monstrous frame appears among people, they react like Frame-breakers and try to destroy it. In revenge, it indulges its wish to "tear up the trees, spread havoc and destruction" (136), at one point replaying the effects of industrialization in one night by turning a rustic cottage and garden into a Black Country of smoke and desolation. It finally asks Frankenstein to build it a mate, promising they will go off into the wilds of South America and avoid human contact. But his maker, after some indecision, refuses, because he has already witnessed the natural hatred between man and the man-machine he has created.

Frankenstein, like Byron, examines what man's ingenuity might cost him in the future; he decides that to create a Mate would mean "a race of devils would be propagated on the earth, who might make the very existence of the species of man precarious and full of terror. Had I a right, for my own benefit, to inflict this curse upon everlasting generations?" (165) Thus the Gothic curse reemerges, tied to the contemporary fear Byron expressed that technology will be its modern embodiment, that the natural antagonism of man to machine must mean the destruction of one or the other.

All this links *Frankenstein* to another, larger concern of the Gothic novel—the threat to society of revolution. At the Peterloo massacre, the overreaction of the authorities was provoked by the overtones of what had happened in France only a few decades before. The workers, 60,000 strong, marched for suffrage while carrying banners emblazoned with such provocative slogans as "Unity and Strength" and "Liberty and Fraternity"—

provocative, at least, to those for whom the memory of the guillotine was recent.

Later in the century, *Frankenstein*'s Monster continued to be used, in political cartoons, for example, to depict the body politic turned ugly and dangerous, a convenient symbol of the frightful spectre of revolution in England or Ireland (see Baldick). Moreover, visualizing the populace as one "person" assembled from the bodies of many goes back much further that Mary Shelley's time. The famous frontispiece of Thomas Hobbes *Leviathan* (1651) shows the state as just such an "artificial man" composed of all men, embodied in the image of sovereignty.

In part, Mrs. Shelley's monstrous creature made from many other humans adapts the image to suggest to those fearful of revolution the dangers of mob rule. Early in the Industrial Revolution, in the politically auspicious year of 1776, an industrialist boasted to James Boswell, "I sell here, Sir, what all the world desires to have,—POWER" (Jennings 73). In the broadest sense, *Frankenstein* examined what technological and political power could create, and how it could redound on its creators.

Thus, the implications of technology and the factory system, as well as the fear of what reaction to that system could do to the state itself, all are echoed in the complex relationship between Victor Frankenstein and his Monster. Frankenstein is both the industrialist and slave in his factory; his creation is both machine as substitute for man, and men united to form a machine. Behind them both is uncertainty and fear, and a sense of urgency about what time will mean for technology. Thus the future is the focus of *Frankenstein*, as the past was for the Gothic novel. (The human relationship to time itself changed as a result of the Industrial Revolution, when the age-old rhythms of work were replaced with the relentless and regular motions of the machine.)

Mary Shelley recalibrated Gothic fictional time — the traditional tale of terror begins and ends in a medieval past, while her story begins in the present and concludes with the Monster "lost in darkness and distance" but not definitely dead. Thus, the horrors of the past were explicitly reflected in the present and left unresolved to threaten the future. The Monster survived the novel in popular art forms as well, its many resurrections on stage and screen beginning only five years later with Richard Brinsley Peake's melodrama *Presumption, or the Fate of Frankenstein*.

The long life of Mary Shelley's Monster in all of its protean power is clear evidence of the vitality of her vision, as is the continuing popularity

*Opposite:* **The image in *Frankenstein* of the useless machine made of human parts was echoed in the treadmill of Victorian prisons. From: Mayhew and Binney, *The Criminal Prisons of London* (1862). Reproduced by permission of Harvard College Library.**

of the novel itself. There are many reasons for *Frankenstein*'s survival, among which is the survival and flourishing of the age of the machine. Throughout the Victorian period, industrialization was a source of pride and poverty: "the cotton mill was the symbol of Britain's industrial greatness; the cotton hand, of her greatest social problem" (Landes 42). Frankenstein's Monster, pleading for acceptance and the right to reproduce while laying waste to both man and nature, and his maker, torn between his duty to humanity and his self-glorification as creator, effectively conveyed that conflict through the powerful vehicle of fantasy.

Another aspect of industrialization was also transforming life early in the nineteenth century; just as industry changed the awareness of time, the revolution in transportation revolutionized the notion of space. As early as 1809, Richard Thevithick had demonstrated a railroad train in Euston Square; in 1814 George Stephenson built a locomotive to use at a colliery — the prototype for those that would, in a few short years, lead trains along tracks criss-crossing Britain. Ships, too, were beginning to be powered by steam; the first one crossed the English Channel in 1812. In 1819, the year after *Frankenstein* was published, Percy Shelley observed the casting of a steam cylinder for a ship and wrote to the maker, "Your boat will be to the Ocean of Water, what this earth is to the Ocean of Aether — a prosperous and swift voyager" (Jennings 159). The dawning age of powered transportation promised to shrink geographical distances and, at the same time, expand each person's universe.

Similarly, Mary Shelley expanded the traditional dimensions of Gothic fictional space; the claustrophobic confines of the underground labyrinth become in *Frankenstein* a pattern of pursuit that covers much of the known world. In the novel (unlike any of the films), the Monster follows Frankenstein from Switzerland up the Rhine through Germany, to England and then to the Orkney Islands, where Victor begins and then abandons his second creature. Then, after Frankenstein's own bride is murdered by the Monster, he pursues it across Europe and Russia and across the Polar wastes.

There seems little reason for all this travel; in part it occurs to indulge Mrs. Shelley's desire to include Romantic "set-pieces" of natural description. But also it keeps the story in almost constant motion, a speeded up rhythm associated from the start of the Industrial Age with the advent of the machine. At the same time, throughout this world spanning pursuit the Monster materializes like a ghost, first haunting its maker's life, then luring him to his death. In bringing the Gothic maze out of the castle cellar and enormously increasing its scope, Mary Shelley makes clear the relationship of her tale of terror to the safe and walled-in world of the horror stories that helped inspire it. There are no limits to her labyrinth and no real end to the pursuit — the path of scientific discovery upon which Frankenstein embarks is endless and unbounded, and it continually conceals the potential for Gothic horror.

At the end of his journey Victor Frankenstein has reversed day for night, living only in dreams of his dead family, yet still ambivalent about the act of creation that led to their destruction. He expresses those doubts to Robert Walton, another explorer stuck in the Polar ice cap on his own voyage of discovery. In fact, Walton is the narrator of *Frankenstein*, relating a series of stories-within-stories. Thus, we first learn of his own failure at finding "domestic affections" and his subsequent obsession to distinguish himself by finding a warm Paradise he believes is hidden beyond the frozen Northern sea.

The irony, of course, is that his travels only take him further from all human contact, just as Frankenstein's obsession to create a "new race of beings" estranges him from the race of human beings around him. While Walton's ship is stuck in the ice, he meets Frankenstein in pursuit of the Monster. Walton listens to and later records Frankenstein's story, which includes his account of what the Monster told him of its life.

The plot thus echoes the pattern of the many Gothic tales that contain sub-plots and legends interrupting the narrative. The difference in *Frankenstein* is that the stories Walton hears are not tacked on, but are integral to the structure of the novel. In fact, as it moves around the world, *Frankenstein* also moves inward, from the witness Walton to his alter ego Frankenstein to his double the Monster. Each tale tells us more about all the participants and is filtered through more of their voices (thus the Monster tells his story to Frankenstein who tells it to Walton who writes it to his sister in a series of letters which constitute the novel which we read). It is a complex and "mechanistic" structure, revealing the inner workings of both the plot and the personalities of the characters, suited to the underlying metaphor of man as machine.

The reader, in sorting through the stories within stories, is forced to take the novel apart, to explore its inner structure, to participate in Victor Frankenstein's work as monster maker. As he collected the parts of cadavers and put together his creation, we are presented with disjointed narratives we must fit together to create *Frankenstein* for ourselves. Thus, we are implicated in the central dilemma of the novel. Just as Victor remains wedded to his creation and repelled by it at the same time, we read on, keeping the story (and the Monster) alive as we continue to turn the pages.

At the end of the novel, the Monster, like the machine, still lives— neither Victor Frankenstein nor Robert Walton nor the reader can kill it off, despite the fear it engenders in all who gave it life. It is last seen heading for the North Pole, promising to destroy itself but reanimated every time the myth re-emerges in our culture.

After Walton witnesses the death of his only friend Frankenstein, then meets the Monster directly and hears its version of events, he reluctantly abandons his own journey, deciding that he cannot risk the lives of his rebellious crew. We leave him as we have been left, in mid journey. The novel ends, like so many Gothic tales, with the representative of a new generation witnessing the destruction of the old. Walton turns back from a path as futile and dangerous as Frankenstein's, away from ruthless scientific discovery and toward the humanity he had abandoned. Yet his ambivalence makes it clear that others will be sure to continue down that path, just as generations of readers, piecing its narrative together over and over again, continue to keep *Frankenstein* alive.

*Frankenstein* as myth has itself traveled well though space, time, and the evolution of technology, from one young woman's "waking dream" to millions of books published in hundreds of languages, to theater and films and popular culture from breakfast cereal to T-shirts. Mary Shelley gave it the impetus, but the power to sustain the myth has come from the way it continues to give form to our fears, among them our ambivalence about the Industrial Revolution. The paradoxical nature of the Monster and its maker, the way the structure of *Frankenstein* makes us read it, the mass production of what Mary Shelley called her "hideous progeny" in all of its forms from art to kitsch, capture our mixed feelings as humans living in a world made by us, but seemingly made for machines.

By the mid-nineteenth century, machines had helped make Britain the richest and most powerful nation on earth, deemed worthy of a celebration the likes of which the world had never seen. Still, the questions raised in Mary Shelley's novel continued to be asked, as her story and other frightening fiction continued to evolve. For, despite the self-satisfaction that marked the public face of Victorian England, most were aware that around and beneath them was a half-hidden Gothic landscape. The children of the horror story, like the Monster in *Frankenstein*, also remained at the edge of popular perception, their vitality insured by the uncertainties undermining the fragile structure of Victorian progress.

# Part Two
# Reading the Landscape (1851–60)

*Chapter Three*
# The City Imagined

> From the form of the city, the style of its architecture, and the economic functions and social grouping it shelters and encourages, one can derive most of the essential elements of a civilization.
>
> —Lewis Mumford

By the middle of the nineteenth century the traditional Gothic horror story had become a backwater of popular fiction, though the cultural contradictions and societal tensions it mirrored were, if anything, heightened. Mid-Victorian England, the center of the industrialized world, had been literally remade by technology; cities mushroomed as rural areas depopulated, while new structures from factories and churches to railroad bridges and stations changed the shape of the landscape.

Around shining monuments to private wealth and public weal appalling slums also flourished, a constant reminder of the human cost of the emerging modern world and a constant threat that the entire edifice could be toppled from below. The Victorian city as constructed and imagined embodied radically different visions of reality; it ranged from a building that had the mass appeal of popular literature to a popular novel that used architecture as its central metaphor. Like all popular art, the shape of the new Victorian landscape came to have its own meaning, expressing in glass, iron and stone the hopes and fears of its audience.

In 1851, the Victorians themselves set out to construct a symbol of what they believed their culture had achieved, a Great Exhibition of the Works and Industry of All Nations. The shape that housed the hundred thousand exhibits of art and manufactured objects was, like the grandiose castles of the creators of Gothic literature, designed to be both a real place and the embodiment of a fantasy, the architectural equivalent of a work of the imagination. A glass building that enclosed space while paradoxically denying its own existence as a solid structure, it also denied the other traditional tenet of architecture—permanence. Transient as a dream, after one summer it was supposed to exist only in the memory of millions. Even though the Hyde Park site was soon given back to nature, the Exhibition gave a significant fraction of the British population an architectural text to read and remember, a summing up in one space of the accomplishments and aspirations of a society proud of them both.

That same year, England's greatest novelist, Charles Dickens, and her first great sociologist, Henry Mayhew, also used a visionary architecture to construct models of Victorian culture. Their aims and methods paralleled those of the organizers of the Great Exhibition, but the results were quite different. Dickens and Mayhew put on exhibit in their writings aspects of England normally hidden from view, housed in an old and familiar literary structure left largely untenanted since the 1830's — the dark and dungeoned castle of the horror story. These two architectural visions, the Crystal Palace of iron and glass and the Haunted Palace of words and pictures, stood in counterpoint, radically opposed models of the lives and landscape that surrounded them.

In fact, as we shall see, though the creators of the Crystal Palace tried to banish the dark fears outside their walls, a shadow persisted. The realities they ignored — the miseries of the mass, the cruelty and exploitation inherent in the social order, and the danger of a collapse into chaos — entered the palace of light under the surface, nearly out of sight, but nevertheless proving the futility of denying the truths behind the images of horror. For the building and its contents, like any work of literature, had a subtext — patterns and images that, from the moment the project was undertaken and the plans published, threatened to erode the fragile facade of self satisfaction embossed upon its gossamer walls.

In 1849, spurred by the success of the Paris Exposition of French Industry, a group of Victorian visionaries in the Royal Society of Arts, with Prince Albert as eager patron, conceived of a vast Exhibition to be held in a temporary building erected for the purpose in Hyde Park. Art, technology, and design would all be represented; huge machines would share space with sculpture, furniture, and the decorative arts. It was to be the greatest world's fair ever seen, testimony to the material progress of all nations, led of course by the British Empire.

But the British organizers of the Exhibition seemed at first unequal to the task. A competition to produce a design for the building led to nearly 250 rejected submissions. With time running short, the Building Committee submitted its own design. This "temporary structure" was to be composed of 15 million bricks and surmounted with an enormous iron dome two hundred feet in diameter; it failed to fulfill all three requirements set out in the original competition — reuse, rapid construction, and low price. The storm of derision that greeted the publication of the design in the *Illustrated London News* on June 22, 1850, seemed about to sink the entire project.

The Commission's design was a failure not merely because of its consummate ugliness, inappropriateness, and disproportion, but because of

The Official Committee Design for the Great Exhibition (plate by Berlyn and Fowler, 1851): This was the plan the public hated, described as "an elephant stepping on a railway shed." Reproduced by permission of the Board of Trustees of the Victoria & Albert Museum.

how all this was read. As an architectural statement, it inadvertently revealed the social order. A classical and decorative dome reminiscent of the classically educated and leisured ruling class sat heavily on brickwork more appropriate for the mills of the industrial classes, and seemed to crush it. (Someone aptly described the design as "an elephant stepping on a railway shed.") The factory system made the Exhibition possible, though the Commission's cast iron dome and endless tiers of identical bricks didn't glorify it, but reflected the gross inequalities and grim esthetics of modern industry. (A decade later, on Brompton Road, the persistent Commission constructed a smaller version with two more modest cast iron domes. It was promptly dubbed the "Brompton boilers" and so thoroughly disliked it was dismantled and removed in 1867.)* At the moment that the Great Exhibition seemed destined to become the great embarrassment, it was saved by a former gardener who designed an enormous, beautiful, and technologically daring structure in just nine days. Joseph Paxton was a Victorian success story, one of the few members of the working class able to rise by luck, brilliance, and determination. Employed at the Horticultural Gardens at Chiswick, he often chatted with the Duke of Devonshire while opening the gate for him. Soon he became the Duke's head gardener at Chatsworth, a

---

* Nearly a century later, Hitler's architect Albert Speer designed a somewhat similar domed horror in Neo-Classical style to be the centerpiece for a Berlin world's fair to take place after the Nazi victory. The symbolism was similar as well.

### 3. The City Imagined

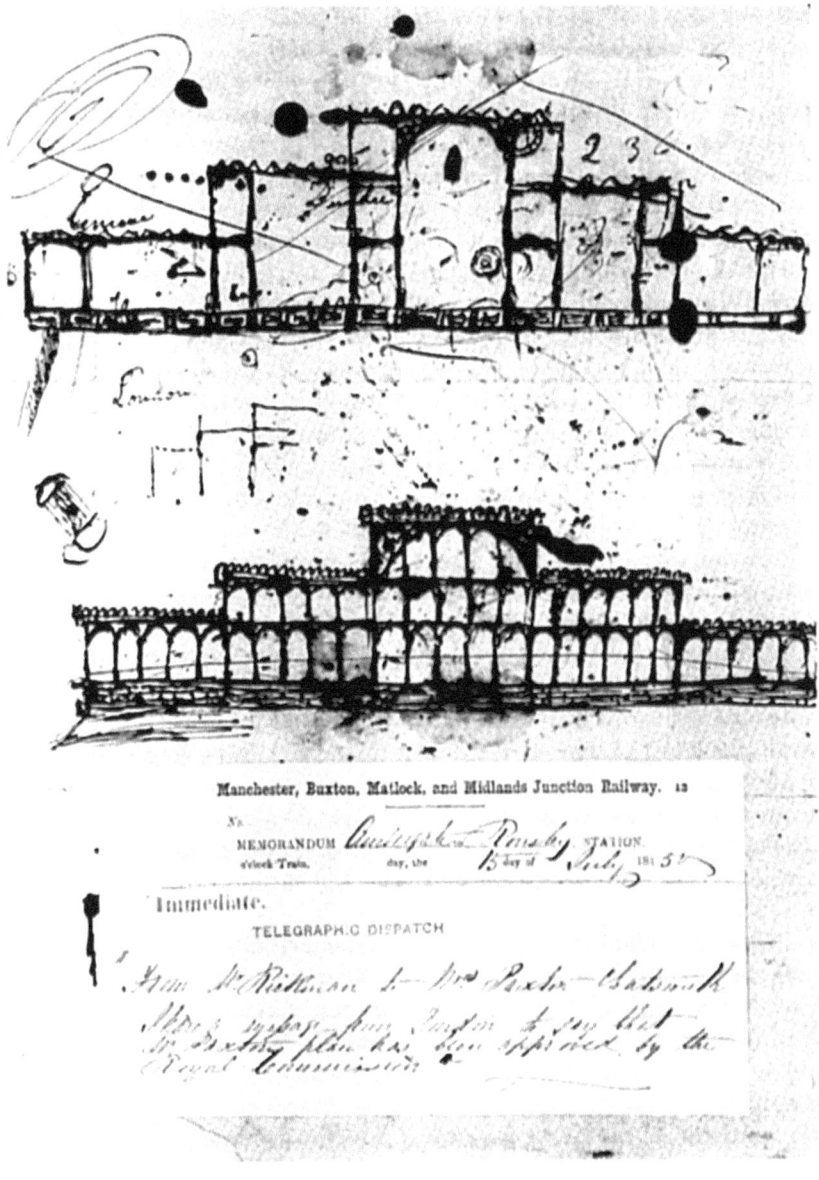

Joseph Paxton's famous blotting paper sketch of his revolutionary last minute design for the Crystal Palace (1851). Reproduced by permission of the Board of Trustees of the Victoria & Albert Museum.

designer of greenhouses and fountains, and finally manager of the Duke's affairs and railway investor at a time when fortunes were made.

Paxton's entire career was, in retrospect, preparation for the moment when, at age 47, he sat in a railway carriage with Robert Stephenson, the celebrated Victorian engineer and railroad magnate who was also a member of the beleaguered Building Committee. As Paxton ate his lunch out of a paper bag, Stephenson scrutinized plans for the Exhibition Hall. Although the submission was very late, Stephenson was enthusiastic. But the Building Committee still hesitated. Then, in a bold and prescient move, Paxton "leaked" the design to the *Illustrated London News,* which printed an engraving of his building on July 6, 1850 with the comment, "Mr. Paxton ventures to think that such a plan would meet with the almost universal approval of the British public, whilst it would be unrivaled in the world" (Kohlmaier 305). He was right on both counts. The response was so overwhelmingly positive that the Committee had no choice. When Douglas Jerrold, writing in *Punch,* gave it a name—The Crystal Palace—the success of Paxton's daring scheme and the Exhibition itself were assured.

Paxton's palace, the most famous building of the nineteenth century, housed a vast array of goods that testified to Victorian ingenuity and accomplishment. But at the same time, the structure itself embodied an ideal, one radically opposed to both the practicalities of cast iron and brick and the Gothic aesthetic of stone towers and dank dungeons. It appealed, as Gothic designs once had, to the fantasies of an entire culture, but (on the surface at least) to their wishes rather than their fears. The tremendous public support given to Paxton's design made clear that something about it was extraordinary, exerting an almost magical lure. The name itself—the Crystal Palace—lifted a rather mundane exhibition of statues and steam engines, trains and tapestries, fountains and furniture, to the realm of romance.

Designers like Paxton were engineers, not architects; their structures were dictated by the potential of new materials to solve structural problems. While working on his sketches, Paxton watched the raising of the third tube of the great iron bridge across the Menai Straits, one of the engineering marvels of the century. Railway tunnels, bridges, and factories, like the slums that propagated around the centers of industry, imposed a new aesthetic on the landscape. It was this new architecture, the seedbed of modernism, that provided the impetus for the Crystal Palace. The rejected design of the Building Committee might have more accurately portrayed the social structure behind industrialization, but the Crystal Palace celebrated the fairy tale promise of the factory system, while using materials and methods dictated by industrial considerations of mass production, low cost, and reusability.

The prevailing aesthetic in public buildings was as unsuitable as the

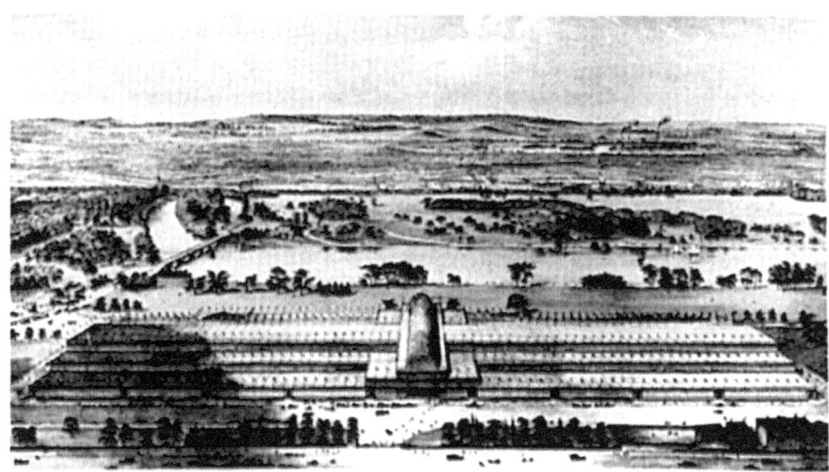

Birdseye view of the Crystal Palace, showing Paxton's innovative use of modular construction on a vast scale. Reproduced by permission of the Board of Trustees of the Victoria & Albert Museum.

Commission's rejected design, for it drew its inspiration, not from the possibilities of the present, but from the remnants of the past. Traditional architecture was engaged in what was known as "The Battle of the Styles," between classicism and medievalism. Massive public building projects such as the British Museum, built by by Sir Robert Smirke from 1823–47, and the Houses of Parliament, rebuilt by Charles Barry between 1840–65, carried out the conflict on the largest scale.

Both architectural styles were more than methods of construction and ornamentation; they articulated in stone two quite different visions of England.

Classicists saw order, stability, and rationalism as paramount. The past had handed down clear and universal rules that governed the shape of things and guaranteed their permanence. As a repository of England's heritage and the spoils of an Empire that compared itself to Greece and Rome, and as a marble metaphor for learning itself, the British Museum's classical design was apt. It was testimony to the attitude, persisting until nearly the First World War, that the proper training for those who would grow to run the Empire was to teach them little more than Greek, Latin, and good sportsmanship.

Victorian Gothicism conveyed a more complex message. Its most ardent proponent was Augustus Welby Pugin, who decorated Barry's Houses of Parliament with an attention to detail that included Gothic style umbrella stands and bell-ropes. A devout Catholic, Pugin headed what was known as the Ecclesiologist movement, designing churches throughout England as medieval structures with ornate interiors, embodying what he called a "sublime and picturesque utility." Pugin's own vision of England was expressed in his book *Contrasts* (1836), where, in a series of essays and drawings, he compared the uniformity and beauty of medieval English buildings with the ugliness of their modern equivalents.

Classicism for him was "pagan" or "heathen." His form of Gothic architecture was a religious text; in it, he saw "the faith of Christianity embodied and its practices illustrated." He dreamed of a neo-Gothic revival, with every public building in the style of the Middle Ages, "the *only rational* architecture, that which can fit itself to all purposes, vulgar or noble" (3). This Christian rationalism, in tune with Evangelical as well as Ecclesiastical thinking, he hoped would be accompanied by a revival of faith and a rejection of the excesses of nineteenth century materialism.

The popularity of medieval architecture a half century earlier was, of course, due to an entirely different set of values. Gothic literature, like the Gothic structures built by its founders—Walpole's Strawberry Hill and Beckford's Fonthill Abbey—was not inspired by Catholic or Evangelical piety but by English Romanticism. The fantastic architecture of this imaginary England was, as we have seen, decayed and often in ruins, redolent more of the feudal than the spiritual. Lovers of the picturesque were drawn to what was wild and disordered—irrationality expressed in landscape or stone. Their medievalism meant images of absolute power and moral decay, a labyrinth of possibilities and terrors enshrouded in gloom.

Gothic visionaries saw the world, nature, and the self as potentially dangerous and largely unexplored. The ruin time had wrought to Gothic masonry implied both an underlying instability in the present and a feeling that the future would not echo the past, but slowly destroy it. Such structures were undermined, as well, by the dark labyrinths that wound beneath them, concealing horrors behind every turning. The architecture of Gothic literature was diametrically opposed to the classicist's faith in stability and order, as well as the light and optimism that filled and fueled both the centerpiece of the Great Exhibition and Pugin's vision of a revival of medieval piety and purpose. When the gloom and terrors of the Gothic castle returned in literature and sociology, they dominated the dark corners of the mid-Victorian landscape, around and beneath the "official" monuments to faith in the past and hope for the future—turning the modern city into the text for a tale of terror.

Thus engineers, designers, and creators of popular fiction all used architecture to express radically opposed visions of England. At mid century, the Great Exhibition suddenly appeared as a spectacular and influential model. It was an engineer's model, and its radical design—winning out over hundreds of classical, medieval and mundane competitors—promised that new materials and methods of construction could remake the urban landscape. Paxton's building, designed to last for one summer, survived, reerected elsewhere, for almost a century, remaining the first and most grandiose symbol of the aesthetic of the modern world.

Pugin's aesthetic of church inspired medievalism was barely represented in Paxton's palace. Although he was a Commissioner of the Exhibition, Pugin's designs were relegated to a small Medieval Court in the furniture section. The next year he suffered a bout of violent madness, threatened the life of a friend, and was confined for a time in Bedlam. He died that September at the age of forty. Pugin's self-destruction — curiously reminiscent of the fate of so many Gothic villains — was probably unrelated to the blow struck at his lifelong obsession, though other arbiters of taste tended to react almost as strongly.

The painter and poet William Morris' outrage at the style of Paxton's building and the vulgarity of its contents led him to retreat to Oxford to try to recreate an idealized Middle Ages through art, crafts and literature. He even commissioned his own structure, a house in old English style at Bexley Heath. Thomas Carlyle called the Crystal Palace a "strange edifice" and the Exhibition a "monstrous place;" John Ruskin, the Victorian high priest of taste, published the first volume of his master work praising Venetian Gothic, *The Stones of Venice*, the month the Exhibition opened, and defiantly began the second volume on May 1, 1851 — Opening Day. He had little use for the aesthetic of engineering, or for Paxton's Crystal Palace, dismissing it as hardly worthy to be considered a building at all.

Ruskin called it an overgrown cucumber frame, and that's exactly what it was. When working as a gardener, Paxton had been dissatisfied with the design of greenhouses, which used heavy woodwork and nearly opaque glass. For twenty years, he had experimented with ways to bring in sunlight, even inventing a machine to fabricate window sashbars. The result was a series of hothouses, culminating in the Great Conservatory at Chatsworth, built between 1836 and 1840, which covered nearly an acre. In 1849, designing a building to house a giant water lily he had coaxed into flowering, he experimented with the lightest of structures — hollow iron columns supporting expanses of glass. Although greenhouses were built throughout Europe at this time (the Palm House built in Kew Gardens by Richard Turner and Decimus Burton between 1844–48 still stands) Paxton saw the potential for using modern materials and methods to house more than botanical specimens.

The Crystal Palace was not only a beautiful building, constructed entirely of ironwork tracery and panes of glass, but an engineering triumph. Because of the interchangeable, prefabricated parts, the entire structure was put up in twenty two weeks and taken down even more quickly. This was possible even though the proportions were staggering — the building covered nineteen acres enclosing 33 million cubic feet of space, with almost

**Photograph of South Transept of the Crystal Palace, by Owen and Ferrier (1851). Reproduced by permission of the Board of Trustees of the Victoria & Albert Museum.**

two miles of galleries, almost three hundred thousand panes of glass, 30 miles of gutters, and 202 miles of Paxton's patented window sash bars (Kohlmeier 306)! Throngs of spectators paid just to watch it go up. They marveled not only at the enormity of the project, but also at the ingenious

Photograph showing the North transept, the famous tree, and the floor, beneath which children gathered garbage (1851). Reproduced by permission of the Board of Trustees of the Victoria & Albert Museum.

construction techniques (including wheeled carts for the glaziers that moved along window sashes doubling as tracks, and hollow columns that also served as drainpipes). The novelty of its construction methods, the audacity of its design, made it more than just another building, or even another work of modern engineering. It was a statement that defined a new age.

Still, the uneasiness with that age is evidenced by the fact that it took nearly a century for architects to use Paxton's innovations widely. Paxton himself was so taken with the idea of glass and iron construction that he later advocated, as Pugin did with Church Gothic, that his designs be adopted wholesale, proposing vast covered parks, buildings, and boulevards that were never built—even a private home made almost entirely of glass. In fact, though the concepts underlying the Crystal Palace had far reaching influence (it was the precursor of the ubiquitous "glass box" of the mid twentieth century), the only structures built in the nineteenth century that resembled it (aside from greenhouses and winter gardens) were those other temples to progress, the new railroad stations. In 1868, the St. Pancreas railroad station and its adjoining hotel were completed. The absurd contrast between the station, with its 243 foot wide roof of glass and cast iron, and the hotel, in High Gothic masonry and spires, made clear that for decades to come the new engineering concepts would be considered fit only to house the machines of the new engineers.

However, the Crystal Palace did become the model for many exposition centerpieces to follow. Like the glass halls of the Paris World Exhibitions of 1855 and 1900, the giant molecule of the 1955 Brussels Worlds Fair, or the Main Pavilion, White City, Trylon and Perisphere, Space Needle, Unisphere and Wonderwall of a century of American expositions, it was a grandiose public statement. Coupling massive proportions and radical materials to imagination and impermanence, the Crystal Palace, like its successors, tried to tie technology, art and industry to the evanescent appeal of fantasy.

At the same time, by their very insubstantial and outlandish design, these cities of the imagination hinted at the fragile nature of the dreams that gave them shape and at the distance those dreams still were from the contemporary structures just outside their gates. Visitors to a century of worlds' fairs have been dazzled by visions of a better tomorrow, but at the same time reminded that the flimsy structures around them would soon be rubble, broken promises of a future that never quite arrives, while the grimmer world they return to carried on.*

Glass walls and ceilings would, of course, never suit a place where dark secrets need be kept, but were perfect for an exhibition such the one housed in the Crystal Palace. Not only did the design let in daylight, it

---

*The Crystal Palace itself did survive the Exhibition. It was rebuilt on an even more grandiose scale at Sydenham, in South London, where it remained as a much loved pleasure palace until a devastating fire in 1936. Paxton's building was believed totally lost until 1985, when pieces of the original structure that had not been reassembled were found in a dusty warehouse in London, forgotten for over a century.

blurred the line between outdoors and in, between nature and the enclosed interior space that defines architecture. Leigh Hunt called it more a bazaar than a palace; all the marvelous goods—from working steam engines to household furniture, locomotives to table decorations, massive sculpture to miniature paintings—were displayed in a space as close as one could get to the open air. In fact, when critics objected to cutting down some trees that stood on the site, Paxton modified his design, adding a huge glass transept to enclose them; thus Nature joined the display of Art and Industry. (According to a rumor that circulated at the time, the trees were infested with sparrows, which threatened to leave their mark on the spectators. Shooting them was out of the question, with acres of glass all around, and trapping them seemed impossible. The Queen herself was said to have gone to the Duke of Wellington, hero of Waterloo, for advice. The old warrior reportedly solved the problem with three words: "Try sparrow-hawks, ma'am".)

In Paxton's glass building, light was shed on every corner of the Victorian world. This was a building without a basement, with no dark corners, with no past. In the galleries were miles of labyrinths, but all above ground, clearly marked, and with no unpleasant surprises. And it generated its own texts. The *Official Catalogue* published after the Exhibition ended duly recorded every possible statistic, down to the numbers of buns consumed (1,804,698). The authors even overcame their reticence and, in the interest of thoroughness, informed the public that 827,820, or 14 percent of the visitors, paid to use the conveniences "in addition to an equal if not larger proportion of gentlemen who made use of the urinals, of which no account was kept" (an oversight that clearly troubles the authors).

This compulsive recordkeeping was very much a part of the age. In 1833 the Royal Statistical Society had been founded, while Charles Babbage founded the Statistical Society of London a year later. The Crystal Palace Exhibition became a demonstration of the power of statistics and led to the First International Statistical Congress three years later. For the next twenty years the compiling of tables and numbers (inspired by the growth of the insurance industry, the use of the census, and numerous fact finding Royal Commissions) became a passion of the times.

The recordkeeping at the Crystal Palace reinforced the implied message of the Exhibition and the building itself—everything (or nearly everything) can and should be open to view, understood rationally and scientifically; doing so will banish the darkness of the soul and the ignorance of the species. Both the practitioners of the new science (such as Adolphe Quetelet, who invented what he called "moral statistics") and the Exhibition organizers shared the same hopes; by shedding light on the breadth of human accomplishment, by understanding the patterns that underlie human activity from the trivial to the profound, war and other forms of human misery would be made obsolete. Thus, the material progress celebrated in this vast structure gained a spiritual justification.

When Paxton added the soaring transept to accommodate the trees, what was originally designed to be a rectangle became a huge cross. The building now resembled a church, or more exactly, what one historian, Edward Rolt, called "a great cathedral dedicated to the worship of material progress" (139). The opening of the Exhibition on May 1, 1851, was described by the newspapers as a solemn spiritual event, with *The Times* even comparing the Queen surrounded by the representatives from around the world to "the day when all ages and climes shall be gathered round the Throne of their Maker."

Moreover, as a palace Paxton's building encouraged another dream, that progress would banish poverty and create a new aristocracy open to all humankind. William Thackeray, in his breathless ode to the Exhibition, celebrated the event as symbolic of the awakening of England from its sleepy agricultural past, the creation of a new rational order that nonetheless harks back to a medieval fantasy:

> A quiet green but few days since,
> With cattle browsing in the shade;
> And here are lines of bright arcade
> > In order raised!
>
> A palace as for fairy Prince,
> A rare pavilion, such as man
> Saw never since mankind began,
> > And built and glazed!

The common theme of the commentaries after the Exhibition closed was that it was bound to usher in a new era of prosperity, mutual understanding, and peace. The *Athenaeum* of October 18 recognized there was a grimmer world outside the fantasyland of the Crystal Palace, but concluded:

> The tale of Hyde Park in 1851 will fall on the page of history. Fallen thrones will lie around it: here the Saturnalia of power, there the wild excesses of popular freedom ... everywhere anarchy, repression, conspiracy, darkness, dismay and death. In the midst ... rises up the great figure of the Crystal Palace to redeem the age.

Thus the optimism of the Victorian spirit was the substance from which the Crystal Palace was created; its tremendous success in the summer of 1851 showed that people wanted to believe in those dreams, or at least to keep dreaming. That such feelings were fantasies soon became evident. Although many felt the Crystal Palace would usher in a new age of architecture, it had little immediate influence on the Gothic revival, which continued unabated. Paxton's triumph remained an architectural aberration precisely because of the element of fantasy that made it possible.

And there were those who, from the start, feared the dream of the Crystal Palace could become a nightmare, who read a frightening message in the palace of glass. Critics of Paxton's design (including *The Times* and the Astronomer Royal) were convinced that it would collapse in the first gale. When a windstorm that came up during construction caused no damage, Paxton's design was vindicated. To set to rest lingering doubts about the strength of the building, he had carts full of cannonballs trundled down the galleries. Still, people worried. On opening day, a military salute was planned; one school of thought held that the noise of the guns would cause every pane of glass to shatter, shredding the Queen and the throngs who came to watch her declare the Exhibition open. These fears point up the other side of the message of the Crystal Palace—the building, like the vision that inspired it, was seen as a castle in the air, destined to come crashing down from an act of nature or the sounds of war.

Belief that the Exhibition foretold an aristocracy for all was also quickly shattered. Though Paxton wanted admission to be free, this revolutionary idea was soon rejected. There were even different days with different admission prices, to keep the upper classes from mingling with the lower orders. In fact, near the end of the Exhibition when a handsome profit was assured, the Commissioners not only refused to allow free admission on certain days, but would not allow the price to go below one shilling, thus effectively shutting out the vast underclass eking out an existence within a mile or two of Hyde Park.

Among the exhibits were further hints that the promises of Victorian materialism did not extend to all who had made it possible. Engineering marvels were the centerpiece of the Exhibition. Highly polished and decorated steam engines powering the exhibits were works of kinetic art and visible symbols of the power of technology to transform the lives and landscape of England. Nowhere was the price paid for progress in human lives and misery made clear. One example: in the previous twenty years, more than six thousand miles of rails, bridges and tunnels had been thrown across the land—one of the greatest engineering feats in history. Yet the human costs had been enormous. Building one railroad tunnel in 1845 took the lives of more workers, in proportion to the size of the force, than were killed at Waterloo. Christopher Hobhouse has written of the exhibits, "Perhaps the spirit of the age was best exemplified in a mine-cage designed to prevent 'destruction to property' in case the rope snapped" (73).

The artistic side of the Exhibition had its own disturbing subtext. Everyone who has examined the collection from the vantage point of a later time has commented on the remarkably hideous furniture and household

58    Part Two: Reading the Landscape (1851-60)

I: Two popular mid-Victorian images, of the chained nude and the veiled woman, dominated the fantasy worlds of art and popular literature in the form of statues of slaves and stories of veiled ghosts. They also were reproduced in the darkest corners of reality—in the subterranean worlds of mines and prisons.

*Veiled Female Prisoner at Surrey House of Correction* (1862). Reproduced by permission of Harvard College Library.

*Top: Half naked girl chained to a Mine Cart,* from the *First Report of the Commissioners of the Children's Employment Commission, on Mines* (1842). Reproduced by permission of Harvard College Library. *Bottom: Veiled Slave,* by Raphaele Monti, from the Crystal Palace Exhibition of 1851. Reproduced by permission of the Trustees of the Wallace Collection.

items. Every inch of the most mundane object was encrusted with ornamentation, stamped out by the new mechanical processes at little cost. Thus, the idea of an aristocracy of everyman was translated into unrestrained vulgarity for the middle class. The new manufacturing processes also brought uselessness within the reach of many. Visitors were treated to vast arrays of bric-a-brac, certified as "artistic" or "ingenious," and ranging from a pocket knife with eighty blades and a centerpiece containing representations of dogs and dead rats (a design of Prince Albert), to cunning arrangements of stuffed frogs, kittens, and rabbits.

In an exhibit labeled "Military Engineering" was a direct reminder of the outside world of "darkness, dismay, and death" that the Exhibition excluded and was supposed to banish—a selection of shackles, leg irons, manacles, fetters, and handcuffs made for export to the American slave states. The items in the sculpture galleries suggested a similar interest closer to home since many (including the most popular piece of art in the Exhibition, Hiram Power's "The Greek Slave") depicted nude women in chains. Like the rest, Power's work is totally undistinguished except for the titillation value of its subject matter; in the words of the caption, written by the sculptor, "the figure is that of a young and beautiful Greek girl, deprived of her clothes and exposed for sale before the licentious gaze of some wealthy Eastern barbarian." The irony of this line may have escaped Powers, as Victorians believed they gazed with artistic and not licentious passion. However, he ends his caption with another curious remark: "The chains on her wrist are not historical, but have been added as necessary accessories."

Two other much admired works were Le Chesney's study of an eagle attacking a nude woman and John Bell's bronze statue of *Andromeda Exposed to a Sea Monster* with the figure attached to a rock by what looks like a bicycle chain. Other statues included more Greek slaves, a *Circassian Slave Exposed in the Market* and R. Monti's *Veiled Slave* (needless to say, according to Victorian sculptors, slaves were almost always beautiful young women)*. The most colossal work of art was Professor Kiss's zinc statue *The Amazon*, with the half nude figure under attack by an enormous tiger. What passed as art was, then, dominated by sexually charged images of nude women captives, humiliated or threatened by symbols of masculine power. Underlying it all may have been a male fear of emasculation by women, since a much admired piece, G. Geef's *Lion in Love* (based on a painting by Camille Roqueplan), depicted a semi-clothed woman using huge marble

---

*Though much in the minority, male nudes were represented, often by figures of Prometheus or St. Sebastian. They, however, presented special problems to the Victorians. After the statues were moved to Sydenham, a "committee of 13 prominent persons" protested the affront to decency of the male nudes, and they were all emasculated with a hammer and chisel.

nailclippers to declaw a dangerous lion she has captivated by her beauty.

The Crystal Palace Exhibition became then, an enormous work of popular culture that expressed both the product of conscious wishes and the disturbing sexual and sadistic imagery of the unconscious. But this was no individual nightmare. It was the collective vision of an entire culture. The Utopia in Paxton's glass case had some unpleasant, but seemingly "necessary accessories"; wealth was built upon technological power and human misery, while female beauty was based upon representations of shame, slavery, and subjugation. As in the age of the Gothic novel, the hidden side of society and the lives of individuals were united by powerful imagery.

The distinguishing characteristic of the horror story—a woman held captive in a castle and pursued by a man with dark designs upon her—was echoed in the marble motifs of the Victorian nude. A commentary on *The Veiled Slave* makes it clear that at least one observer, though sharing the sexism of his time, clearly recognized that something was odd about an aesthetic ideal that repeatedly connected women and slavery: "We confess ourselves no advocate for that style of art which avails itself of the beauty of the female form for the purpose of exhibiting the debased consequences of the misplaced power of her natural protector" (Beaver 61).

Because of the transparency of the walls of the Crystal Palace, paintings were banished, thus depriving visitors of the mainstay of the Royal Academy—photographically painted nudes. In painting and literature as well as sculpture, naked females were bound, humiliated and tortured for the rest of the century, distanced from contemporary reality only by the guise of a classical, historical, or mythological subject. Andromeda, chained to her rock and threatened by a sea monster, was always popular, the subject of paintings by Edward Poynter, Fredric Leighton, and Gustav Dore among others. Dore made over a quarter million pounds between 1850 and 1870 with paintings and engravings on subjects such as Andromeda or Paola and Francesca—the latter, called *The Tortured Lovers* (1863), was perhaps his most successful work. It was rapturously described by the Rev. Francis Kilvert, blissfully unaware of the de Sadean nature of his praise of the

> beautiful girl stripped naked of her blue robe and stabbed in the side under the left breast.... The naked girl is writhing and drawing up one of her legs in an agony.... The anguish of death is stamped upon her white and sharpening, yet still lovely features, but her soul is rapt above her pain in an ecstasy of love [Pearsall, *Nights* 128].

The connection between visions of slavery and the shape of the social structure had been noted directly, if in a somewhat different context, by a workman at a public meeting a few years before the Great Exhibition. He compared his state to that of the slaves of the West Indies: "I am a slave to the classes above me . . . I work hard, and cannot get food for myself and my children . . . I am whipped in the belly, while the black slave was only beaten on his fat back" (Dodds 11). John Stuart Mill, in *The Subjugation of Women* (1869), linked image and reality even closer when he described the Victorian wife as ". . . the actual bondservant of her husband, no less so, as far as legal obligation goes, than slaves" (462).

Thus, one powerful set of images—of domination, humiliation, torture and bondage—continued to recur, reminiscent of the worst excesses of the age of the horror story, and a reminder of the darkest corners of mid-Victorian society. They united an artistic vision of beauty, the patriarchal household, secret passions like the "English vice" of flagellation and the enormous subculture of prostitution, and the wage slavery of an entire class chained to the contrivances in the new factories. In addition, being tied and whipped was a regular activity in the British Navy and English public schools (one day in June 1832 at Eton, eighty boys were flogged). It was also a standard legal punishment administered to children for a variety of offenses from petty larceny to "repeated misconduct." The late Victorian explorer and journalist Henry M. Stanley recalled that when he was a child in St. Asaph's workhouse in the 1850's a boy was flogged to death by a schoolmaster (Chesney 19).

What was revealed to a close reader of the images, objects, and language that defined mid Victorian culture behind the glass facade was a tale of terror that threatened the fragile fantasy of civilization presented to the crowds who thronged to London in the summer of the Crystal Palace. In fact, the idea of the crowd itself became a source for another set of fears, another reason that the promise of the Great Exhibition was left unrealized, another stepchild of the horror story.

During the 140 days that the Exhibition was open over six million tickets were sold, including three quarters of a million season tickets; it is estimated that about 17 percent of the entire population of Great Britain at the time came to the Crystal Palace. These enormous masses of people (as many as 110,000 on a single day) remembered the Exhibition as one of the great moments of their lives and indelibly stamped the message of the Crystal Palace on the culture of the second half of the nineteenth century. They were a remarkably well mannered horde, with very few violent incidents on record. Beforehand, however, many had anticipated great danger. The Prince of Prussia was allowed to attend only after a long struggle; his father felt a revolutionary disturbance inevitable.

Charles Babbage, who put models of his "calculating engines"—the ancestors of the computer—on display, recorded the fears of Londoners, who not only objected to the noise and disturbance, but anticipated an outbreak of the plague and, worse, believed that London would be overrun by revolutionaries who might take possession of the city. The Duke of Wellington shared these concerns and advocated the use of 15,000 troops to keep order (Babbage 29). In some respects, the fears were justified. Luddites no longer attacked the factories, but many other mass popular movements seemed on the verge of turning into rebellion. Workingmen's associations were formed by builders, bakers, tailors, and other groups in the laboring classes; the anti–Temperance movement was fueled by enormous meetings of discontented workers; reestablishment of the Roman Catholic hierarchy in England in 1850 led to huge anti–Popery demonstrations.

The greatest threat to the established order in mid century was the Chartists, a mass movement of workingmen who petitioned for universal male suffrage. In 1841, the Chartist cause seemed to have died out after a threatened general strike, a wild riot in Birmingham, a march on London, and a confrontation with authority that left a dozen men dead and some 400 in prison. Then, three years before the Great Exhibition, the movement threatened to revive when mass meetings were scheduled and a final, huge petition was sent to Parliament demanding voting rights for the disenfranchised six sevenths of the adult male population.

This was also the year, 1848, that half the thrones in Europe were rocked by revolution, while Ireland also was in the midst of revolutionary fervor spurred by the devastation of the "Hungry Forties." Authorities reacted to the Chartist demonstration with troops and 170,000 special constables; the Bank of England was surrounded with artillery and sandbags. In the face of such opposition, the movement petered out.

These periodic mass demonstrations and riots were often put down by the authorities by an equally massive show of force. In 1830, starving laborers destroyed property in sixteen English counties; over a thousand rioters were imprisoned or transported to Australia, and nine were hanged. One of these was a nineteen year old, "whose chief offense was that he had hit a prominent financier with a stick and severely damaged his hat" (Richter 16). Although such Draconian punishments had largely disappeared by the 1850's, the fear of class war that had inspired them remained. The conventional picture of a stable Victorian era is wrong. Frustration with the slow pace of social and political reform and reaction to the harshness of economic injustice continually stirred the populace, often to riot.

The site of the Great Exhibition itself afterwards became the scene of some of the largest public disorders in the century. In 1866 and 1867, huge crowds calling for reform assembled in Hyde Park. The first of these demonstrations was met by over two thousand constables and soldiers attempting to enforce the ban on public speaking in the park. The next year, a gathering of one hundred and fifty thousand people overwhelmed the authorities, who stood by. From then on, Hyde Park became the site of mammoth public meetings. One tangible result of these confrontations, which established the right of the people to use the parks to exercise free speech, is the Speakers' Corner.

The ruling classes feared these continual mass demonstrations, for in the *vox populi* they heard a mob capable of destroying the fragile structure of society. When a mass meeting of a working men's society was announced in 1866, Lord Ellenborough invoked the memory of the fall of the French monarchy, adding that the demonstration "means Revolution and nothing less, and under the circumstances that object would be accompanied by the sacking of London. It must be met accordingly" (Richter 57). (In fact, in 1886 a mob of unemployed workmen stoned the aristocratic gentlemen's clubs in Pall Mall, led by a socialist agitator carrying a red flag and preaching revolution.)

Even when crowds gathered only for entertainment, they sometimes displayed an undertone of barely suppressed violence. The other great exhibitions of the period were public executions, not outlawed until 1868. In 1849, when two notorious murder cases ended at the scaffold, as many as 100,000 people attended the spectacles, some arriving by special excursion train. They watched either from the streets or from rooms overlooking the scaffold and rented for the occasion. Their loutish behavior was for many a foretaste of what could happen in Hyde Park two years hence.

In fact, on November 12, 1849, *The Times* announced the proposed Great Exhibition and invited the world; the next day, its account of the execution of Fredrick Manning and his wife for the robbery and murder of her lover begins by comparing it to just such an event: "For days past . . . the immediate neighborhood had presented the appearance of a great fair, so large were the crowds of people collected there, and so intense the state of excitement in which all present seemed to be." Among this mass of humanity were "thieves, low prostitutes, ruffians, and vagabonds of every kind . . . with every variety of offensive and foul behavior"—such is the report in *The Times* of another member of the crowd, Charles Dickens, who was appalled by the spectacle. He saw in the mood of the mass and the horror of the proceedings a vision of mankind "fashioned in the image of the Devil."

Dickens' letter contains both images of horror and a warning that the crowd is a threat to the survival of society itself:

> I believe a sight so inconceivably awful as the wickedness and levity of the immense crowd collected at the execution this morning could be imagined by no man . . . the shrillness of the cries and howls . . . from a concourse of boys and girls . . . made my blood run cold. I do not believe any community can prosper where such a scene of horror as was enacted this morning outside Horsemonger gaol is presented at the very doors of good citizens.

## 3. The City Imagined

The mobs that threatened the social order throughout the period were the obverse of the orderly masses at the Great Exhibition, evidence that there could be another, more horrifying face to the crowd. A model of Victorian prosperity, the Crystal Palace stood in the center of a century of popular discontent and disruption. It is no surprise that free admission was never permitted; imagining huge numbers of poor people set loose in a glass palace caused many to see the spectre of disaster.

Fear of the crowd gone mad was no doubt fostered by the phenomenal popularity of a book published in 1841 (and still in print today), Charles Mackay's *Extraordinary Popular Delusions and the Madness of Crowds*. Mackay chronicled mass delusions and movements in history, from the Crusades to alchemy, the witch mania to the Tulip mania, with the accent on the terrifying detail and the instructive anecdote, designed to "show how easily the masses have been led astray . . . even in their infatuations and crimes" (xxvii). Even though Mackay's only discussion of contemporary England is benign—he examines the "Popular Follies of Great Cities" in a short last chapter—the implications of the book as a whole must have been threatening to mid Victorians. The year after the Great Exhibition, Mackay wrote a preface to a new edition that expressed those fears directly:

> In reading the history of nations, we find that, like individuals, they have their whims and their peculiarities; their seasons of excitement and recklessness. . . . We find that whole communities suddenly fix their minds upon one object, and go mad in its pursuit" [xix].

In the era of the Great Exhibition, new forms of popular literature fed the fixations of the mass reading public, as Gothic literature had earlier in the century. Each of the notorious murder cases was followed in the newspapers, with every sordid detail recounted; afterwards, penny broadsheets were sold in enormous quantities (over 2 million in the case of the Mannings) detailing the crime and the last moments of the criminals in prose and verse. The Manning case had a particularly huge impact in part because of the sexual overtones and the conviction of a woman; "sensation" novels about female poisoners, such as Mary Braddon's *Lady Audley's Secret* (1862) were soon to become all the rage. The case also had the familiar architecture of the Gothic story—sketches of the Manning house pointed out the spot under the kitchen floor where the victim had been found, buried in quicklime, partly decomposed and with eighteen severe head wounds. A public weaned on the gruesome discoveries in secret places that laced the cheap bluebooks known as "shilling shockers" was back in familiar territory.

The horror stories that replaced the fantastic tales of medieval superstition and supernatural terror were of two types. Apart from the feeble remnants of Gothic literature were stories of contemporary crime—fiction and non-fiction—that also emphasized gruesome discoveries and dark secrets. Although they had their heyday at mid-century, none survived beyond their time. But there was another way the language of the tale of terror was translated for a new audience—in fiction and non-fiction that dealt with the condition of the crowd locked out from the Crystal Palace, only hinted at within its walls. Those works became structures to contain the fears that lurked behind the facade of Victorian optimism, building materials for another kind of visionary architecture more in tune with the realities of the modern world.

In both realistic fiction and sociological analysis, images familiar to the devotee of horror stories—the dark labyrinth, family curse, haunted castle and shocking discovery—were given new life. No longer confined to a fantasy which took place in a safely remote time and place, Gothic images now illuminated contemporary reality. Next to the Crystal Palace stood the Haunted Palace; by mid century it was an institution large enough to hold all those locked out of Paxton's structure, all those denied a place in the Exhibition's vision of a bright and shining future.

*Chapter Four*
# Beneath the Crystal Palace

> Seeing the dark and impenetrable slums, I see our civilization as a thin film lying over a volcanic pit. Some day the pit will break through and devour us all.
> —Charles Kingsley

Among the crowds at the Crystal Palace was Charles Dickens, who visited it twice. Although Joseph Paxton was his friend and Dickens admired the technical skill that went into designing and constructing the building, what was inside the glass walls bothered him. He wrote his assistant William Henry Wills that he had an "instinctive feeling against the Exhibition of a faint, inexplicable sort" (Mackenzie 237). Dickens was not hostile to science and technology (John Ruskin called him "a leader of the steam-whistle party *par excellence*") but he did object to huge systems that reduced people to ciphers and, most of all, to smugness and self-satisfaction. In a letter to Mrs. Lavina Wilson, Dickens joked about the "horror" he found in the Great Exhibition and, particularly, in the enthusiasm others expressed about it:

> I have a natural horror of sights, and the fusion of many sights in one has not decreased it. I am not sure I have seen anything but the fountain and perhaps the Amazon. It is a dreadful thing to be obliged to be false, but when anyone says, 'Have you seen...?' I say, "Yes" because if I don't, I know he'll explain it, and I can't bear that!! [Dickens, *Letters* I 257]

At this time Dickens was at the height of his career, having just published *David Copperfield* and in the midst of launching his magazine, *Household Words*. The month after visiting the Exhibition he moved into his new house in Bloomsbury and began thinking about his next novel, a work much different from the human comedies and family histories that marked his rise to popular acclaim. It was to have a plot with "sensation novel" elements of murder, mystery, and detection, and the dark setting of Gothic fiction. Instead of focusing on the travails of one individual, it would trace the cross currents generated by masses of people victimized by the economic realities and corrupt legal system of mid-Victorian England.

Dickens' admiration for the technical ingenuity of the Crystal Palace and his reaction to the excesses of the Great Exhibition it contained no doubt helped shape his own vast and intricate undertaking. He experimented with many possible titles, among them *Tom-All-Alone's* and *The East Wind*. What he settled on makes clear that he was constructing his own alternate architecture that, like the glass envelope of the Crystal Palace, would encompass his novel and hold it together. His marvelous construction, like Paxton's, both contained and symbolized a world. But, from the stark sound of the syllables of its name to the nature of the exhibits within, it was clear that Dickens' model was the microcosm of a different universe. His structure was closer in design to the dark castles of horror stories and their successors—Victorian prisons and workhouses. In opposition to the Crystal Palace, Dickens built his own monument to mid-Victorian culture—*Bleak House*.

The first lines of the novel, written as Paxton's enormous building was being dismantled, are among the most famous in Dickens. They not only set the mood for what is to follow, but show that he intended to use the subterranean images of the horror novel—darkness, the past, the labyrinth, and the mystery in the center of it all—to lead his readers into his own Exhibition:

> London. Michaelmas Term lately over, and the Lord Chancellor sitting in Lincoln's Inn Hall. Implacable November weather. As much mud in the streets, as if the waters had not but newly retired from the face of the earth, and it would not be wonderful to meet a Megalosaurus, forty feet long or so, waddling like an elephantine lizard up Holborn Hill. Smoke lowering down from chimney-pots, making a soft black drizzle, with flakes of soot in it as big as full grown snow-flakes—gone into mourning, one might imagine, for the death of the sun.
> Fog everywhere.... The raw afternoon is rawest, and the dense fog is densest, and the muddy streets are muddiest, near the leaden-headed old obstruction ... Temple Bar. And hard by Temple Bar, in Lincoln's Inn Hall, in the very heart of the fog, sits the Lord High Chancellor in his High Court of Chancery [1].

The High Court of Chancery, the great edifice at the center of Dickens' novel and his city, is wreathed in primeval fog and darkness, mud and smoke—in polar opposition to the light and clarity that permeated the glass city of Great Exhibition. The atavistic atmosphere is enhanced by the presence of the dinosaur, which reflected contemporary interest in the writings on the giant lizards of the Mesozoic by another of Dickens' friends, the naturalist Richard Owen. Dickens' reconstructed dinosaur also serves a darker purpose; it suggests, like the Gothic atmosphere itself, the pervasive influence of the past, the feeling that not much has changed in the state of humanity since the dawn of creation. Also, since the bones of extinct creatures had been discovered deep in the earth, Dickens' dinosaur lumbering through the London darkness further connects the vanished past and the dismal present with images of entombment, of the black world under our feet.*

Comparing the dim drizzle of soot to a city in mourning "for the death of the sun" and the mud to the condition of the Earth at its birth erases time, implying that the world will be much the same at the beginning and end of history. This rejection of progress, or at least of the ability of history to ameliorate the human condition, stands opposed to Victorian optimism but is very much akin to the feeling that pervades the world of Gothic horror. The modern critic Robert Darnton gets much the same impression when he resurrects the image of crumbling architecture so familiar to the Gothic imagination to see in these lines "a pervasive sense of moral rot clinging to decrepit institutions" (109).

The subject of *Bleak House* is the injustice at the heart of society; Dickens' focus is on the building in the heart of the fog, the High Court of Chancery, which was designed to administer inheritances, to transmit the legacy of the past. It thus becomes a symbol of the impossibility of creating a new world unencumbered by what has gone before, of making the dreams of the Crystal Palace real. The stagnant, impenetrable, and muddy atmosphere which pervades this place is also evidence of the failure of the system to be accessible to those it is supposed to benefit. What the pathetic would-be heirs of the Jarndyce and Jarndyce case seek here is shrouded in the opaque rituals of the law, buried in words and yellowing documents, impossible to find. And so they wander this antique institution, sometimes for a lifetime, vainly trying to make their way past the countless legal "exhibits" and find a way out. Instead, their guides, the lawyers, lead them deeper into the labyrinth.

*Bleak House* thus unites an ironic counterpart of the Great Exhibition with the atmosphere and tradition of the tale of terror. Characters in the book from throughout the social strata seek to to claim their long promised but elusive inheritance—one of the themes of the first Gothic novel, Walpole's *The Castle of Otranto*. In that story, the castle to be inherited self destructs at the end, just as in *Bleak House* the Jarndyce legacy is finally consumed by legal costs and collapses. Both stories use the conventions of concealed identity and the impotence of figures of moral authority and build

---

* *Curiously enough, the year Dickens placed the Megalosaurus in his landscape, Prince Albert suggested that when the Crystal Palace was reconstructed in Sydenham it be populated with models of prehistoric creatures. Under Owen's supervision, the sculptor Benjamin Waterhouse Hawkins created life size dinosaurs; when the Crystal Palace reopened in 1853, Owens, Hawkins and nineteen guests celebrated with a New Years' dinner inside the belly of Iguanadon.*

the plot upon a shameful family secret. Both legacies are cursed and can destroy anyone who ensnares himself in their labyrinthian coils. (Mr. Jarndyce, the "father" who cannot help the heirs claim their estate, calls the suit "the family curse ... the horrible phantom that has haunted us so many years" [393].)

But Dickens places his tale of horror in the Victorian present. He also widens the scope of his story, dealing with a cross section of society caught in what one deranged litigant calls "the system." Dickens examines the subject of inheritance in its largest sense by asking the question implicit in Victorian self examination: Who has the right to the riches of society? (The proper distribution of wealth is also the theme of many of the sub-plots: Mrs. Jellyby's and Mrs. Pardiggle's misdirected charity, Mr. Boythorn's and Mr. Carstone's odd ideas about money, the failure of the government to compensate Dr. Woodcourt for an act of heroism, and a piece of gold given a poor street sweeper by a mysterious veiled lady.)

The architectural canvas of *Bleak House* contains more than one haunted castle; we visit a collection of structures within the overall structure of the novel. Each is built from horror story designs and adapted to the author's realistic purpose. The noble Dedlocks live in Chesney Wold, an estate that features a ghost who confines her activities to a Ghost Walk (behavior straight out of the shilling shockers) and is even connected to an Otranto-like curse: "I will walk here, until the pride of this house is humbled" (69). The home of the philanthropic Mrs. Jellyby and her neglected children is a crumbling pile of dangers, with stairs so worn "as to be absolute traps," doors impossible to open, and the "constant apparition of noses and fingers in situations of danger" (32). The office of the Law Stationer Mr. Snagsby may be haunted at night by his dead partner, while his wife's "complainings and lamentations" sound like "a shrill ghost unquiet in its grave" (180). Even the lawyers' offices in London would not be out of place in a Gothic romance. Miss Esther Summerson, the heroine, describes her arrival there in language that any devotee of the horror novel would immediately recognize:

> We drove slowly through the dirtiest and darkest streets that ever were seen in the world ... until we passed into sudden quietude under an old gateway, and drove on through a silent square until we came to an odd nook in a corner, where there was an entrance ... like an entrance to a church. And there really was a churchyard, outside under some cloisters, for I saw the gravestones from the staircase window [22].

Bleak House itself is a reversal of the Gothic castle; the home of the kindly John Jarndyce, it is a refuge, not a prison. Yet even here, Dickens uses the horror story motif of the labyrinth in a long description of the layout of the rooms. As in countless tales of terror, the heroine describes how she "lost herself in passages" filled with surprises like "mangles and three-cornered tables . . . and something between a bamboo skeleton and a great bird-cage." She concludes that one gets back to the main hall "wondering how you got back there, or had ever got out of it" (50). The house has now taken on the benevolent aspect of John Jarndyce, but when his father, who killed himself over the hopelessness of the Jarndyce suit, lived there, the house shared that personality. The younger Jarndyce recalls, "When I brought what remained of him home here, the brains seemed to me to have been blown out of the house, too; it was so shattered and ruined" (73).

Thus, Dickens uses the alternate architecture of the horror tale to tell a story that remains in the realm of the possible and in the world of his contemporaries. The line between horror fantasy and social realism was, however, sometimes pretty thin. The most Gothic of his buildings is the store of Mr. Krook, brother of the Lord High Chancellor. Like the court of Chancery itself, Krook's store is a place where everything enters and nothing leaves. Here the mysterious scrivener Nemo dies, and here the mad Miss Flite lives, waiting for the judgment in Chancery that will set her and her caged birds free.

And here too is Krook himself, who presides over a charnel house of waste—sacks of womens' hair, collections of old bones that suggest to visitors the bones of legal clients, heaps of rusty keys and yellowing law documents. Krook is "cadaverous and withered; with his head sunk sideways between his shoulders, and the breath issuing in visible smoke from his mouth as if he were on fire within" (39). Called, like his brother, the Lord Chancellor, he and his store mirror the entire corrupt system; they show Dickens adapting a familiar set of Gothic conventions to direct his readers from the realm of nightmare to a vision of reality.

Throughout the novel, images from the horror story become vehicles for revealing inner truths, the darkness behind the light. But Dickens had to be careful not to violate the conventions of his art. In the Gothic novel, the supernatural became the way to make everything possible; even in Ann Radcliffe's novels, where the supernatural is explained away, the remoteness of the setting made the flimsiest explanations plausible. But this new use of horror demanded that the images remain just that—ways of seeing what is real. Although Dickens' wrote a number of ghost stories aside from *A Christmas Carol*, in a realistic novel like *Bleak House*, everything that happened had to remain in the realm of reality.

Thus, Krooks' "fire within" was an acceptable metaphor for his Satanic nature; when, later on, Dickens describes him as "with a spirituous heat smouldering," the impression is strengthened. However, Dickens then foreshadows the end of the Jarndyce suit and suggests the system itself is destined to self-immolate by having Krook die of spontaneous combustion. This was a bit too unlikely for the readers of *Bleak House*, and Dickens was forced in a public correspondence with George Henry Lewes to defend the scientific possibility that someone could burst into flames and be totally consumed.

This controversy makes clear how the discourse of the Gothic tale came to be used in both realistic fiction and nonfiction. Imagery was drawn from Gothic romance, but its reference was to the here and now, with the supernatural only used metaphorically. In Dickens, for example, there is little direct evidence of a higher spiritual realm arranging the signs and portents for the benefit of the characters—a staple of the Gothic works of Walpole, Beckford, and Lewis among others. Dickens does, however, depend upon coincidence in all of his novels to propel the plot and connect the characters, a convention that implies a similar world beyond the fiction and serves much the same purpose. And, specifically in *Bleak House*, we get the feeling throughout that the destinies of the living characters have been shaped, like those in Gothic fiction, by the wishes of the dead. John Jarndyce manipulates them all through the medium of his will, while Nemo, the impoverished scrivener who once loved Lady Dedlock, still can destroy her life after his death.

Therefore, the apparatus of the horror story in both Romantic fantasy and Victorian realism enabled the reader to discover another reality beneath the apparent world around him, one that questions the comfortable assumptions of society. The pervasive power of the dead to control the living, found in Gothic ghosts, *Frankenstein*'s Monster, and the corpses in *Bleak House*, reinforces the feeling implicit in the tale of terror—that the real power on this earth lies with those buried in it. The dark labyrinth of the Gothic castle, the world-spanning travels of Frankenstein and his Monster, and the lifelong wanderings in a foggy legal maze of the would be heirs in *Bleak House* evolve one image for a similar purpose, to create a visual analog for confusion and helplessness—in this case of a society which seemed to have lost its moral direction.

*Bleak House* explores these themes on a the largest scale; each of the haunted castles is linked to a central structure, Lincoln's Inn Hall, the home of Chancery. In that building (and in Krook's store, its counterpart) lies the destiny of all the characters. But the ultimate Gothic Castle in the novel is contained in no one building; it is the system that contains and connects them all, from the magnificent estate of Chesney Wold to the horrid slum of Tom-All-Alones. Dickens tells us that Chancery, the bureaucratic embodiment of injustice, "has its decaying houses and its blighted lands in every shire; its worn-out lunatic in every madhouse, and its dead in every churchyard" (3).

Like the glass envelope of the Crystal Palace, Dickens' novel is an invisible structure, encompassing the breadth of Victorian society, summing up its failures as the Great Exhibition collected its successes. *Bleak House* contains the depth of society as well, and thus it is shrouded in darkness, not bathed in light, pervaded by images of darkness at noon and of the vast labyrinth that underpins and connects everyone. The characters are caught in the maze of injustice represented by the unending Chancery lawsuit; continually, within those dark passages, people from all levels of the social order discover each other. They also slowly realize that they are all under the same transparent roof. The title of the novel itself is the name of one of the buildings within it, but it also signifies the book the reader holds, the structure of ink and paper that contains Dickens' microcosm of the world in which he lived.

*Bleak House*, with its hidden wills, crime, and undercurrent of violence, helped spawn many less sophisticated works which used the same elements purely for entertainment value. In these novels, the Gothic formula was used to enhance the melodramatic atmosphere. Like the "shilling shockers," they were produced and consumed quickly. The difference is that the source of horror became contemporary incidents—murder, mayhem, blackmail and the mystery of lost inheritances. But unlike Dickens' novel, these tales lacked the complex undercurrent of social commentary and symbolic connection which gave *Bleak House* the ring of a deeper truth. They did, though, often employ a character Dickens developed with great skill in his novel, the one character who could tread the dark labyrinth with assurance—the detective.

In *Bleak House*, Chief Inspector Bucket is introduced as another Gothic figure. When first seen in the law office of Mr. Tulkinghorn, he is something of an apparition: "there is nothing very remarkable about him at first sight but his ghostly manner of appearing" (234). At the same time, Bucket is one of the first detectives in English fiction, ancestor of Conan Doyle's Sherlock Holmes. He solves one murder, uncovers another mystery, and leads his characters through the darkest corners of Victorian London. But his function, unlike that of other fictional detectives, is not to use his powers of deduction to stitch up holes in the fabric of society.

Instead, he is a tour guide through the depth and breadth of the multilayered Victorian world of *Bleak House*, serving to show people from all classes how they are connected—the aristocratic Lady Dedlock to the poor scrivener whose name means "no one," the lawyer Tulkinghorn to the maid Hortense, the destitute street sweeper Jo to them all. At the end of the novel, Esther Summerson is led by the detective "with great rapidity, through such a labyrinth of streets that I soon lost all idea of where we were" (827). But Bucket knows where each "slimy turning" leads; he knows also that at the end of the maze Esther will unveil the final horror—the body of her mother.

Inspector Bucket is the thread that ties all the characters together or, more aptly, shows them they are all in one bucket. The real secret he uncovers is the world of poverty and despair others refuse to see. His actions are not always benevolent or corrective. He is sometimes cruel or unfeeling and contributes indirectly to the neglect and death of the most helpless figure in the book, Jo, a street urchin who barely survives by sweeping a path across the filthy streets for passersby in return for a few pence. But Bucket makes the characters all witnesses to the horrors of urban life and suggests their own complicity in such suffering.

Dickens' literary models for Bucket no doubt included Poe's C. Auguste Dupin and the memoirs of France's Inspector Vidoq. But the most immediate source was Inspector Field of London's new Detective Department. On June 14, 1851, a few weeks before he toured the Great Exhibition, in a piece in *Household Words* entitled "On Duty with Inspector Field," Dickens wrote of their nocturnal tour of London's worst slums. Field takes them through a "maze of streets and courts," illuminating the darkness with his lantern and impressing the author with his ability to tread the labyrinth with assurance. The places they see are all dark and forbidding, described as if they were underground lairs of a sub-human species: "confined, intolerable rooms, burrowed out like the holes of rats or the nests of insect vermin." He calls one place "Rats' Castle." Within these cellars the visitors are assailed by unearthly smells ("stricken back by the pestilent breath that issues from within") and face visions ("a spectral figure rising, unshrouded, from a grave of rags"). The goal of this Gothic quest to a graveyard of the living is not to arrest any of the numerous small time thieves and other malefactors they encounter; it is to show that there are those who know the abyss and can return from it intact.

Dickens was also interested in traditional detective duties, actually visiting the scene of a murder in 1849 and criticizing the quality of police work; in Paris, his favorite haunt was the city morgue. But it is the detective as guide to the urban Hell which is the most relevant use of the Gothic pattern to expose the underworld of Victorian culture. For not only Dickens, and not only novelists, used the imagery of the horror story to explore and illuminate this darkness.

II.

Although, as the publisher Charles Knight complained in 1845, the "cheap bookseller's shops are filled with such things as *Newgate, A Romance, The Black Mantle, or the Murder at the Old Jewry, The Spectre of the Hall, The Love Child, The Convict* and twenty others, all of the same exciting character" the most powerful tales of terror were found elsewhere. Like the authors of the early Gothic "shilling shockers," the writers of these mid-Victorian horror stories were often anonymous; their works were also called "blue books" and illustrated with lurid engravings (sometimes condemned as unsuitable for young ladies to view); they detailed horrors that both fascinated and repelled, and many were serialized in newspapers and twopenny periodicals.

The titles, however, revealed the difference. One of the best sellers of 1842 was *The Sanitary Condition of the Labouring Population of Great Britain.* Another was called the *Report of the Result of a Special Inquiry into the Practice of Internment in Towns* (1843). The most horrifying were the first and second reports of the Children's Employment Commission (1842-43). All of these government documents spurred the glacial process of reform. (It took twenty five years of legislation to restrict a child of nine to a sixty-nine hour week and that only in cotton mills!) They also provided ammunition to those who wished for revolution (Friedrich Engels used their research to write *The Condition of the Working Class in England in 1844* — the year he met Karl Marx in London). And, for the huge reading public that devoured them, they provided many of the same thrills as had their Gothic predecessors.

The nature of their appeal is made clear in an article from an 1850 issue of *Punch,* where William Thackeray, the novelist who as a boy thrilled to the horrors of the shilling shockers and as a man composed an ode to the wonders of the Great Exhibition, comments on revelations about the poor:

> A picture of human life so wonderful, so awful, so piteous and pathetic, so exciting and terrible, that readers of romances own they never read anything like to it; and that the griefs, struggles, strange adventures here depicted exceed anything that any of us could imagine . . . we are of the upper classes; we have had hitherto no community with the poor . . . until . . . some clear-sighted energetic man travels into the poor man's country for us, and comes back with his tale of terror and wonder.

Thackeray reads sociology as if it were fiction; though he mentions a higher purpose (community with the poor), the thrills are uppermost. His vision of the author as a traveler into a remote land (which was, of course, all around him) is another echo of the original tale of terror. These new horror stories satisfied the Victorian demand for realism and desire for reform, as well as a passion for self laceration that often accompanied anguish over the condition of England. At the same time, experience could be read as a Gothic novel. Readers like Thackeray could vicariously participate in the horrors portrayed, aware that this was "real" and happening around the corner, but insulated by the similarity of what they read to the fantastic fiction with which they were familiar. Thus, a new audience eavesdropped on the lives of the poor while exiling them to a fictional landscape once peopled by the medieval characters of Gothic fiction. Yet, readers recognized (as they had done when encountering the ghosts and ghouls of Gothic romance) that this cast of unearthly spectres was also somehow speaking to them.

Along with the proliferation of government committee reports came investigations by individuals into this troglodyte world. Dickens had been one of the first in his *Sketches by Boz* (1836–37), though his tone is less horrific than full of boyish enthusiasm. Between 1841 and 1844, Charles Knight put out in weekly numbers almost 2500 pages of *London*, covering subjects ranging from Roman ruins to street sounds and the history of sewers. In the following twelve years the even longer (and notoriously gruesome and unreliable) *Mysteries of London* and *Mysteries of the Courts of London* entertained readers with what at least purported to be G. W. M. Reynolds' investigations of vice, squalor, and cruelty among the urban poor. Reynolds' books were the most shamelessly lurid, though all these accounts succumbed to some extent to the readers' need for Gothic thrills more than to the journalists' desire for accurate reporting. However, the most horrific revelations that emerged in these decades were not about the metaphorical London underworld at all, but exposed the literal intervention of the dead in the lives of living, a Gothic theme if ever there was one.

In the four years beginning in 1843 a surgeon, George A. Walker, published in pamphlet form a series of letters he had written to the *Morning Herald* and lectures he had given to the Mechanics' Institute, and unleashed a storm of controversy. His subject was the horrific state of the burial grounds in London; his style was given to vivid anecdotes in nauseating detail. Because far too many dead were crammed into far too little space, some truly Gothic situations arose. Walker tells of one churchyard where over twelve thousand bodies were crammed into pits, the uppermost corpses covered with only a few inches of earth and, in one place, directly beneath the wooden floor of a chapel. As he puts it "a SUNDAY SCHOOL was held over this abominable receptacle of putrid and decaying mortality" (2nd series, 13). Worst of all, he documents the noxious and sometimes fatal effects of breathing "the emanations of the dead" and then points out that, because of inadequate burial and constant reinternments, people throughout London "breathe on all sides an atmosphere impregnated with the odour of the dead ... the soil of the ground is saturated, absolutely saturated, with human putrescence" (*Internment* 6).

His revelations were clearly the basis for Dickens' description of the burial ground in *Bleak House,* a place full of rats and piles of bones, where a poor law scrivener's body was interred so near to the surface that, in the streetsweeper Jo's words, "They was obliged to stamp upon it to git it in" (278). Unlike other investigations into the underside of Victorian life, which insulate the reader by traveling from the regions of respectability into unknown corners of a Gothic city, Walker (like Dickens) sees the dead directly invading the domain of the living, and implicates all the people of London in a corruption that taints the very air they breathe. Reading the city around them as a tale of terror, writers like Dickens and reformers like Walker were drawn to the Gothic vision of an underground world around the corner and beneath our feet. To find the lost medieval landscape of horror, writers and reformers needed only to look beneath the surface of the modern city, and not very far beneath it at that.

The year of the Crystal Palace and *Bleak House* also saw published in book form the most famous and influential of these private investigations — the first volumes of Henry Mayhew's *London Labour and the London Poor*. Mayhew was an ex-playwright and journalist (one of the founders of *Punch*), who had declared bankruptcy in 1847. In the next two years he published a number of short and successful comic novels in collaboration with his brother Augustus, including *The Greatest Plague in Life, or the Adventures of a Lady in Search of a Good Servant* and *When to Marry and How to Get Married*. Then, in September 1849 in the *Morning Chronicle*, appeared Mayhew's "Visit to the Cholera Districts of Bermondsey" the first of seventy-six such 'letters' (Thackeray's glowing comments are about these pieces).

The success of these remarkable insights into the lives of the poor, enhanced by Mayhew's ability to let his subjects speak in their own words, led him to begin publishing his findings in his own twopenny weekly in December 1850. The four volumes he eventually collected (with the help of others) are divided into those who "will work," "can not work" and "will not work," and cover the range of activities that kept the poor alive, from street performers and collectors of debris to sellers of everything from baked potatoes to crockery, from crippled beggars and street crossing sweepers like Jo in *Bleak House*, to prostitutes, thieves and vagabonds. Each is carefully described and cataloged as in the Great Exhibition; for example, his section on street sellers is divided into sellers of fish; of fruits and vegetables; of game, poultry, rabbits, butter, cheese, and eggs; of trees, shrubs, flowers, roots, seeds a branches; and so on. Thus, while crowds of visitors admired the exhibits in the Crystal Palace, an equally large number were guided in much the same way through weekly tours of the urban slums.

Although Mayhew is our source for many details about life in London in the mid-nineteenth century, his sociology is not always accurate or consistent. His background as a playwright and novelist was as much an influence as his journalism; the power of his writing comes from the drama he creates from the voices of the poor and the shape he gives to their stories. Mayhew's tone is very different from that of the government reports; we sense his presence in all of his conversations and are moved to pity and terror more by the voices he records than by reams of official statistics. Though he, like the Parliamentary commissions and "moral statisticians," is drawn to numbers (at one point he tries to calculate the number of pounds of horse manure deposited daily in the streets of London), his accounts of individuals give his work enduring power and keep it in print today, over a century after it first appeared.

Each of the stories he tells is filtered through the consciousness of the writer, Mayhew, who is well aware of the power of Gothic imagery. One of his most wrenching stories concerns the "pure finders," among the poorest of the poor, who spend their days collecting "pure" (dog manure) to sell to tanneries for a few pennies. He seeks out one of these "unfortunates" in a room seemingly at the end of the world, yet at an address familiar to any resident of London:

> In the wretched locality . . . lying between the Docks and Rosemary-lane, redolent of filth and pregnant with pestilential diseases, and whither all the outcasts of the metropolitan population seem to be drawn, either in the hope of finding fitting associates and companions in their wretchedness . . . or else for the purpose of hiding themselves . . . from the world — in this dismal quarter . . . I discerned, after considerable difficulty, an old woman, a pure-finder.

Mayhew's difficult quest goes beyond finding the woman; he has trouble even seeing her. She seems almost less than human, an object able to blend with the debris and darkness of her room:

> I opened the door, the little light that struggled through the small window, the many broken panes of which were stuffed with old rags, was not sufficient to enable me to perceive who or what was in the room. After a short time, however, I began to make out an old chair standing near a fire-place, and then to discover a poor old woman resembling a bundle of rags and filth stretched out on some dirty straw in the corner of the apartment.

Mayhew patterns this moment directly on the "discovery" scene of the typical Gothic horror story, where the heroine's curiosity leads her to draw aside a veil and enter a dark chamber in which is slowly revealed a tableau of horror.

From the moment Emily St. Aubert first gazes on Montoni's Gothic castle in Radcliffe's *The Mysteries of Udolpho,* or the veil on Frankenstein's bed is drawn aside to reveal the face of the Monster, seeing has been a powerful metaphor in the tale of terror. To struggle to see what chooses to remain in darkness is to bring to consciousness that which each of us, and society, wants to keep in obscurity. One wonders how many of the millions viewing the exhibits at Paxton's Crystal Palace really saw the shackles manufactured for the slave trade or the meaning behind the statues of women in chains.

Dickens uses the same metaphor of vision and the same set piece in *Bleak House* when Tulkinghorn enters the "spectral darkness" of a destitute law scrivener's "foul and filthy" room. As in countless shilling shockers, Tulkinghorn's candle chooses this moment to go out, leaving the room illuminated by only the "gaunt eyes" of two ghostly holes in the drawn shutters. In that dim light he gradually comprehends that the figure stretched out on the bed is the skeletal corpse of Nemo, once the lover of Lady Dedlock, who has fallen so low in the world that he has taken on a name that means "no one."

In *London Labour and the London Poor*, the spectral figure also turns out, to Mayhew's "astonishment," to be what he calls a "superior woman"— the daughter of a milkman ("very well off") who somehow lost her way in the struggle for existence through no fault of her own. She in turn tells a story, reminiscent of *Bleak House,* of a fellow "pure finder" who died in poverty and, on the day of the funeral, was identified as the heir of a great estate. We then learn of another pure collector who once held a lucrative situation as a servant but fell through drink and "is now so reduced that he is ashamed to be seen." All three stories may be true in varying degrees, but Mayhew, like the novelist he was, is clearly shaping them. The horror of what he sees is enhanced by the histories he relates; like Dickens, Mayhew reanimates a convention of the tale of terror to show his readers the connection between themselves and these seemingly subhuman creatures—one misstep and the abyss waits for all.

As in the government reports, investigations by individuals like Mayhew emphasized the wretched condition of the poor crowded into the maze of streets and courts of the city. Like the heroines of Gothic romances, the investigators peered into the darkness to uncover scenes of horror. The spectres they saw had a human history, but had become ghosts condemned to an unearthly existence—actual counterparts of Jo, the street sweeper in *Bleak House,* who has "always been a-moving and a-moving on, ever since I was born" (319) but keeps returning to haunt the black slum of Tom-All-Alones. Their testimony in those reports, like Jo's in the inquest on the death of Nemo, became a curse upon society. And like Jo's plaintive words, the most damning curses were delivered by children.

*The Second Report of the Childrens' Employment Commission: Trades and Manufactures* (1843) recorded the words of thousands of children working in trades from pottery to papermaking, listing their statements in long appendices that are more devastating than the carefully considered statistics and conclusions in the report itself. For example R. D. Grainger recorded the testimony of "No. 61," Mary Brooks, a nine year old from

Nottingham who worked from 6 a.m. to as late as 9:30 p.m., six days a week, in lace manufacturing:

> Has been a threader for two years and a half ... has no regular time for meals; gets tired sometimes at night; they often are sleepy at night; often has the head ache; sometimes sleeps well and sometimes not. Her legs ache but not often. Her eyes often pain her very much and sometimes run with water. Sometimes she sees "pretty things" when she shuts her eyes at night.
>
> her<br>(signed) Mary x Brooks<br>mark<br>(appendix f 14)

Although moments like this can move us still, Mayhew's ability to create literature out of such materials gives his horror stories a special power. We sense in his words, and in those he records, the life of the streets as well as its death and the human spirit that endures in the worst adversity. His admiration for the persistence and skill of some of these denizens of the darkness shows most clearly in the most Gothic passages, when he explores the secret lives in London's sewers.

Beneath the labyrinth of London was another—the ancient and extensive sewer system, flooded twice each day by the Thames tide and fraught with dangers. In a section entitled "Of the Subterranean Character of the Sewers," Mayhew shares with his readers vivid descriptions of their construction and contents, gleaned from official surveys. Thus we learn of the filth that filled them (from dead cats to dead people), and of the ceilings covered with "hangings of putrid matter like stalactites three feet in length." He is also careful to inform us that sewers under the slums and workhouses and those under the most "fashionable squares" are equally horrendous. Thus all of London was united by its underground arteries and by the same noxious smell that arose from drains in every quarter.*

Though it was illegal to enter the system, a band of scavengers made a living scouring the darkness for salable trash and bones. They contended with the dangers of being drowned when the tides flooded underground cul-de-sacs, buried in collapsing brickwork, overcome by "noisome vapours," or (in Mayhew's words) "beset by myriads of enormous rats, and slaying thousands of them in the struggle for life, till at length the swarms of the savage things overpowered them, and in a few days afterwards their skeletons were discovered picked to the very bones."

Mayhew's stories of survival in what he calls "this foul labyrinth" are

---

*In 1858, the smell from the Thames and the sewers that drained into it got so bad that there were plans to evacuate the government to Hampton Court. Though known as "The Great Stink," the smell was only somewhat worse than usual.

more the stuff of Gothic myth than Victorian realism. We may doubt his tale of killer rats the size of cats, or of the Londoners who, through the sewer grates, sometimes could hear the faint echo of the screams of trapped scavengers reverberating through the darkness. Even he doubts the truth of his "strange tale" of a "race of wild hogs inhabiting the sewers in the neighbourhood of Hampstead." These "fabulous monsters" may not have existed, but they share with the other inhabitants of the sewers the aura of the supernatural. Readers of Mayhew could believe that literally beneath their feet existed a world that would not be out of place in any tale of horror.

Like the best of the tales of terror, *London Labour and the London Poor* took its readers to another realm. Whether above ground in the dark squalor of the slums (often compared to a troglodyte world) or literally in the subterranean bowels of the city, London became part of a Gothic universe. In fact, the mythology of the tale of terror was used by writers like Mayhew or Dickens because it fit the sense of horror they felt. No longer were spectres and ghosts, monsters and mazes confined to a remote castle in a remote time; within the structure of contemporary society, Victorians had created their own Gothic castles.

This was true in more than a metaphorical sense, for some public buildings of mid-Victorian England were explicitly designed as horror stories in stone. As a result of the Poor Law Reform of 1834, the indigent who wished assistance from the state had to present themselves at the iron gate of the workhouse that stood in every large town, where they were led into a warren of cold stone buildings, stripped and searched, dressed in uniforms, segregated by sex, and severely restricted in their contacts with the outside world. The idea was to make life in these "prisons for the poor" as unpleasant as possible and thus discourage malingering. As a result, poor families starved rather than enter the workhouses, places they called "Bastilles"—places that came close to recreating the Gothic castle that dominated the fictional landscape fifty years before.

Prisons came even closer than workhouses to reproducing modern equivalents of medieval fortresses. Pentonville prison, opened in 1842 as a model for penal institutions, was built in mock Gothic style, an ironic echo of the architectural fantasies of Walpole or Beckford, complete with towers, battlements, and portcullises. Like Strawberry Hill or Fonthill, the structure proclaimed to inmates and passersby that it was a modern place where medieval values survived. What had changed, of course, was the scope and purposes—Walpole and Beckford were aristocrats indulging in an eccentric hobby, while the creators of Pentonville had (intentionally or not) cast in stone the grim intentions of an entire society. In the name of modern penal reform, prisons found their models in the Middle Ages, in the castles that to readers of Gothic fiction meant dark secrets and silent suffering.

Predictably, both workhouses and prisons came under scrutiny by reformers. Although some provided tolerable living conditions, a Parliamentary Commission of 1845 found, for example, that the inmates of the Andover workhouse, given the task of crushing animal bones to create fertilizer, "were eating the rotting gristle and marrow to supplement their deficient rations" (Rosenberg 79). When Henry Mayhew visited a London prison in 1856, he watched nearly five hundred men work in a huge bare room, decorated only with slogans such as "It is Good for a Man That He Bear the Yoke in his Youth." They were under the infamous silent system, which robbed them not only of their liberty, but of their humanity. Mayhew writes of what he calls "the goblin character of the sight" with imagery that reminds us of the human machines of *Frankenstein* and the Industrial Revolution and of the ghosts of Gothic horror:

> The building was full of men, and as silent as if it merely contained so many automatona.... To behold those whom we had seen full of life and emotion ... reduced to the inanimateness of the statue, is assuredly the most appalling and depressing sight we can look upon.... Not only is the silence as intense and impressive as that of death itself, but the movements of the workers seem as noiseless and therefore unearthly, as spectres [Mayhew and Binney 311].

In some prisons such as Pentonville the wish to stamp out all communication between inmates meant combining enforced silence with what was called the "separate system." Prisoners were kept apart as much as possible (including in chapel and the classroom) and, when together, were forced to wear masks or veils. The concept recreated the veiled horrors which haunt the halls of the shilling shockers, and suited the Gothic atmosphere of the place (it also drove many inmates insane). The connection wasn't lost on Mayhew, who describes the eyes of one inmate "appearing through the two holes cut in front, and seeming almost like phosphoric lights shining through the sockets of a skull" (141). Once again, experience was seen (literally this time) through the eyes of Gothic fantasy.

By the middle of the nineteenth century, a growing number of writers tried to throw light upon the dark corners of the contemporary world. And the language of realism was simply inadequate to describe what those explorers saw. Meaning came by reading the world with the tools of the tale of terror. In the Gothic universe already existed places and creatures, mythology and emotions, equal to the task. Given a new focus, that apparatus made the Victorian tale of terror immediate and inescapable. At the same time, by using such language and imagery the creators of the new literature of fear were guaranteed a huge audience that had grown up, like William Thackeray, hooked on horror and eager to rediscover its guilty pleasures in the guise of social reform. The evolution of the landscape of terror from an ersatz medieval world to a way of seeing the urban darkness both heightened the thrill of fear and brought it uncomfortably close to the readers. Just as many Gothic tales were variations of one story, the many lurid and terrifying vignettes in Mayhew and others kept telling readers of unearthly creatures who nonetheless resembled them, creatures buried alive in the lower depths, contending with a medieval array of terrors in the struggle to survive.

## III.

This underground labyrinth of despair extended beyond the confines of the Victorian city. Outside the west entrance of the Great Exhibition, visitors encountered a single block of 24 tons of coal from the Duke of Devonshire's mines. Those about to enter Joseph Paxton's shining city were thus shown the source of power for the symbols of progress arrayed within; they also were reminded of a part of England persons of sensibility tried to forget—the Black Country.

This district, aptly situated around the medieval ruins of Dudley Castle in southern England, had become the greatest iron producing area in the world at the time, abundant in iron ore, coal, sand, and limestone. It was also a bleak wasteland, the closest place on earth to Hell. John Nasmyth, although an engineer and an architect of Victorian progress, could see the cost when he described its sublime Gothic landscape:

> The venerable trees struggle for existence under the destroying influence of sulphureous acid; while the grass is withered and the vegetation everywhere blighted. I sat down on an elevated part of the ruins, and looked down upon the extensive district, with its roaring and blazing furnaces, the smoke of which blackened the country as far as the eye could reach.... We may fill our purses, but we pay a heavy price for it [Rolt 120].

The scene also reminds us of the fog and smoke shrouded district around Dickens' Court of Chancery, and indeed, even before finishing *Bleak House,* Dickens turned to this setting for his next novel. This book also had a spare title of two single syllables, a concern with the common humanity that binds all classes of society, and an interest in the effect of the system upon individuals. This time, however, the setting is a factory town in the Black Country called Coketown.

*Hard Times* also has its Gothic moments—the house of the schoolmaster Gradgrind, Stone Lodge, looks like its owner and reflects his unyielding belief in a world without dreams; the machines in Josiah Bounderby's factory are living monsters that never sleep; the villain Harthouse is clearly allied to Satan himself and pursues the heroine Louisa with the thoroughness of any Gothic villain. And the movement of the characters is down. The near ravishment of Louisa, the heroine, is compared to her descent of a long staircase, while Stephen Blackpool, the honest weaver lost in the Black Country, ends his life at the bottom of an abandoned mine shaft, in the Gothic realm of mid Victorian England, buried alive in the darkness beneath our feet.

Blackpool's death at the bottom of the abyss called the "Old Hell Shaft" reminded Dickens' readers of the blackest secret of the Black country. Just as the urban slums had a worse "underworld" beneath them in the sewers, the Black Country and other areas like it in England, Scotland and Wales had their own subterranean realms where, according to the Census of 1851, over a quarter of a million men and boys labored in constant danger. The mines were perhaps the most dangerous and dreadful places of occupation, where workers not only contended with the possibility of sudden burial alive or suffocation, but also faced with a near certain future of disease and disfigurement.

The reports of the *Commission for Inquiry into the Employment and Condition of Children in Mines and Manufactures* (1842) made clear, in words and woodcuts, the horror faced daily in the darkness by men, women, and children, some as young as four years old. In many mines children spent up to sixteen hours a day drawing coal tubs through underground passages, some no more than a yard in height. Typical was the testimony of Margaret Leveston, six years old, a coal bearer in the East of Scotland, who "makes 10 to 14 rakes a day; carries full 56 lbs of coal." The subcommissioner adds that "one journey is designated a rake; the height ascended and the distance along the roads together, exceed the height of St. Paul's Cathedral" (91–92).

When this report was read to the House of Commons in 1842, some members wept openly, and a bill was passed to correct the worst abuses. The House of Lords, however, attacked the bill as an interference with the free labor market. More concern was expressed about the indelicacy of the woodcuts, which showed that because of the heat and poor ventilation men and women worked nearly nude, some chained to the carts they pulled. At a time when people looked with admiration at the chained nudes depicted in the sculpture at the Crystal Palace, accurate renderings of analogous contemporary suffering were condemned. Like the woodcuts that had embellished the more lurid shilling shockers, the illustrations that accompanied the Parliamentary Reports were read as pornography. As one subcommissioner put it, "any sight more disgustingly indecent or revolting can scarcely be imagined than these girls at work—no brothel can beat it" (24).

Finally, an amended bill became law; women and girls were forbidden to work underground, largely on the grounds of indecency. Males ten and over were still allowed into the mines. Nothing was done about their working conditions, even though the report was explicit about the effects of such labor: stunted growth, a crippled gait, the likelihood of lung disease and joint inflammation. Tom Mann, a Welsh labor leader at the end of the century, recalled what it was like to be ten years old and work underground in 1866, almost a quarter century after this "reform" was enacted:

> A piece of stout material was fitted to the boy around the waist. To this there was a chain attached, and the boy would hook the chain to the box, and crawling on all fours, the chain between his legs, would drag the box along and take it to the 'gob' where it would be emptied. Donkey work it certainly was . . . the boy had to crawl on hands and toes dragging his load along in worse than Egyptian darkness. Many a time did I actually lie down groaning as a consequence [Burnett, *Useful Toil* 55].

The difficulty in passing meaningful reform pointed up the great gulf between the privileged and the poor, the sense that England was really two countries, physically near each other, but as far apart in sensibility and suffering as Heaven and Hell. In the year of the Great Exhibition, the symbol of Victorian culture at its zenith, one prison held 239 children under the age of fourteen (a few as young as five), sentenced for offenses such as stealing a few shillings, some bits of food, or, in the case of two boys ages ten and eleven, for spinning a top (Mayhew and Binney 388, 416)! Everywhere in a society that built monuments to its modernity was evidence that something terrible was undermining the foundations.

The styles of architecture created or imagined by Victorian engineers, architects, and writers contained their visions of England. Classicists and lovers of church Gothic looked to an idealized past for inspiration; engineers like Joseph Paxton saw salvation in the future. All wished to see England rebuilt; by changing its shapes, they hoped to transform its substance. But despite many attempts, the buildings of Victorian Britain couldn't recast the reality of what went on around and underneath them.

In the 1850's the industrialist and philanthropist Titus Salt built Saltaire on the outskirts of Bradford, a model city for the 4,000 employees of his mill; he hoped its sturdy and spacious houses, broad streets, and attractive squares would be copied throughout industrialized Britain. The Utilitarian philosopher Jeremy Bentham had his own architectural vision. He saw the poor living in a country wide network of workhouses, producing goods and creating wealth. The buildings themselves would be arranged in a system he called the "Panopticon"—a circle of buildings with a central watchtower, enabling a small staff to oversee a large workforce. Salt's model never replaced the slums, while Bentham's was echoed only in the plan of Victorian prisons and madhouses.

The most famous of those lunatic asylums, Colney Hatch, began as another architectural statement of Victorian optimism. Opened only two months after the Crystal Palace, it also was inaugurated with great fanfare, described as the first of a new kind of asylum that would treat the insane with compassion. Mental patients had, until then, been shut away in filth and squalor, restrained and mistreated, or simply left to rot. Now, the Italianate facade, the six miles of corridors and rooms carefully decorated with domestic touches, and the formal gardens and farm of Colney Hatch were deemed essential to the patients' rapid recovery, an orderly microcosm that would soon be reflected in the minds of the inmates. In the past, visitors paid to see the grotesque antics of lunatics in places like Bethlem Hospital (the infamous Bedlam); now, places like Colney Hatch hosted dances and Christmas balls—another image of order to present to the inmates and the outside world (Dickens attended one of the first, in 1851).

But the mirror of a sane world so carefully cultivated in such exhibitions was as artificial and transitory as the Great Exhibition itself; before long the new asylums were grossly overcrowded and the lives of the inmates, if less brutalized, were as hopeless and powerless as ever. Legions of the insane (primarily female) remained buried in paternalistic institutions, the societal equivalent of the attics and cellars where madwomen were sequestered in Gothic fiction. Even Colney Hatch, like the Crystal Palace, turned out to be a temporary structure; by 1857 it was disintegrating along with the dreams of its planners, sections of its walls and roof cracked or collapsed, an inadvertent Gothic ruin, the inspiration that brought it briefly into shape condemned as a "colossal mistake" (see Showalter 101).

The city modeled by writers like Charles Dickens and Henry Mayhew with the materials of the tale of terror came closest to structuring an enduring metaphor for all of Victorian reality—as a decaying edifice embodying a system whose power was illegitimate and ill used, with secrets hidden in every corner and gruesome scenes disclosed to anyone curious enough to penetrate the all pervading darkness. It was a Gothic castle that was mostly dungeon and labyrinth, a subterranean realm inhabited by the poor, the criminal classes, and the dead. Whether the metaphorical underworld of the lawless cities, the societal dungeons of the prison, workhouse, and asylum, or the literal labyrinths of sewer and mine, the undermining force of an underground England was felt everywhere. The upper rooms of respectable society reeked of the pervasive smell Walker describes, a "Great Stink" redolent of physical and moral corruption, of secrets imperfectly hidden, of dead that refused to remain buried.

There, too, could be heard echoes of the screams Mayhew said emanated from the sewers of London, heard also in the voices of the poor captured by the writers who descended into the malodorous darkness. Like the fictional castles that inevitably succumbed to an ancient curse and collapsed, the Gothic model of Victorian society always seemed to be tottering, about to fall to the forces that cried out from beneath it. Like the famous sketch of the Crystal Palace that Joseph Paxton drew on a scrap of blotting paper, the old tale of terror provided the outline for a new literary construction that summed up the horrors of the age.

After examining these contradictions—the proximity of wealth and poverty, the Gothic world of the dark labyrinth under the feet of and around the corner from the Victorian world of progress, prosperity, and self-satisfaction—one aspect of Joseph Paxton's Crystal Palace becomes particularly ironic. Although that building had no basement, it did have a floor made of wooden boards covering a crawl space. The boards were laid a half inch apart so that a typical example of Victorian ingenuity, a "sweeping machine consisting of many brooms fixed to an apparatus on light wheels," could quickly brush debris beneath the building (ffrench 105). To prevent combustible materials from building up underneath the floor, a squad of small boys was employed to work in the crawl space collecting garbage. Thus, while millions of visitors walked the sunlit halls of the Crystal Palace admiring the achievements of their civilization, beneath their feet, in nineteen acres of semi-darkness, children labored in the dust.

Part Three
# Myths and Mysteries (1886–97)

*Chapter Five*
# The Proximity of the Past

> Move upward, working out the beast
> And let the ape and tiger die
> — Alfred, Lord Tennyson

> The criminal: an atavistic being who reproduces in his person the ferocious instincts of primitive humanity and the inferior animals
> — Cesare Lombrosio

At the same time the Crystal Palace embodied Victorian dreams about the shape of the future, it inadvertently mirrored the social structure of the present and marked the moment when man began to examine his origins in the distant past. In 1851, the year of the Great Exhibition, the term "prehistoric" first appeared in print; Richard Owens and Benjamin Hawkins created the first full scale models of dinosaurs for the reconstructed Crystal Palace at Sydenham a year later. Before the end of the decade, Darwin's *Origin of Species* (1859) implied that man and dinosaurs were not the result of separate acts of creation.

Further blows to Victorian belief in man's uniqueness and nobility were delivered soon after, when Thomas Henry Huxley showed his contemporaries in words and pictures the similarity between man and the lower primates in *Man's Place in Nature* (1863), John Lubbock combined imagination and evolution in the extremely popular reconstruction of a brutal past, *Pre-historic Times* (1865), and John McLennan argued in *Primitive Marriage* (1865) that the sacrament of monogamy had evolved from a prehistory of sexual promiscuity. When Darwin fulfilled the prediction contained on the concluding page of *Origin of Species*, that "much light will be thrown on the origin of man and his history" with *The Descent of Man* (1871), Victorians were confronted in full measure with their heritage and forced to weigh dreams of a bright future against nightmares of a dark past.

As far back as 1699, Edward Tyson had described a chimpanzee as a "pygmie," "no man, nor yet the common ape; but a sort of animal between both." But in a pre-evolutionary world, this was taken as further evidence of the intricate construction of the Great Chain of Being, with each link separate and humans favored by God above the rest of creation. When, however, in the Victorian era the first reports of gorillas came to England, they were depicted (erroneously but in concert with contemporary Darwinian thinking) as both the immediate ancestors of man and brute killers. A skeleton and skull that had been dug up from Neander valley of Germany in 1856, with its low forehead, small brain cavity, and heavy brow ridges, began to be accepted not as the remains of a modern mental defective but as a distant relative of its discoverers.

Imaginative reconstructions of man's prehistory were inspired by evolutionary theory and anthropological discoveries, but shaped, at least in part, by the pattern of the past and the view of man's nature found in the tale of terror. The ancient curse that stained the noble lineage of the tortured protagonist of such stories was paralleled in the belief in a dark destiny determined by the biological heritage of humanity. The power of the dead to control the living, a theme from Walpole to Dickens, gained new significance as popularizers of science argued that modern culture was built on the survival of ancient barbarism. Augustus Pitt-Rivers, an influential anthropologist, contended that all material goods evolved from weaponry (armor became clothes, clubs became tools), while weapons themselves had been created in imitation of the claws and teeth of predators and the stones and clubs he believed had been used by apes. His speculations reached a wide audience when his collection of primitive artifacts was exhibited in the South Kensington Museum in 1879, and, subsequently, at the Pitt Rivers Museum in Oxford in 1885 (see van Keuren).

An even more well known scientist, Cesare Lombrosio, argued that criminal behavior and madness were reversions to the primitive, evidence of atavism or degeneracy. The seed of the caveman or the pre-human brute was thus believed to lie dormant in both society and the individual, further justifying the repression and cult of respectability that was so much a part of late Victorian life. Secret pleasures and more serious crimes, long castigated as sin by the religious establishment, now became in the popular mind scientific evidence of the survival of the beast. Victorian hypocrisy, prudishness and evasiveness, seen then and now as the distinguishing characteristics of the age, became more than ever what one historian has called "cultural defense mechanisms in a time of upheaval" (Gay 420).

We have seen how the architecture of horror fiction was created to house the fears of its audience, just as the Crystal Palace later tried to encase its dreams. By the end of the century, evolutionary science and its popularizers had created new anxieties which the structure of the horror story could easily be remodeled to accommodate. And, in little more than a decade, three fictional characters did give new life to the tale of terror—

life that endured to become a vital part of modern popular culture. Robert Louis Stevenson's Jekyll/Hyde, Arthur Conan Doyle's Sherlock Holmes, and Bram Stoker's Dracula were born in 1886, 1887, and 1897 respectively. Something about each of their stories has continued to speak to our culture with the force of legend, not only inspiring further cycles of adventures as ancient myths did, but also putting in the form of fantasy the central concerns of the age.

Another character came to public consciousness at the same time, at the center of a story as fantastic in detail as horror fiction but recorded by journalists as fact. Like the fictions, the story of Jack the Ripper has evolved in popular culture over the last century through similar means and for similar reasons. As we shall see, these four figures, whether they existed in literature or in life, became exemplars of the Gothic power to shape experience into patterns that confront fears about the immediate future with beliefs about the deep past.

In the three fictions — *The Strange Case of Dr. Jekyll and Mr. Hyde,* the Holmes stories, and *Dracula* — representatives of a scientific and rational contemporary universe often help liberate, and always battle, darker, older forces that threaten to tear apart the fabric of civilized society. The conflict is played out as variations on the age old (and Gothic) theme of the double — as tenants of one body in the case of Jekyll and Hyde, as alter egos in a battle of wills in the cases of Holmes and the arch-criminal Moriarty, or vampire hunter Abraham Van Helsing and "king vampire" Dracula. Though they mirror each other, one half of each pair is in some way an atavism, a throwback to a brutal past. The heroes Holmes and Van Helsing, like the discontented doctor Henry Jekyll, engage in what is essentially a spiritual battle of modern civilization against "prehistoric" criminality. In all three cases, the main characters feel within themselves the power of a primitive legacy they struggle to overcome. Just as the fictional domain of fear expanded in the previous half-century to encompass all of society, in these evolutionary outgrowths of the tale of terror the span of time has increased, reaching back further than the vestiges of medievalism to the obscure origins of man in prehistory.

Moreover, these late Victorian myths (like *Frankenstein*) share a mistrust of the solitary individual. Jekyll's first crime is his preoccupation with self and scorn for group values, while Hyde appears only when the city around him is silent and deserted. Dracula puts others under his power, but he has no real companions; he lives in his castle and travels in England alone. We learn little of Moriarty, but can assume that he, too, though at the head of a criminal organization, is without civilized companions, a dictator served by human appendages. The adversary of these dangerous individuals is always a group, a civilization in miniature, the primitive horde tamed by history and culture.

The builders of prisons and the architects of the Western Front also recreated, intentionally or as a consequence of war, the central Gothic symbol of forbidding castles and haunted ruins. The prisoners of soldiers must have felt as if they were living in the landscape of the horror story.

The ruins of the Cloth Hall, Ypres (1916). This was a medieval architectural jewel, bombed to ruins in World War I. It dominated the devastated British zone known as the Salient, giving all who saw it the feeling that they had entered a sublime and fictive universe. Reproduced by permission of the Imperial War Museum, London.

Although the mid-Victorian fear of mass madness and mob rule continued, the influence of Darwin and other less reliable thinkers like Lombrosio and Pitt-Rivers encouraged the belief that the natural state was a constant struggle for survival between individual organisms, that only by working together could humans avoid the bloody battle that marked the lives of all other creatures. In *Dr. Jekyll and Mr. Hyde*, a small group of people confront Edward Hyde after a particularly vicious incident, while Jekyll's friends and associates — his lawyer Gabriel Utterson (and his friend Richard Enfield), colleague Dr. Lanyon, and butler Poole — are most vulnerable when alone, coming together when they try to control events. Hurrying through the windswept streets with Poole for his climactic confrontation with Jekyll/Hyde, Utterson "had never seen that part of London so deserted ... never in his life had he been conscious of so sharp a wish to see and touch his fellow-creatures" (72). Dracula is also defeated by a close knit band, who succeed only when they coordinate their efforts. (Holmes is somewhat of an anomaly, standing as he does above the crowd of mere mortals. Still, he would be lost to cocaine and depression without Watson, while he needs people to bring him cases and police to serve as foils.)

Companionship then, becomes a defense against reverting to a Hobbsean state of anarchy, or (more aptly) a Darwinian struggle for survival. The success of each group thus replays the rise of civilization itself and its function in controlling the rapacious self-serving instincts that were believed to have dominated prehistory. In fact, in each of these tales history is created, recorded by those who make it. Thus, *The Strange Case of Dr. Jekyll and Mr. Hyde* contains written statements by two of the participants, Sherlock Holmes' cases are all written up by Watson (a fact Holmes comments on more than once), while *Dracula* is composed of the materials for a history — diaries, newspaper clippings, journal entries and the like. This emphasis on the novel as a collection of documents is part of a long tradition, (it comprises the narrative of *Frankenstein* as well), but here it takes on new meaning. The act of writing and the survival of documents is, in all three myths, discussed directly, part of the significance of the texts and not merely the method of transmission. When prehistory ended, man was forced to account for his actions; to late Victorians, deprived by Darwin of a special creation, the creation of history became the dividing line between human and brute, the indisputable mark of civilization.

Among the many written records in *Dracula*, there is no document by

*Opposite: Exterior of the City Prison at Holloway.* **A mid-Victorian structure, like other "modern" prisons Holloway was complete with Gothic battlements and grim dungeons — a medieval throwback that revealed the primitive impulse behind contemporary penology. Reproduced by permissions of Harvard College Library.**

the vampire himself; Moriarty and Holmes' other criminal adversaries leave no record of their machinations, while the only writings of Hyde are a few brief notes and blasphemous comments scribbled in the margins of one of Jekyll's pious books. These individuals are incapable of contributing to the making of history, which draws all its potential readers into the group that, through the acquisition of knowledge, rises above the primitive. By the act of reading these tales, the audience declares itself on the side of civilization, among those whose literacy is a bulwark against a reversion to a prehistoric, pre-literate state.

Although villains like Dracula, Moriarty, or Hyde may be capable of speech, their failure to leave written records puts them closer to the abyss before history, the undocumented and brutal existence believed to have been lived by caveman and ape. Dracula and Moriarty are classified by their adversaries as examples of what van Helsing and Holmes call the "primitive criminal brain," who, along with the "ape-like troglodyte" Hyde, are living throwbacks to a primeval past, evidence of the continued survival of anarchical and brutal tendencies that the new science had found lurking in and threatening modern culture. Although Hyde seems content with his own cruel and private pleasures, he too is, as we shall see, mysteriously tied to a shadowy and anarchical world that threatens everyone. Both Dracula and Moriarty are portrayed as openly planning to replace modern England with a social structure from the brutal past. Dracula's goal is to turn loose an army of vampires, to become the "father or furtherer of a new order of beings," while Moriarty is the spider at the center of a vast web of underworld activity undermining the civilized system of law and order. In all three cases, a social model of restraint and cooperation is under siege from primeval, criminal chaos.

The power of these tales comes, as well, from a technique they also share—the representatives of a shadowy past are precisely placed in an identifiable present. All three depend strongly upon specific locales from London streets to English towns to wild but actual regions in the backwaters of Eastern Europe. Letters addressed to Holmes and Watson still arrive at the site of their lodgings; we are given real street names for the homes of Jekyll and his friend Utterson, and can precisely follow with a map and calendar the movements across space and time of the characters in *Dracula*. The primeval forces of darkness are linked even closer to the contemporary world, as the technique of the tales combines Gothic elements with mundane and familiar settings. To the readers of these stories, able to visit the specific places mentioned while drawn to the seductive evil of characters like Dracula, familiar geography became less physically and psychically safe.

Thus, the late Victorian tales of terror continue the movement of horror from the remoteness of the medieval castle to the reality of modern

Europe. Yet they remain what we call fantasy, not "realistic" fiction or fact. But realism is always only a matter of degree; these myths said something real about human fears, perhaps more true than the scientific theories that inspired them. Lombrosio's evidence for a criminal physical type, like Pitt Rivers' careful displays of the evolution of armor and weapons into clothing and tools, have long been rejected as fantasy—but fantasies like *Dracula* are still very much with us. Earlier in the century, literature labeled "non-fiction"—the explorations of urban slums and reports of the working conditions in mines and factories—used the apparatus of fantasy, the imagery and language of the Gothic novel, to convey a deeper truth than facts and statistics could. In giving form to feelings of horror and unease, as well as to wishes, dreams and fears, both what we call fiction and non-fiction used the same tools for a similar purpose.

At the end of the century, at the time Henry Jekyll, Edward Hyde, and Sherlock Holmes were created, journalists in London told their readers about events and a character that seemed a composite of the most fantastic features of those myths. They learned that, hidden at the center of the city, yet outside the constraints of civilization, was a mysterious and anomalous individual. Like Moriarty or Hyde, he seemed to possess superhuman powers, could elude his pursuers with impunity, and engaged in activities marked by a primitive criminal brutality. Pursuing him was a vast group of people led by the guardians of civilized behavior and including amateur detectives with ingenious (and often wildly improbable) solutions to a baffling mystery.

The collection of accounts comprising the history of these events (which even includes some crude and disturbing letters by the criminal himself) combines moments that seem supernatural with real and particular places that can still be visited. And behind it all is a uniquely threatening and horrible truth, half hidden in the shadows of the tale. Yet Jack the Ripper existed; his victims, five East End prostitutes, really died, and died horribly. In this case, savagery and irrational action seem to have triumphed conclusively over law and order; the mystery of the perpetrator's identity is still unsolved, his motive still unknown.

Popular fiction about horror and crime were a staple of late Victorian reading, but only a handful of stories attained the status of myth. Real examples of horror and murder were just as common as fictional ones; most crimes, like most such fiction, only captured public attention for a brief time. In 1887, the year before the Ripper murders, the Whitechapel District where they occurred recorded some five hundred inquests into unexplained deaths (Cullen 7). Although most authorities attribute no more than five deaths between the end of August and the beginning of November, 1888, to the Ripper, the murder of prostitutes was common enough that the count of his victims has been put as high as fourteen, and crimes committed over a period of many years bracketing this period have been claimed to have been his work. Even during the months the Ripper was active, the papers reported similar but unrelated crimes such as the "Whitehall mystery"—parts of a woman's body kept turning up in the Thames. Something about those crimes known as the Ripper murders stood out from the rest, creating a public sensation unparalleled in the century, with echoes that still resound in the popular mythology of crime.

Sherlock Holmes, who first appeared that same year in *A Study in Scarlet*, stands as an equally enduring symbol, not of unsolved crime, but of inevitable detection, protecting the social order from a whole range of assaults, including theft, espionage, blackmail and murder. However, Conan Doyle's tales, though similar in many ways to the other myths, lack the nightmare element of irrationality that might explain the phenomenon of the Ripper and its relationship to the fears haunting late Victorian life.

The assumption behind detective stories is that scientific analysis (what Holmes calls "reasoning backward" and compares to the ability of a student of prehistory to reconstruct a creature from a single bone) can explain all human behavior, and thus that crime is pursued for rational (or at least understandable) motives. Holmes, like an evolutionist, begins with an effect and reasons back to the chain of past events that caused it. He is seeking, as many theorists influenced by Darwin were seeking, the causes of violence by examining its traces and reconstructing its history. Like Lombrosio and others, who found clues to criminal behavior in the physical attributes of the criminal, Holmes always discovers material evidence that enables him to explain the otherwise inexplicable. Holmes is a member of a now discredited breed of Victorian scientist (from phrenologists who read character in bumps on the head to anthropologists who measured intelligence in the dimensions of the skull), confident that if one only looked close enough at the material world, the dark secrets of the psyche would be revealed.

Only much later, in 1902 with *The Hound of the Baskervilles*, did Conan Doyle approach the emphasis of the other myths upon irrationality and anarchy. There, far from the metropolis of London and on the edge of the Great Grimpen Mire, Holmes and Watson encounter the Gothic castle and dream landscape so familiar to horror story devotees. There, too, are found the Gothic family curse, an atavistic escaped criminal, and the source of fear in the unleashing of brute violence. Close to the dwellings of primitive man (where Holmes lives for a time) and the power of ancient superstitions, Watson, at least, begins to doubt that every human action can be explained by the process of logical deduction.

Holmes never does; perhaps for this reason the mystery of the Ripper never entered the casebook of the master. The brutality and ritual butchery that marked these crimes (the Ripper not only slashed and mutilated his victims; he stole their uteruses) raised too many disturbing questions. It is hard to imagine Holmes looking for clues among the remains of the Ripper's victims; nor can we imagine a motive that would be detectable to a man who knows all there is to know about cigar ash, but almost nothing about the darker recesses of the human heart.*

Although Sherlock Holmes was the creation of a man who, later in life, came to believe in ghosts and fairies, Arthur Conan Doyle could never bring himself to accept the Gothic vision of reality. It took a different kind of detective and a different kind of detective fiction—the Gothic mystery of *Dr. Jekyll and Mr. Hyde*—to create a model for the fears of latent primitive and purposeless violence that came to the surface in the frenzy over the faceless criminal known as Jack the Ripper.

II.

Robert Louis Stevenson's short novel, *The Strange Case of Dr. Jekyll and Mr. Hyde* was, in itself, a publishing phenomenon; when it appeared in 1886, it quickly became the most widely read, discussed, and quoted work in English. Then, less than two years later, the Ripper murders seemed to replay the fantasy of Dr. Jekyll's mysterious and brutal secret life in the reality of London's East End. Why Stevenson's novel captured the public's imagination, and why the Ripper soon did the same, becomes clear when we look at both as mysteries and as myths. A famous author and a nameless criminal together confirmed the late Victorian fear that respectable people, without the restraints of civilization, could easily revert to savage violence.

Stevenson's story has the moralizing quality that Victorians loved, helping to account for one aspect of its immediate popularity—as a source for sermons. But there is more to it than that. The real message seen in the events of this clearly fantastic tale reflected the sense of unease that permeated the time, the feeling that life was more than a struggle between good and evil, right and wrong—it was the old Gothic battle between seeing and not seeing, between accepting and denying our own essential natures, between a generation hoping for a bright future while fighting off the barbaric remnants of a brutal past.

Robert Louis Stevenson certainly believed that what he was writing at

---

*The acknowledged creator of the fictional detective, Edgar Allan Poe, was faced with a similar challenge when a woman was found murdered in New York. Poe attempted to have his detective, C. Auguste Dupin, solve the crime in a three part story called "The Mystery of Marie Roget." His elaborate theories were proved wrong and he was forced to withhold and rewrite the final episode to conform with a much less logical reality. Future detective writers realized that just as Holmes "reasoned backward," their stories must be written backward, with the solution in hand.

the end of 1885 at Skerryvore, his house in Bournemouth, was a Gothic story that spoke to everyone, despite its modern setting and veneer of science. Like the first such tales, written over a century before, it began in a nightmare and was written at breakneck speed, thus keeping it close to the subconscious source of inspiration. Though his wife asked him to recast and deepen the moral message of the first version of what he called his "fine bogey tale" (which he promptly threw into the fire), the revision took only three days. Stevenson himself, in a letter to his friend W. H. Low, called the published version a "Gothic gnome" which "came out of a deep mine, where he guards the fountain of tears . . . the gnome's name is *Jekyll and Hyde*; I believe you will find he is likewise willing to answer to the name of Low or Stevenson (2 January 1886, *Letters* II, 10).

When it appeared in January of 1886, *The Strange Case of Dr. Jekyll and Mr. Hyde* was an incredible sensation, selling forty thousand copies in a few months, read by everyone, quoted in the pulpit, discussed in the popular press. Yet, as one reviewer, James Ashcroft Noble, recognized, it was ". . . simply a paper covered shilling story, belonging, so far as external appearance goes, to a class of literature familiarity with which has bred in the minds of most readers a certain measure of contempt" (*Academy* 23 Jan. 1886, 55). But, obviously, this "familiar" tale was somehow extraordinary; Stevenson had, consciously or not, brought up from that mine something quite rare, valuable and illuminating.

In examining *Jekyll and Hyde* we must first rid ourselves of the misconceptions of over a half century of films. Hyde, for example, is not the hideously ugly creature we have come to expect. Although he exhibits "ape like fury" and is of less than normal stature, the horror of his appearance comes in the loathing everyone who sees him feels. Richard Enfield, the first man to describe him, can say only, "There is something wrong with his appearance; something displeasing, something downright detestable. I never saw a man I so disliked, and yet I scarce know why." It is his moral degeneracy that shines through, not any obvious physical deformity. Dr. Henry Jekyll, for his part, is not a young and good man tragically led to destruction by careless experiments; he is middle aged, with his own dark past, who deliberately sets out to create an impenetrable mask to shield his nocturnal activities from view.

And those activities are not, Stevenson tells us, simply sexual promiscuity; the closest he comes to defining them (in a letter) is to say that Hyde was

> not, Great Gods! a mere voluptuary. There . . . no harm whatever in what prurient fools call 'immorality'. . . . [Hyde] is the essence of cruelty and malice and selfishness and cowardice, and these are the diabolic in man—not this poor wish to love a woman, that they make such a cry about [quoted Eigner 150].

The story itself is no clearer; Jekyll speaks of "pleasures" that "were (to say the least) undignified," while Hyde, before the murder that climaxes and ends his secret life, is seen striking a woman selling matches and heedlessly knocking down a child. But the places he frequents in the London darkness and what he does there are left obscure.

Some of the activities left undescribed may have been relatively innocuous. After all, the lawyer Utterson, through whose eyes we see much of the action, denies what gives him pleasure with Evangelical fervor; he drinks gin "to mortify a taste for vintages; and though he enjoyed the theater, had not crossed the doors of one for twenty years." (None of this is overstatement; the son of the Evangelical James Stephen says that his father "once smoked a cigar, and found it so delicious that he never had one again" [Annan 14].) Still, though Stevenson himself never condemned sexual dalliance (and in fact wrote poetry in praise of it), there is a strong suggestion that whatever Jekyll went to such pains to conceal may have been, from the first, more than what he (or we) would call innocent.

Most importantly, the relationship between the two is not the "split personality" that has come to be labeled as "Jekyll and Hyde." As has been pointed out many times, Jekyll is not all good, nor is Hyde all evil. Self righteous, imperious, with a face of a "slyish cast," Jekyll, before liberating Hyde, admits he was "committed to a profound duplicity of life." Hyde, though Jekyll sees him at one point as "wholly evil," does evoke some sympathy when, at the end, Poole hears him "weeping like a woman or a lost soul." (Vladimir Nabokov has argued [184] that Hyde's desire to return to Jekyll's form is another sign of the spark of good within him, though his only motive seems to be self preservation. Still, he does have a spark of Jekyll in him at all times, which is not quite the same thing.)

The dark secret of Jekyll and Hyde is, then, not that one person splits in half, but that two very different and complete individuals share one house and one body. By the end of the book, the relationship between Jekyll, Hyde, and the elusive narrator of "Henry Jekyll's Full Statement of the Case" who speaks of both with equal detachment, becomes, as we shall see, very mysterious indeed.

Familiarity with the outcome of the tale has caused us to forget that *The Strange Case* is a mystery, complete with detective, the lawyer Gabriel Utterson, who at one point says that, in pursuing Hyde, he shall be "Mr. Seek." However, this detective is singularly incompetent; every deduction he makes is wrong, and the solution finally has to be presented to him in a manuscript written in Jekyll's hand. In this case, the tools Holmes uses so well are singularly ineffective. In fact, that short manuscript contains what is remembered as the story of Jekyll and Hyde; the vast majority of the book chronicles Utterson's failure to make sense of the events before him, and the devastating consequences when another of Jekyll's friends, Dr.

Lanyon, is also shown the solution by Jekyll himself. Utterson's and Lanyon's experiences form the bulk of the tale; the novel is really about their incomprehension as much as it is about Jekyll's new understanding.

Jekyll's forbidden knowledge, coupled with Utterson's and Lanyon's difficulty in discovering it, together make this "strange case" so powerful. Both a detective case and a case in abnormal psychology, it constantly escapes pinning down by the lawyer's methodical logic. Utterson is utterly confounded by the "supernatural" answer that one man can change into another, given, as in the Gothic novels of Ann Radcliffe, the flimsiest scientific rationale. Holmes would be baffled as well, since Jekyll's impossible pharmacological "solution" falls outside the acceptable logical conventions of realistic detective fiction.

In Conan Doyle's fictional world criminals can be understood because their actions are understandable; the supernatural (like the irrational) is banned because it admits a world beyond logic, where motives are as murky as methods. Thus the actions of both Jekyll and the Ripper would be beyond Holmes' power to explain. But such mysteries fit squarely in the horror tradition, which from the start portrayed amateur investigators unraveling mysteries whose threads extended to the edge of what is possible, and beyond. The revival of the Gothic mystery in *Jekyll and Hyde* and *Dracula*, like the fascination with the real mystery of Jack the Ripper, suggests that the conventions of Conan Doyle's tales of Sherlock Holmes failed to account fully for the complexities of human motivation.

Conan Doyle continually affirms the power of observation and logic to see and hold back the darkness; we know Holmes will always figure out the most extraordinary and inexplicable events — from hiring a red headed man to copy an encyclopedia to repeating a nonsense verse through the centuries — giving them purpose and thus making them safe. In the Gothic mysteries, detectives like Utterson fail (in *Dracula*, the woman the heroes swear to protect dies because of their bungling) when they don't realize that what the supernatural represents — irrational, primitive and purposeless activity — is ultimately unknowable. They can succeed only after they follow vampirehunter Abraham van Helsings paradoxical advice (delivered in his characteristic broken English) "to believe in things that you cannot."

Even without Jekyll's impossible drugs and their "power to shake and pluck back that fleshly vestment, even as a wind might toss the curtains of a pavilion" Utterson would fail to comprehend the truth. For his assumptions about both Jekyll and Hyde are based upon his inability to believe that anyone like Jekyll could love anyone like Hyde, much less create a different and detestable persona and announce "This, too, was myself." Many of Utterson's wrong guesses are over what kind of "strange case" he is investigating. At one point he believes it to be criminal (Hyde blackmailing Jekyll), at another point medical (Jekyll suffering from "one of those maladies that both torture and deform the sufferer"), at another point mental. Dr. Lanyon's testimony contains yet another kind of "strange case" — the drawer of chemicals Jekyll asks him, in a desperate note, to fetch from his locked laboratory when he is imprisoned in the body of Hyde.

Lanyon also tries to play detective, examining the drawer full of drugs and the notebook of dates and cryptic comments, and concluding with the conviction that he "was dealing with a case of cerebral disease." In Lanyon's presence, Hyde removes the drugs from the drawer and performs the transformation. Lanyon's narrative ends after his account of this moment, when the real secrets in this strange case are revealed. Comprehending the effects of the drug gives Lanyon a glimpse into a primitive heart of darkness, the survival of prehistoric man within ourselves, and destroys his desire to live.

The chemicals themselves are Stevenson's own rational solution to the mysteries of Jekyll's experience, his attempt to place the impossible within a scientific framework. Like the elaborate contrivances Ann Radcliffe used to explain away the ghostly manifestations in novels like *Mysteries of Udolpho* and *The Italian* nearly a century earlier (and the defense of spontaneous human combustion Dickens introduced to explain the inexplicable self destruction of Krook in *Bleak House*), Stevenson's appeal to a universe of understandable cause and effect is unconvincing and, finally, like the drug itself, inadequate.

The drug begins to lose its ability to bring Jekyll back, while Jekyll starts to become Hyde spontaneously. In the final chapter, "Henry Jekyll's Full Statement of the Case" (which is far from a full explanation), the narrator attributes this to chemical causes — a new drug supply which lacks some unknown adulterant. Yet it is more likely that the center of the Jekyll/Hyde character has shifted from the discontented doctor to the troglodyte Hyde emerging from his cave. When the essence of the self joins Hyde, Jekyll becomes a mask increasingly difficult to sustain. In the films, after Hyde's death, Jekyll reemerges; in the book, the body remains Hyde's. Throughout the story, Stevenson points up the inadequacy of all rational methods of solving this "strange case" — the detective, the doctor, the scientist, the author himself — all are confounded by the complexity and elusiveness of human possibility.

In fact, there are other mysteries left unilluminated at the end of the novel. Not only do we not know precisely the nature of the forbidden pleasures Jekyll pursued in secret and Hyde continued with impunity, we also are unclear about the one crime of Hyde's we do witness, the savage murder of Sir Danvers Carew, M. P., clubbed to death by Hyde in an "ape like" fury. We never find out why he was killed, whether he knew Hyde or not, and why, according to a witness, this "aged, beautiful gentleman" looked at Hyde with "old world kindness of disposition, yet with something high too, as of a well founded self-content"—in short, without the loathing that seemed to affect everyone else who encountered Hyde.

Utterson, earlier called "the last reputable acquaintance and the last good influence in the lives of downgoing men," is informed of the murder because a sealed letter with his name and address was found on the victim. We never find out what's in that letter, although the other two sealed letters to Utterson in the story (from Lanyon and Jekyll) contain horrifying secrets. Whatever it contains, Utterson has "no sooner seen it" and been told of the circumstances than he announces "I shall say nothing until I have seen the body.... This may be very serious." He seems to be alluding here not only to Carew's death, but to something beyond it that his death may reveal. The policeman who finds the body, his eye "light[ing] up with professional ambition" exclaims, "This will make a deal of noise." But on these mysteries, Stevenson gives us only silence.

Since he displays a very un–Holmesean wish not to know too much, Utterson makes a strange detective. He commences his search for Hyde's connection to Jekyll after a conversation with his friend Richard Enfield on the unhealthy consequences of asking too many questions:

> You start a question, and it's like starting a stone. You sit quietly on the top of a hill; and away the stone goes, starting others; and presently some bland old bird (the last you would have thought of) is knocked on the head in his own back garden and the family have to change their name. No sir, I make it a rule of mine; the more it looks like Queer Street, the less I ask.

Gabriel Utterson replies, "A very good rule, too," and the two vow never to talk of Hyde again. This fear that unraveling one thread could destroy the fabric that holds respectable society together is another barrier to Utterson's search for truth. In the course of his investigation, "a bland old bird," Sir Danvers Carew, is indeed knocked on the head in mysterious circumstances, while Dr. Lanyon pays for his curiosity with his life.

The focus on Jekyll's transformation to Hyde and his subsequent self-destruction, the core of every retelling of the myth, has diverted attention from these other unanswered questions. The mystery of Jekyll/Hyde remains, as does the identity of Jack the Ripper; both are connected to the obscure secrets and fears at the heart of late Victorian England. These unanswered questions help explain the survival of all three Gothic mysteries—Jack the Ripper and *Dracula* as well as Jekyll/Hyde. Unlike Arthur Conan Doyle, the journalists who told of the Ripper and the writers who made Dracula and Jekyll/Hyde live leave us doubting that rational deduction can explain the enigma of human behavior.

The elusive mysteries of *The Strange Case of Dr. Jekyll and Mr. Hyde* evolved from the fears that inspired the Gothic impulse from its inception.

## 5. The Proximity of the Past

The private horror of the duplicitous doctor finds its echo deep within each of its readers, while reflecting the instability that threatened the survival of the entire social structure. Utterson, Enfield, Jekyll, Hyde, Lanyon, and even the unfortunate Sir Danvers Carew are somehow united, victims of secrets revealed and keepers of secrets, protecting a larger truth from each other and themselves.

Like the creators of Dracula and the Holmes stories, Stevenson unites the private and public realms with a focus on specific places that underlies Utterson's ambivalent quest for knowledge. The movement of characters from one place to another—whether it is districts in London, parts of one house, or even between bodies—illuminates the conflicts that underlie Stevenson's story and account for its phenomenal success. Not only is the distant past close to civilized man, but brutal and primitive life abuts the centers of civilization. Stevenson examines the city itself and the contrast between the poverty and plenty that exist side by side; he makes Jekyll's home a house with two entrances, near each other but so different that few suspect they are connected, and finally, he defines Jekyll's crime as seeing his own body as a place to be entered and left at will.

Like the horror tales that inspired it, Stevenson's "fine bogey tale" unites society, the family, and the individual, as well as past, present and future. By understanding how the very proximity of places and the metaphor of movement give meaning to the tale, we can see what John Fowles may have meant when he used that same metaphor of space to declare (in *The French Lieutenant's Woman*) that *The Strange Case of Dr. Jekyll and Mr. Hyde* is "very possibly the best guidebook to the age."

Many of the other guidebooks to that age—books that deal with the shape of the city in nineteenth century England—emphasize the closeness of wealth and squalor, respectability and vice, safety and danger. Within adjacent streets in late Victorian London, the average life expectancy of the inhabitants could vary as much as from 38 years to 12 (Young 21). As far back as the late eighteenth century, someone walking through London would be struck by these contrasts:

> One moment the vista might be of noble colonnade, bow-windows and gleaming door knockers ... the next, if you chanced to take a careless turning, it was to find yourself among gin shops and pawnbrokers and broken down dwellings of such squalor that they literally oozed filth [Low 3].

The consequence of a wrong turning in late Victorian London could be more perilous:

> a stone's throw from the prosperous Strand are courts and passages ... where it is risky for the casual visitor to penetrate even in broad

daylight.... Everyone knows the nightmare casbahs, swarming with disease and crime, behind the busy streets [Chesney 5].

In Stevenson's native Edinburgh, the contrast was highlighted by the shape of the city itself; the poorest area, the once prosperous Old Town, overlooked the wealthiest:

> Towering over the New Town on the South, flanking it to the east, and a short walk from its smart West End were the rendezvous of criminals and prostitutes . . . areas of an underground that the decent preferred to forget. And at any moment, turning the corner from a dense slum or breasting a cobbled slope, one might catch sight of green hills or the glint of water [Calder *RLS* 4].

Stevenson himself, in his "Picturesque Notes" (1878), described how "The poor man may roost up there in the centre of Edinburgh, and yet have a peep of the great country from his window; he shall see the quarters of the well-to-do fathoms underneath, with their broad squares and gardens" (*Works* I 279).

This emphasis upon what one writer has called the "grotesque proximity" between the wretchedest members of society and the richest and most powerful (Chesney 105) underlies *The Strange Case of Dr. Jekyll and Mr. Hyde*. It opens with an account of one of the regular Sunday rambles around London of Utterson and his friend Richard Enfield, which takes them to the "by-street in a busy quarter" where Enfield once encountered Hyde. The street is a study in contrasts, standing out from its "dingy neighborhood" like "a fire in a forest." Neither wealthy nor poor, its collection of middle class shops is compared to "rows of smiling saleswomen," while the "sinister block of building" that stands between them has a "blind forehead" and "blistered door" where tramps and vandals shelter.

Personifying places, giving landscapes implicit narratives, is, as we have seen, a characteristic of the horror story and the notion of the sublime that underlies it. The door, of course, conceals the laboratory from which Hyde emerges for his obscure excursions through the sleeping city. But the "smiling saleswomen" are also masks, suggesting that Jekyll is not the only one to veil his true feelings behind a false front. Later, we learn that these ostensibly very different places are so packed together that "its hard to say where one ends and another begins."

The difficulty of defining where places are and how they relate is pointed up in the course of Enfield's story. He met Hyde near the door after returning from his own obscure destination, "coming home from some place at the end of the world, about three o'clock of a black winter morning." Later, Hyde enters the door and returns with a check, signed by a gentleman whom we later learn is Jekyll. At the time, Enfield has doubts about the authenticity of the signature, since he can't believe Jekyll could live in such squalor, and besides, knows his address; "he lives in some square or other." Of course, the square is just around the corner; the laboratory is Jekyll's back door.

Jekyll's front door, which leads to the "pleasantest room in London," is similarly personified, and again as a mask, wearing "a great air of wealth and comfort, though it was now plunged in darkness." The house itself is the last one "still occupied entire"; the rest of the square is a study in urban Gothic, "decayed," with the buildings turned to flats. The inhabitants also have mysteries to conceal, mysteries also connected to places. They are "map-engravers, architects, shady lawyers and agents of obscure enterprises." All are united by their professional interest in charting the shape of the land, of buildings, of human lives.

Thus, doors and buildings again become important, defining by their appearance and location the relationship between places and personalities, while they connect two dissimilar but proximate realms. Stevenson recognizes this, calling the first chapter "The Story of a Door," and beginning Enfield's tale of his encounter with Hyde with the lines,

> "Did you ever remark that door?" he asked; and when his companion had replied in the affirmative, "It is connected in my mind," added he, "with a very odd story."

The story that follows finally ends, at least for Utterson, when he and Poole smash down the inner laboratory door that guards Jekyll's secret and find the body of Hyde.

Doors also traditionally guard the secrets of the self in dreams, another horror story landscape where different places exist in grotesque proximity. Utterson dreams of Enfield's tale as a "scroll of lighted pictures," alternatively seeing Hyde crush a child at every street corner and a "room in a rich house" where a door opens and Hyde awakens the sleeper (as the Monster awakened Frankenstein). These two scenes shift in ever increasing frequency, until Utterson is forced to "haunt" the mysterious door, hoping to see Hyde and end his own nightmares.

Utterson's dream extends the fictional landscape to the dark recesses of the self. The story occurs simultaneously in an external world and in the fears and fantasies of the dour and repressed Gabriel Utterson. When he tracks Hyde to the slums of Soho, it seems to the lawyer to be "like a district of some city in a nightmare." The darkness is mirrored in his own thoughts, which are also of "the gloomiest dye." He, too, "becomes conscious of that terror of the law, and the law's officers, which may at times assail the most honest." The fog that alternatively lifts and obscures his vision creates scenes like the scroll of lighted pictures of his dreams, since each new vision is different, "changing glimpses" illuminated by "lamps, which had never been extinguished."

Lamps and fog alternate throughout the story, images of illumination and concealment that mirror the conflict Utterson feels (shared by society as a whole) between wanting to know the truth and being afraid to find out. As in *Bleak House,* the city is defined by darkness and mist, blackness that has moved from the Gothic basement to every corner of the urban atmosphere. At one point, fog even begins to "lie thickly" inside Jekyll's house, forcing the doctor to light both a lamp and the fire. Enfield's tale emphasizes the "black winter morning" contrasting with "street after street, all lighted up as if for a procession, and all as empty as a church;" Uttersons' nightmare moves swiftly "through wider labyrinths of the lamplighted city;" Utterson finally meets Hyde on a night when the streets are "as clean as a ballroom floor; the lamps, unshaken by any wind, drawing a regular pattern of light and shadow." Even Carew's murder occurs on a night "brilliantly lit by the full moon" though later "a fog rolled over the city."

Such contrasting dream images are found elsewhere in late Victorian literature, most notably in James Thompson's very popular poem about the urban Hell, "The City of Dreadful Night" (1873), where

> The street-lamps burn amidst baleful glooms,
> Amidst the soundless solitudes immense
> Of ranged mansions dark and still as tombs....
> (I)
>
> Although lamps burn along the silent streets;
> Even when moonlight silvers empty squares
> The dark holds countless lanes and close retreats
> (III)

The feeling of precariousness that these images evoke, of the small civilized circle of light in a dark and dangerous expanse of space and time, helps account for the power of Stevenson's novel. He was able to connect individual anxieties to the fears of an entire culture, turning his own "waking dream" into a collective nightmare. In *Dr. Jekyll and Mr. Hyde,* the images of darkness and light illuminate the larger questions, but still surely owe much to the nightmare that gave birth to the novel and to Stevenson's own childhood fears, when his world was limited to the dimensions of his sickroom. One of his earliest recollections was of his nurse, Alice Cunningham:

> I remember with particular distinctness, how she would lift me out of bed and take me, rolled in blankets, to the window, whence I might look forth into the blue night starred street lamps, and see

## 5. The Proximity of the Past

where the gas still burned behind the windows of other sick-rooms. These were feverish, melancholy times: I cannot remember to have raised my head or seen the moon or any of the heavenly bodies; my eyes were turned downward to the broad lamplit streets and to where the trees of the garden rustled together all night in undecipherable blackness ["Memoirs of Himself" XXV 225].

In the supernatural absurdities of the Gothic novel, the horrifying realism of mid Victorian sociology and literature, and in the myths of the last decades of the century, these images of darkness and light, obscurity and revelation, ignorance and knowledge, recur. From Catherine Morland wandering into forbidden rooms in Northanger Abbey to the journalist and detective peering into the dark corners of the urban slums to Utterson haunting a doorway hoping to "but once set eyes" on Edward Hyde, vision has both led to scenes of horror and dispelled their terror.

During the nineteenth century, the range of that vision expanded in both space and time. In the Gothic novel, the heroine stumbled upon the skeletons hidden in one family's closet; her dim candle revealed the secrets of one evil nobleman's dark past. By the end of the century, darkness covered the entire landscape; penetrating it revealed horrors that implicated all of society. The dead controlled the living, not as spectres or through curses and legacies, but by the sheer force of genetic inheritance extending back to prehistory. The solution to the mystery of *Dr. Jekyll and Mr. Hyde*, like the answer to the parallel enigma of Jack the Ripper, can be found when we examine them as manifestations of the shadow cast by an undying past, of the brutality unleashed when the light of civilization is averted, of the Gothic power of blackness.

*Chapter Six*
# Dr. Jekyll and Jack the Ripper: The Power of the Will

> Man's physical organism is played upon not only by the physical conditions about it, but by remote laws of inheritance, the vibration of long past acts reaching him in the midst of the new order of things in which he lives.
> —Walter Pater

The connection in the public mind between *The Strange Case of Dr. Jekyll and Mr. Hyde* and the notorious case of Jack the Ripper had some unfortunate consequences; Richard Mansfield, an American actor appearing in 1888 in a stage production of the novel, was forced to cut short its run with a benefit performance for the homeless of the East End after he kept being fingered by playgoers as the killer. Although not everyone was quite so literal in identifying Stevenson's art with late Victorian life, it is clear that the reading public used the pattern of Dr. Jekyll's story to piece together a narrative from the horrifying evidence left behind by Jack the Ripper.

*Dr. Jekyll and Mr. Hyde* became a blueprint for speculation about the murders because both events—fictional and factual—conveyed, graphically and undeniably, a sense of the precariousness of a culture caught between outward respectability and secret violence. They also seemed to prove the survival of what Walter Pater called "the remote laws of inheritance" and others called "the beast within"—the legacy of a brutal evolutionary heritage expressed in the insatiable demands of a ruthless will. In many subtle ways, the powerful artistry of a bedridden author and the primitive actions of an elusive maniac were parallel creations; each gave form to the fears hiding in the late Victorian urban darkness.

Dr. Henry Jekyll becomes Edward Hyde because he wants the perfect disguise, freedom to indulge in what he calls his "undignified pleasures" without hindrance. The drug is the answer, a clearly supernatural device that cloaks Jekyll in anonymity, protecting him from detection and disgrace. With the fear of exposure gone, Jekyll's activities as Hyde soon turn monstrous. The few examples we observe all occur in a "strangely deserted"

London. Jekyll, then, becomes man without the constraints of society and the bonds of personal obligation; complete freedom, combined with isolation from censure and civilization, becomes the real formula for his transformation from forward thinking scientist to the hideous throwback that is Hyde.

Although we never learn the exact nature of these "pleasures," clearly violence is at their center, violence displayed on three occasions by Hyde, and referred to in Stevenson's comment that Hyde was the "essence of cruelty and malice and selfishness and cowardice" (Eiger 150). Stevenson's reluctance to be explicit tinges whatever Hyde did with added horror supplied by readers' imaginations; part of the power of the tale is that the audience must participate by visualizing their own variations of those obscure and nefarious activities. As in the tale of terror, the veil drawn over the most shocking moments ostensibly protects the readers, but actually gives them freedom to indulge their most private fantasies in the solitary landscape of the mind—the real domain of Jekyll's alter ego.

But that may not have been Stevenson's only motivation. He had written another story on the same theme the previous summer, "The Traveling Companion"; it was rejected by an editor as "a work of genius but indecent" and destroyed by Stevenson as "foul, gross, bitter, ugly ... a carrion tale" (Brown 247). Possibly the lost tale made explicit what its successor was shrouded in darkness; the act of putting such fantasies directly into words proved too unsettling for both author and editor. The equation behind the particular terrors of *Jekyll and Hyde* is, then, that freedom and anonymity can turn a hypocrite into a beast whose crimes become literally unspeakable.

Jack the Ripper's nocturnal pastimes were also deemed indescribable; newspapers dwelt on their savagery and brutality but withheld vital details, going only so far as to state that "certain organs" were missing. Concealing the exact nature of his crimes behind the Victorian veil only made his acts more mysterious and subject to a similar creative embroidery of rumor and speculation. This sense of mystery was heightened by the seemingly inexplicable circumstances surrounding the attacks. Unlike the other criminals who filled the sensationalist press, the Ripper had a strange and almost supernatural power to commit his crimes with impunity and in anonymity. He operated in one of the busiest districts of London, killing two women in one night, four in open streets not far from policemen and passersby. Yet the closest Scotland Yard ever got was when Major Henry Smith, the Acting Police Commissioner for the City of London, ran through the dark and tangled streets of Whitechapel a few minutes after one murder to see the last dregs of bloody water draining out of an outdoor basin where the invisible criminal had washed his hands.

What the *Daily News* called the "most agonizing of the East End mysteries ... the utter paralysis of energy and intelligence on the part of the police" (11 Oct. 1888, 5) was not a symptom of inactivity. Though the government posted no large reward (as had been done six years earlier when Lord Cavendish was the victim of the Phoenix Park murders) a huge public outcry had results. Police were out in force (sometimes dressed as prostitutes); they rounded up large numbers of suspicious characters, all of whom were quickly released, and even employed two champion bloodhounds, Barnaby and Burgho, who promptly got lost in a fog. Nothing worked. The crowded streets of the East End always seemed to be deserted when the Ripper struck, while what evidence did exist led everywhere and nowhere.

Although many people claimed to have seen the Ripper with his victims, their descriptions rarely tallied. A reporter for the *Daily Telegraph* summed up the problem:

> Each informant is firmly convinced the man she saw was the Unknown ... but as the description varies in each case it is quite plain that they cannot refer to the same person. According to one he is a thick-set, clean shaven man; another states that he is a pretty tall man, with dark whiskers and a beard, a third speaks of him as shortish with light whiskers. Altogether the descriptions are so confusing that they afford no guide to any officer [2 Oct 1888, 3].

Everyone did agree on one "fact" that informs us of the wish to locate evil on some undefined "other"—whatever his features, the man the witnesses saw looked "like a foreigner." (Of course, knowing the attitudes of Imperial England at that time, it may be more accurate to say that, to these "witnesses," foreigners looked like the Ripper.) The elusiveness of the criminal and the lack of detail about his brutal crimes invited the public to construct their own fictions. And they did, inundating the police and press with explanations of the criminal's motivation and methods of escape, suggesting that many could perform the collaborative act Stevenson had asked of those who read of Hyde's crimes and put themselves, in their imagination at least, in the Ripper's shoes.

While professional and amateur detectives had more theories about the Ripper than Gabriel Utterson had about Hyde, all proved equally fruitless. A leather apron found near one body intensified a search for a suspect nicknamed "Leather Apron," supposedly an employee of a nearby slaughterhouse. The discovery of a strange chalk inscription ("the Juwes [sic] are the men that will not be blamed for nothing") led to anti–Semitic mob violence, but no arrests. For a while it was believed the murderer carried a leather bag of a type that quickly fell from fashion. Others saw him with strange parcels wrapped in newspaper or wearing a Holmsean deerstalker hat. Queen Victoria herself suggested examining the crews of foreign ships docked nearby. Over 14,000 letters inundated police and press, full of armchair theories and harebrained advice.

Suspects were arrested, questioned, and released with monotonous regularity. All the while, the criminal did more than remain at large and continue killing. He advertised himself in a series of letters and poems sent to his pursuers. In them, he dropped clues ("What fools the police are. I even give them the name of the street where I am living"), mocked the armchair theorists ("I'm not a butcher, I'm not a Yid /nor yet a foreign skipper"), promised further atrocities and, worst of all, implied his readers were secret sympathizers ("The next job I do I shall clip the lady's ears off and send to the police officers, just for jolly, wouldn't you?"). He even sent evidence of his crimes: along with part of a kidney cut from Catherine Eddowes and sent to George Lusk, chairman of the Whitechapel Vigilance Committee, came a note reading, "From hell, Mr Lusk, sir, I send you half the kidne I took from one woman, prasarved it for you, tother piece I fried and ate it; was very nice" [sic]. Like later communications from other serial killers, the Ripper letters show a desperate desire for notoriety; what they don't show is remorse, regret, or a wish to be caught and stopped.

Instead, the Ripper created a literature of fear unprotected by the mask of fiction, unelevated by the goal of social reform. Equally gruesome glimpses of reality had been communicated throughout the period, but filtered through narrators who, like Henry Mayhew (or the considerably more lurid G. W. M. Reynolds of *Mysteries of London* fame) served to shape experience with the tools of fiction and stand between the events and those who read about them. The Ripper speaks directly to his readers, implying by his words and literacy (despite the [possibly intentional] misspellings) that he is one of them, acting out the grotesque fantasies that made popular fiction from Gothic romance to penny dreadfuls part of the imaginative life of a mass audience.

The Ripper's mood in his letters is much as Jekyll recalls Hyde feeling after murdering Carew: in an "ecstasy of mind, gloating on my crime, lightheartedly devising others for the future." Like Hyde confidently drinking the potion that protects him with "a song on his lips," the Ripper's voice exudes confidence in a perfect disguise (he writes "How can they catch me now?"). And, of course, in identifying his actions with the wishes of an outraged public ("I shall clip the lady's ears off ... wouldn't you?) he recognizes one reason he is so hard to catch. He isn't the unearthly being of Gothic horror and Victorian journalism, but an outwardly undistinguished member of the respectable mass audience who read about him as they read horror stories, with both fear and fascination.

Jack the Ripper (the name used as a signature on many of the thirty-four letters believed to be genuine) was, however, more than another "boy next door" psychopath, the modern paradigm of senseless murder. His special ability to conceal his actions sets him apart, for he seemed to many to have the supernatural powers of a ghost from Gothic fiction. Anne Chapman was murdered and disembowelled early on the morning of September 8, 1888; *The Times* commented that the murderer "must have left the yard in Hanbury Street reeking with blood and yet . . . he must have walked in almost broad daylight among streets comparatively well frequented, even at that early hour, without his startling appearance attracting the slightest attention" (11 Sept 1888, 6).

Another murder had even more fantastic aspects. Police Constable Edward Watkins circled Mitre Square every fifteen minutes. At one thirty a.m. on September 30, he saw nothing unusual. The next time around, the body of Catherine Eddowes lay on the pavement, throat cut, face slashed, eyelids nicked, disembowelled, with her right earlobe, uterus and kidney missing. She had been murdered near the International Working Men's Club, whose lights were all ablaze, and within three yards of a half open kitchen door that threw bright light upon the yard. Once again the killer vanished in the maze of courts and alleys he must have known intimately; a *Daily News* reporter suggested he might even have used the underground labyrinth of sewers.\*

Then, as now, notorious crimes attracted publicity seekers: supposed witnesses, false confessions, would-be psychics, and amateur detectives with fantastic theories. The extraordinary nature of the Ripper murders brought all of these characters out in force. Even the police were affected, photographing the eyes of at least one of the victims in hopes of catching an image of the killer. The *East London Advertiser* alluded to the appeal of the Ripper phenomena for the public by pointing out the similarity of the events to the mythology behind the horror story:

> It is so impossible to account, on any ordinary hypothesis, for these revolting acts of blood that the mind turns as it were instinctively to some theory of occult force, and the myths of the Dark Ages arise before the imagination. Ghouls, vampires, blood-suckers . . . take form and seize the excited fancy [10 Nov. 1888, 4].

---

\* *Jack the Ripper was not the first criminal to achieve both notoriety and general belief in his almost supernatural powers of concealment. He was sometimes referred to as "Spring Heel Jack," the name given to a criminal phenomenon earlier in the century. This character, who first terrorized the London suburbs in the 1830's, was so named because of his alleged prodigious leaps, supposedly made possible by springs in his boots. The subject of newspaper tales and penny dreadfuls for the next fifty years, Spring Heel Jack was the "Bigfoot" of his day. His "crimes" consisted of leaping over hedges (and, it was sometimes alleged, houses) to plunder and frighten solitary travelers with his "fiery breath" and "eyes of flame." Despite the absurdity of it all, for a time Spring Heel Jack was taken seriously, with police squads and vigilante committees formed to hunt him down.*

Soon, the theory that the Ripper was from the lower classes was abandoned; his letters were seen as imitations of illiteracy, while his crude butchery was taken as evidence of surgical skill. After a coroner solemnly announced the absurd "fact" that an American doctor was paying for uteruses to supply with each issue of a new treatise on female disorders, medical men became suspects, shadowed by plainclothesmen, hauled in at the merest pretext. The conviction that the murderer was a doctor certainly was also due, in part, to the profession of the unfortunate Henry Jekyll. In the century since the murders stopped and the letters ceased, no less than six doctors have been fingered as the Ripper, including a poisoner, Dr. Neill Cream, as well as Sir William Gull, physician to the Royal Family. These theories, as well as those that accuse the Duke of Clarence, heir to the British throne, or his closest friend, James K. Stephen, may be implausible, but they point up one more reason both *Jekyll/Hyde* and the Ripper murders remain in the public consciousness.

As has been noted many times, in late Victorian England the secret lives of respectable Englishmen required the services of an army of prostitutes of both sexes (Mayhew puts the number in London alone at 80,000) some of whom provided special services such as flagellation or procuring children (known as "unripe fruit"). When a gentleman's pocket change was a workman's monthly wages, when the authorities generally looked the other way at the perverse pleasures of the well to do, the relationship between wealthy men and poor women encompassed more than economic exploitation. The Ripper story, like *Dr. Jekyll and Mr. Hyde,* thus fulfilled another function of the Gothic story; they took to horrid excess the private horrors of their readers.

Stevenson was certainly aware of a scandal that broke in *The Pall Mall Gazette,* a popular sensationalist newspaper, a few months before he wrote *Dr. Jekyll and Mr. Hyde.* W. T. Stead, the editor, simply recorded his routine purchase of a thirteen year old girl for sexual purposes from her mother, for five pounds. He then went on to document the widespread practice of child prostitution in England. Stead's articles caused a sensation and did what a Royal Commission set up in 1871 could not do; by the end of the year the age of consent had been raised from twelve to sixteen, procuration was finally a crime, and sex with a child was punished by whipping or imprisonment. Ironically, Stead himself was jailed for three months for spiriting the girl to Paris without her parents' permission (though he clearly did so only to protect her). The stories and subsequent trial caused a "pent-up horror that gripped the whole country while the deadly drama was slowly being unfolded" (Pearsall, *Worm* 375). Exposés like Stead's (reprinted in a pamphlet luridly entitled *Maiden Tribute of Modern Babylon*) titillated their readers and led, slowly, to reforms, but never did away with the secrets behind Victorian respectability.

With very few exceptions, the only check on such excesses was guilt and fear of exposure, the loss of one's good name. Jekyll found the solution; as Hyde, "undignified" pleasures

> soon began to turn toward the monstrous ... drinking pleasure with bestial avidity from any degree of torture to another; relentless like a man of stone. Henry Jekyll stood at times aghast at the acts of Edward Hyde; but the situation was apart from ordinary laws, and insidiously relaxed the grip of conscience. It was Hyde, after all, and Hyde alone that was guilty. Jekyll was no worse; he woke again to his good qualities seemingly unimpaired. . . .

Jekyll, like the Ripper, could for a time sustain two lives without guilt or danger; it was the fulfillment of a fantasy of power and protection that has always existed, but must have been widespread in an age when every brothel and back street had patrons from the ranks of the "respectable" classes. (Peter Gay labels his discussion of late Victorian hypocrisy "A Search for Safety" [405].) Jekyll found not only the perfect disguise, but by becoming two autonomous people was able to reconcile the need to escape respectability with the late Victorian hatred of lying and hypocrisy.

Jekyll's method is his magic potion; the Ripper's means was equally miraculous. As one reporter concluded, "The criminal withdraws himself from all eyes as securely as though he possessed the charm which could make him invisible at will" (*Daily News* 10 Nov. 1888, 4). For a time, both are safe from discovery by others and, if Jekyll's manuscript and the Ripper letters are to be believed, from self reproach. But the consequences are devastating. Hyde's vicious crimes, alluded to by Stevenson (and demonstrated in the brutal murder of Danvers Carew), and the even more sickening activities of the Ripper proved where power without restraint could end.

The last of the Ripper murders seems to bear this out. Mary Kelly was murdered in her squalid lodgings on November 9; this time the Ripper had privacy and a whole night to carry out his inexplicable brutalities. The result was a woman horribly dissected, with internal organs laid out by the bedside, blood and flesh on walls, furniture and floor. This gruesome scene was discovered as the Lord Mayor's Procession was about to begin. Here, too, wealth and poverty were thrown into a cruel conjunction. Part of the festivities included throwing copper pennies from the windows and balconies into the roadway where ragged crowds waited to see the gilded coach and parade of dignitaries: "the fun was to see the street boys, and men for the matter of that, dart across to catch the descending copper or scramble for it in the indescribably filthy kennel" (*Daily Telegraph* 10 Nov. 1888, 3). This time, events were interrupted by newsvendors crying the latest murder, leading to jeers at the police and somewhat spoiling the show.

In many ways, then, the Ripper murders replayed Stevenson's fiction as fact. Neither Hyde nor the Ripper could be described, yet both shared an "otherness" that Ripper witnesses called foreign and Richard Enfield, describing Hyde, could not label:

> He's an extraordinary looking man, yet I really can name nothing out of the way. No sir; I can make no hand of it; I can't describe him. And it's not for want of memory; for I declare I can see him at this moment.

Both criminals operated in a strangely deserted London. In those brief moments when people were absent, civilization and its restraints on savagery also seemed to depart. Both Hyde, annotating Jekyll's pious books with blasphemies, and the Ripper, in his obscene notes to police and press, mocked the respectability of the age. The mystery in both is not merely the identity of the criminal, but his other identity, since hypocrisy is at its heart.

The answer, that a respectable member of the comfortable classes can also be such a monster, eludes those who, in both cases, try to find a solution. That both Hyde and Jekyll's doors lead to the same rooms is the emblem for the dual nature of the central character and the hypocrisy of the age; juxtaposing the pomp and degradation of the Lord Mayor's Show with the horror of the Ripper's final performance makes the same point. (This was not lost on the Ripper's contemporaries; one popular theory was that he was a social reformer, and, in fact, his crimes are credited with spurring the rebuilding of much of the East End.)

Finally, both stories share supernatural qualities; here, as in horror fiction generally, the unknown realm where impossible events happen mirrors the inexplicable in human life. Jekyll's magical ability to change bodies, like the Ripper's equally baffling power to elude description and detection, reflects their shared ability to go beyond the bounds of rational human action. Yet many Victorians also led two contradictory lives, disappearing from civilization when they stepped out for a night's pleasures. (Even Utterson's respectable friend Richard Enfield, when he first encounters Hyde, is returning from "some place at the end of the world," a place that is never defined.)

Of course, the greatest "supernatural" quality they share is the mystery of motivation. When Jekyll and Jack make real the common fantasies of perfect disguise and unlimited power, the nature of humanity, human progress, and the civilizing process are called into question. Actions such as theirs led many at the time (and Freud half a century later in *Civilization and Its Discontents* [1930]) to conclude that, without the restraining forces of social control, man's powerful instincts would erupt in predatory violence.

The many people who tried to make sense out of the Ripper's crimes, sharing the belief in clear cause and effect held by Sherlock Holmes, looked for a reason these particular women were attacked. But the theories (such as a father seeking the prostitute who infected his son with syphilis, or a palace conspiracy eliminating witnesses to the secret marriage of a Royal prince) are without substance. Like the shadowy crimes of Edward Hyde, the Ripper's viciousness is random and unprovoked, his victims the outlet for irrational and destructive energy.

Although the exploration of the double life and the fantasy of perfect concealment and unrestrained power are the obvious connections between Stevenson's novella and the Whitechapel murders, there is more that links the horror story of 1886 with the horrible reality of the autumn of 1888. When we look closely at contemporary beliefs in the power of the will and its relationship to the body, the reason both Jekyll and the Ripper were described as doctors becomes clearer. At the same time, we can better understand why the two criminals—one imagined and the other all too real—were able to walk the same urban labyrinth undetected and, finally, disappear without a trace.

II.

One of the enduring elements of the horror story tradition is, as we have seen, the age old theme of the power of the dead —through a curse, a will, or a ghost itself—to control the future of those still alive. To ignore or attempt to thwart the wishes of that dead voice meant, as early in the modern Gothic tale as in Horace Walpole's *The Castle of Otranto* (1764), madness and self destruction. But the dictates of the dead often also meant disaster. The curse fulfilled, the will of the dead carried out, tended to turn the bequest to dust. In *Otranto*, the story ends when supernatural intervention restores the rightful heir to the castle, as it crumbles around him.

Charles Dickens' *Bleak House* (1853) follows the same pattern. The would-be heirs await the outcome of the Jarndyce inheritance case, but, on the day a newly discovered and decisive will is to be introduced in court, the entire estate is consumed in court costs (just as Krook, the ghoulish hoarder of the lost document, is consumed in a burst of supernatural flame). On this ironic day of judgment, the characters come into their true inheritance, the one all persecuted Gothic heroes and heroines seek—the freedom to go on with their lives. And the novel ends. Even Mary Shelley's *Frankenstein* (1818) leaves us with the narrator Robert Walton hearing the last words of Victor Frankenstein and having to decide whether or not to follow his example of ruthless research or reject the bequest as a curse. Walton's uncertainty, like Frankenstein's, suggests that, as in the Gothic story generally, the legacy of the past has left the future far from secure.

Whether or not there is an actual document, a curse, or merely the genetic fact of inheritance, the reader is made aware of the power of wishes to survive death, to persist as both a lure and a dangerous trap. To be a beneficiary in such tales is a reason for hope, but a foolish one, since it brings pursuit, danger, pain, and ultimately disappointment. To attempt to thwart the wishes of the dead poses even greater danger. The Gothic tale has been defined in many ways, but certainly our explorations so far have made clear that one of its consistent characteristics is the domination of the dead in the affairs of the living through supernatural or legal means — manifestations of the crushing weight of heredity or tradition. So it is no surprise that what Stevenson called his "Gothic gnome," *The Strange Case of Dr. Jekyll and Mr. Hyde* (1886), at its center, explores the power of a strange will.

Gabriel Utterson, as Jekyll's lawyer, is charged with carrying out the provisions of a will he keeps in "the most private part" of that safe where all the secrets of his clients reside. It is a document he refused to help the doctor draft, because it offends him "both as a lawyer and as a lover of the sane and customary sides of life, to whom the fanciful was the immodest" (35). In it Jekyll directs that, should he disappear for more than three months, "the said Edward Hyde should step into the said Jekyll's shoes without further delay" (35). We later learn, of course, that Jekyll means this literally; Hyde is bequeathed not only Jekyll's possessions, but also his body.

Utterson is haunted by what he calls "the strange clauses of his will"; they appear "before his mind's eye, as clear as a transparency" (42) leading him to begin a search for Hyde that ends in another version of the ironic Gothic bequest. When he and the butler Poole break into Jekyll's laboratory, they find Hyde, dressed in the doctor's clothes, and, no doubt, his shoes. But he is dying. Like the heirs to the disintegrating Gothic castle or the rubble of the Jarndyce case, the figure Jekyll has called his "son" has come into a legacy that becomes useless at the moment it is his.

What do we make of Stevenson's use of this pattern? First of all, the fact that Jekyll creates such a will indicates that he is planning to bequeath his body permanently to Hyde, to use his creation not merely as his mask, but as his heir. In the published version, Jekyll speaks only once of having "more than a father's interest" and Hyde having "more than a son's indifference" (89). In an early draft of the novel, Utterson's speculations about the will include the suspicion that Hyde is actually Jekyll's son:

> How should [Jekyll] have chosen as his heir one who was unknown to his oldest intimates? If it were a case of terrorism, why the will? Or again, if Hyde was Jekyll's son, why the proviso of the disappearance? [Lemendorfer 54].

Whether his kinship is real or metaphorical, stated or implied, Hyde's slow growth in strength and stature and his spontaneous appearances, contrasted with Jekyll's degeneration and increasing difficulty in reappearing, serve the Gothic theme of generational change. In many such tales, the dangerous and destructive power of the will is but one manifestation of the general failure to pass power safely from one generation to the next.

Like the prototype of Manfred in *The Castle of Otranto*, Jekyll is both hero and villain, brooding over dark secrets, lord of a castle he has no right to inhabit any longer. Dr. Jekyll's life before Hyde was "already committed to a profound duplicity" (81) — his hypocrisy is evidence that he occupies his body under false pretenses. Hyde, freed from the cave of Jekyll's subconscious, becomes the rightful heir to his body, and the representative of the next generation. At the same time, he is a throwback to the undisguised cruelty of prehistoric man, a "troglodytic" presence in modern London. As in earlier Gothic stories, the young protagonist is bequeathed the future, but it is a mirror of the past. The difference is that, in *Jekyll and Hyde*, the castle is the self, the bequest literally a giving over of the old body to a new tenant.

One of Stevenson's innovations is, then, to treat the body as a thing, something to be bequeathed and inherited, a place that the aptly named Hyde can first use as an occasional refuge, then as a permanent residence. Another is to make explicit the implication in much of the "fiction of inheritance" that the term "will" signifies two things at once — a quality of mind and a document, the force that intends and the instrument for carrying out those intentions. Utterson worries about both aspects of Jekyll's will, at one point saying, "I have been wanting to speak to you Jekyll.... You know that will of yours?" Jekyll replies, "My will? Yes, certainly, I know that" (43).

Influenced in part by the Gothic tradition, Stevenson's notion of the will also draws upon contemporary thinkers such as James Sully, who believed that modern man needs to apply the power of the will to prevent a relapse into primitive emotions and instincts — in short, to prevent the evolutionary legacy from becoming a curse (Block 456). But the shifting signification of body and will central to a thorough understanding of *Jekyll and Hyde* is more complex, and clearly owes much to a German philosopher whose ideas had first been popularized by Edouard von Hartmann in *The Philosophy of the Unconscious* (1869), the most widely read and influential book of philosophy of the century, and whose major work, *The World as Will and Idea* (1818), appeared in its first English translation in 1883. Arthur Schopenhauer's treatise tries to bring together everything from human aesthetics to animal instincts into one system, based upon what he defines as the will and its relationship to the external world.

Schopenhauer's ideas had a profound effect upon a wide range writers and thinkers of the late nineteenth century, from Tolstoy and Turgenev to Zola and Freud. In England, both Joseph Conrad and Thomas Hardy were deeply influenced, Hardy more than any other writer. Charles Darwin quotes Schopenhauer favorably in *The Descent of Man* (1871), though it appears he never read him directly, but obtained his information from an article in the *Journal of Anthropology* (Magee 264). Another such indirect source was an article in an 1853 issue of *Westminster Review* (edited at the time by George Eliot).

The psychologist James Sully, who, as Ed Block shows, was a strong influence on *Dr. Jekyll and Mr. Hyde* and his friend Stevenson in general, was another conduit for Schopenhauer's philosophy in such articles as "Genius and Insanity" (1881) and, no doubt, in their many conversations in the years after their first meeting in 1876. And Stevenson had studied Schopenhauer even before this time. In a letter to Mrs. Albert Sitwell in 1874 he described his prandial pastimes:

> I must tell you of my way of life, which is regular to a degree. Breakfast 8.30; during breakfast and my smoke afterwards till ten, when I begin work ... from one to two, I lunch and read a book on Schopenhauer or one on Positivism [*Letters*, I 192].

Schopenhauer's most relevant and central thesis is that what he calls the will is the driving force behind all existence. "Will" for Schopenhauer, is many things — unconscious energy in the case of animal instinct, electricity, magnetism, even gravity. In humans, the will is the unique way man knows himself: "This and this alone gives him the key to his own existence, reveals to him the significance, shows him the inner mechanism of his being, of his action, of his movements" (129). The body, on the other hand, is what he calls "an object among objects," merely another thing in the material world.

Schopenhauer sees man's mind and body as intimately connected, so that "every emotion agitates the body and its inner constitution directly, and disturbs the course of its vital functions." (132) What's more,

> Every true act of his will is also at once and without exception a movement of his body. The act of will and the movement of body are not two different things objectively known ... they do not stand in the relation of cause and effect; they are one and the same.... The action of the body is nothing but the act of the will objectified [130].

Despite Jekyll's confident assertion, "My will? Yes, certainly, I know that" (43), Schopenhauer argues that much of the will is repressed by our conscious mind, yet still exerts a powerful influence. He states that "man is at once impetuous and blind striving of will (whose pole or focus lies in the genital organs) and eternal free, serene subject of pure knowing (whose pole is the brain)" (262). (It is no wonder that Thomas Mann, among others, saw a profound influence on Freud, even identifying Schopenhauer's will and knowing with Freud's id and ego [Magee 284].) Jekyll's experiments are more than attempts to release a second self; his bodily transformations are, in fact, only manifestations of his real intention — to control his will.

Schopenhauer asserts that "Every true, genuine, immediate act of will is also, at once and immediately, a visible act of the body. And, corresponding to this, every impression upon the body is also ... at once and immediately an impression upon the will" (131) — implying a transforming power not unlike that of Jekyll's potion. This view was paralleled in the widespread belief of evolutionist psychologists that a diseased or atavistic mind was reflected in a distorted physiognomy. Cesare Lombrosio, the chief late Victorian authority on criminality, argued that the criminal mind could be detected by examining the shape of a skull, pattern of hair, even the condition of internal organs. His followers (including Havelock Ellis, who wrote *The Criminal* in 1890) went so far as to declare that, like the "dwarfish" Hyde, criminals were "about 2 inches shorter and 17 pounds lighter than the average English population" (Ellis 94). Both Schopenhauer and Lombrosio believed, for different reasons, that the body could be read like a document, revealing ancestry or desire, an imprint of the past upon the present. Jekyll strives further, seeking the power to alter that document at will.

When, in *Jekyll/Hyde*, Enfield, Utterson, and the crowd of people who confront Hyde are struck with an immediate loathing, they see in his body what Jekyll later calls "the stamp of lower elements in my soul" (118). The reasons are not only philosophical and evolutionary, but also philological. Like Jekyll's written will, which, for Utterson, was an "eyesore" that "offended him," Hyde's body is an offensive material manifestation of Jekyll's wishes for the future, a document that is stamped with evil. His will resides in the most private part of Utterson's safe and simultaneously haunts the back streets of London. Thus, in neat Schopenhaueran circularity, Jekyll's will has turned his body into an object — and the object is his will. (This isn't the only example in the novel of a body becoming a document. After Jekyll's friend Dr. Lanyon witnesses Jekyll's transformation, he visibly degenerates until "he had his death-warrant written legibly upon his face"[57].)

Schopenhauer saw pain as bodily evidence of opposition to the will, and pain inflicted on others as a bodily manifestation of the desire to dominate another's will, "to compel another individual to serve my will instead of his own" (434). When Jekyll first becomes Hyde, he suffers "the most racking pangs ... a grinding in the bones, deadly nausea, and a horror of the spirit" (83); later, when he becomes Hyde spontaneously, the process is much less painful, presumably more in tune with his will. Hyde's compulsion to inflict pain — on a helpless child he tramples, a poor street seller he strikes, an aged gentleman he beats until "the bones were audibly shattered and the body jumped upon the roadway" (47) are clues to the unanswered question in the novel — the cause and nature of Hyde's nocturnal pleasures.

In fact, what Stevenson elsewhere called Hyde's "cruelty and malice and selfishness and cowardice" (Eigner 150) all may stem from his overriding purpose, to assert the power of his will. For Jekyll or Hyde, one's own body and that of others are mere material objects, to be possessed, exchanged, damaged, or destroyed. Pain thus becomes an emblem of domination over others and the self. The witnesses to Hyde's first crime (which Jekyll later refers to as an incident hardly worthy of mention) see him run into a girl of eight or ten and then "trample calmly over the child's body" (31). But not only is his victim merely an object in the road; Hyde himself is seen as a thing: "It wasn't like a man; it was like some damned Juggernaut" (31). Like Hyde, Jekyll is obsessed by his belief in man as a ghost in a machine, striving to make his body serve what Utterson calls "that will of yours."

In this same conversation about his will comes more evidence that Jekyll hates the body and seeks to assert the primacy of will over it. Twice he attacks Lanyon as "hide bound," telling Utterson, "I never saw a man so distressed as you were by my will; unless it were that hide-bound pedant, Lanyon, at what he called my scientific heresies (43)." The pun is obvious — Lanyon's "Hyde" is bound within him. At the same time, he is "hide bound" because he allows his will to be bound by the limits of his body, by his "hide." Jekyll's will, which distresses Utterson, and his scientific heresies, which upset Lanyon, are one and the same; Jekyll's experiments demonstrate his belief that to control his will means he can reshape his body.

If the assertion of will and the hatred of the body are seen as the center of Jekyll's obsessions, much in the novel is clarified. Jekyll's transformations to Hyde and the crimes he commits in that body become more than the tragedy of a man who tries and fails to live the perfect double life. Jekyll wants to dominate the body completely; he hates it for limiting his will and restraining his power. For a while, he believes he has succeeded in defying its limits. As he tells Utterson, "the moment I choose, I can be rid of Mr. Hyde" (44). At Jekyll's moment of triumph, when Lanyon sees him transform, the doctor's features "melt and alter" (80), an echo of the nightmare Utterson has of a figure that crushes a child at every street corner, a figure with "no face, or one that baffled him and melted before his eyes" (37–8) — the body made plastic. The irony, of course, is that the "will" which stamps itself on Jekyll's malleable body is the legacy of a brutal past.

Regarding his own and other bodies as objects, mere instruments of his will, not only explains Hyde's brutalities, but also Jekyll's profession. Stevenson links Jekyll to a particular kind of doctor, and perhaps a particular doctor, one the public believed shared his attitude toward the will, the body and pain. Jekyll performs his experiments in a room reached through a "surgical theatre," a place

> indifferently known as the laboratory or dissecting-rooms. The doctor had bought the house from the heirs of a celebrated surgeon; and his own tastes being rather chemical than anatomical, had changed the destination of the block at the bottom of the garden [51].

Why this seemingly unnecessary detail? Stevenson's equation of Jekyll's chemical experiments with dissection and surgery, and especially placing the dissecting rooms in a separate place with a disguised entrance on a back street, would no doubt bring to mind the "resurrectionist" scandals earlier in the century.

Because surgeons and anatomists were strictly limited in the number of corpses available for dissection earlier in the century, an illicit trade in bodies stolen from graveyards was extensive, including even an export business among England, Scotland, and Ireland. These activities had long aroused public anger, leading to mob attacks on suspected grave robbers, and, in 1828, the inevitable Select Committee Report. In Stevenson's Edinburgh that same year the most notorious case came to light when the infamous Burke and Hare were arrested for smothering a series of paupers and prostitutes and selling the bodies to a highly respected doctor, Robert Knox, who paid good money and asked no questions. On February 12, 1829, a mob sacked and burned Knox's home, but were prevented by the police from lynching Knox himself. Continually harassed, he was forced to leave Edinburgh and died in obscurity. For a time, then, at Dr. Knox's back door, as at Dr. Jekyll's, human bodies became commodities.

In a time and place closer to the writing of *Jekyll/Hyde*, doctors were targets of public anger for a similar reason — this time treating living beings as unfeeling objects. The anti-vivisection movement had gained powerful impetus in the second half of the century (in part, perhaps, because evolutionary theories had established man's kinship with the lower animals [see Turner 60–78]). Testimony before *The Royal Commission on the Practice of Subjecting Live Animals to Experiments for Scientific Purposes* in 1875 had caused a huge outcry. The public was horrified not only by the details of the experiments, but also by the callous attitudes of the vivisectors describing them. One doctor, Emanuel Klein, told of the most gruesome experiments with apparent disregard for suffering, commenting, for example, that he used anesthetic only when the animals' screams "inconvenienced him" (Pearsall 225). According to R. D. French, "the impact of Klein's testimony upon opinion within the Commission and upon the public, after the minutes of the evidence appeared, cannot be overestimated" (Landsbury 429). It came to be commonly believed that vivisectors enjoyed inflicting pain. In 1882, a book attacking vivisection was presented to Queen Victoria; her response mirrored public attitudes: "the subject causes her *whole nature* to boil over against these 'Butchers' (Doctors and *Surgeons*)" (Pearsall 228).

Many of the leaders of the movement to ban vivisection were also agitators for women's rights; they saw in the way doctors treated the passive bodies of animals parallels to their own insensitive treatment by the male medical establishment. Leading anti-vivisectionists such as Frances Power Cobbe and Caroline White also documented cases of surgeons who removed the ovaries of healthy women for menstrual difficulties or ill defined "women's mania," or callously used indigent women in public hospitals like animals in laboratories—for medical demonstrations and experiments (see Landsbury).

In the extensive realm of Victorian pornography, women also became victims or objects, tied to ingenious "saddles," regularly whipped and tortured—treated like experimental animals. Sometimes the connection with doctors is direct, as in *The Amatory Experiences of a Surgeon* (1881) by the pseudonymous "James Campbell." As Carol Landsbury concludes, "Throughout Victorian pornography, the riding master with his whip and the doctor with his scalpel exchange roles" (424).

Victorians were, then, both fascinated and horrified by the way bodies—whether human corpses, living animals, or female victims of male cruelty or fantasy—could become things. Doctors, vivisection and sexual violence also had been linked in a popular novel published three years before *Jekyll/Hyde*—Wilkie Collins' *Heart and Science: A Story of the Present Time* (1883). The villain is a "vivisector," Dr. Benjula, whose experiments are intended to discover a cure for "brain disease." Aside from tormenting animals, he develops a strange relationship with a little girl, Zo Galilee, whom he subjects to mental and clearly sexual torture, tickling her unmercifully or showing her the bloodstained bamboo stick he uses to beat dogs. Collins clearly means to connect Dr. Benjula's activities in his secret laboratory with his equally perverted affections—an equation Dr. Jekyll uses when he dons the cloak of Edward Hyde.

In the popular mind, there was, then, a common denominator linking the activities of doctors, vivisectionists, pornographers, and partakers, like Hyde, in the obscure pleasures of the Victorian secret life—all reduced another body to an object and gained pleasure in subjecting it to the will. In the most extensive relic of late Victorian pornography, the eleven volumes of *My Secret Life* by the anonymous author called "Walter," the reader is struck by how many sexual relationships he has with bodies and how few human relationships he has with people (even though he is infinitely more truthful and complete than the typical pornographer). Walter is obsessed by his own power or the power of his money to subject women to his often bizarre and degrading whims. Colin Wilson comments on one typical scene, where Walter is fascinated by watching himself in a mirror having sex with a ten year old girl: "The image captures something essential about Victorian sex: the male's complete indifference to everything but his own desires" (53) as well as the depersonalized pleasure of simultaneously exercising his will and observing his body.

As Jacques Lacan has pointed out (159ff), the image in the mirror is a mysterious thing to a child, since it is ourselves, yet not ourselves. As we grow up, he maintains that we continue to identify with the reflections of objects, the images of the world around us, the mirror reality where bodies are two dimensional and apart. When Jekyll first becomes Hyde, after watching the ingredients of his potion "boil and smoke together in the glass" (83), his first act as Hyde is to look for a mirror; later, he puts one in his laboratory "for the very purpose of those transformations" (84). Thus, from the start, Stevenson makes clear the change is not complete until Jekyll/Hyde looks in a mirror, until he detaches his self from the image of his self, until, like Walter in *My Secret Life*, he watches the effect of his will on his body.

At the end of Utterson's futile quest for knowledge, he and Poole discover the mirror in Jekyll's dissecting room, which was "but for the glazed presses of chemicals, the most commonplace in London":

> "This glass has seen some strange things, sir," whispered Poole.
> "And surely none stranger than itself," echoed the lawyer in the same tone ... "what could Jekyll want with it?" [71]

What Utterson and Poole see in the glass is not only itself, but also a "hundred repetitions" of the fire, for the glazed drawers of chemicals are also mirrors. Within it as well are "their own pale and fearful countenances stooping to look in" (71).

The mirror in Jekyll's laboratory is the final door in a story about doors. Utterson's friend Richard Enfield first encountered Edward Hyde by the sinister back door to Jekyll's respectable house, in a chapter entitled "Story of the Door" (29); Utterson and Poole gain entrance to the laboratory by breaking in another door that seems alive, a door that "leaped against the lock and hinges" and gave out a "dismal screech" (69). Between those doors stands the locked cabinet concealing Jekyll's mysterious chemicals, while Utterson's study has its own mysteries hidden in his safe.

In the last, glass door in Jekyll's laboratory, Utterson, Poole, and Jekyll see the world and themselves reflected and transformed, a world of surfaces, stripped of the will that makes them live. In a mirror, bodies do indeed become "objects in a world of objects"; as Schopenhauer once declared, "Will is the thing-in-itself, the inner content, the essence of the world. Life, the visible world, the phenomenon, is only the mirror of the will" (354). The danger of seeing the body as merely an object or a reflection is that, as in Hyde's case, pleasures can turn from the "undignified" to the "truly monstrous." Violence directed towards others becomes an expression of power over the outside world, as well as a displaced expression of hatred at the frailty and limits of the self, a rebellion against being "hide bound."

As Hyde loses control of his violence towards others, Jekyll loses control of his own body, finding it no longer subject to his own conscious desires but changing on its own, following the dictates of unconscious drives he is powerless to arrest. Jekyll/Hyde becomes both tormentor and victim simultaneously, asserting his will upon other bodies and losing his own to the same force. At the end, locked in his dissecting room and inside the body of Hyde, he searches frantically for a way out. When Utterson and Poole arrive outside the last locked door, a voice calls out:

> "Utterson! said the voice, "for God's sake, have mercy!"
> "Ah, that's not Jekyll's voice—it's Hyde's! cried.Utterson. "Down with the door, Poole!" [69]

The call is from Jekyll, but the body is Hyde's. Reacting to a voice that the body determines rather than the spirit—the will—behind it, Utterson and Poole show no mercy. In the end, Jekyll's will remains bound to a body, the wrong body, and thus both body and will are destroyed. Hyde's poisoned corpse, a thing "sorely contorted and still twitching" (70) on the dissecting room floor, is the only tangible result of Jekyll's experiments, a doctor's victim reduced to matter by the ironic triumph of the will.

It is tempting at this point to speculate on how Jekyll's struggle with his will is linked to the author, who "could not pass a mirror without a look at himself" (Calder 56), who, "sick and penniless and rather back on the world" (*Letters*, I 375) had the nightmare that inspired the novel. Like many of his works, *The Strange Case of Dr. Jekyll and Mr. Hyde* was written in bed. Since childhood, Stevenson had been frail, feverish, and constantly in danger of an early death from tuberculosis. Earlier in the year, he had suffered one of his worst hemorrhages and returned to Skerryvore not only confined to bed, but limited in his ability to speak and move. He described himself at this time as "a chronic sicklist; and my work cripples along between the bed and the parlor, between the medicine bottle and the cupping glass" (Geduld 95).

In this state, "suffering from continual haemorrhages ... hardly allowed to speak, his conversations being usually carried on by means of a slate and pencil" (Geduld 96) he was inspired to write *Dr. Jekyll and Mr. Hyde*. After writing thirty thousand words in three days and receiving his wife's written objections, Stevenson threw the manuscript into the fire. In three more days another thirty thousand word draft was completed. As his wife recalled, "that an invalid in my husband's condition of health should have been able to perform the manual labor alone of putting 60,000 words on paper in six days seems incredible" (Geduld 96).

Stevenson's famous description of the novel's genesis in "A Chapter on Dreams" uses language that not only recalls Schopenhauer's distinction of body and will, but also suggests how it connects to Stevenson's own physical needs: he "had long been trying to write a story on this subject, to find a body, a vehicle, for that strong sense of man's double being which must at times come in upon and overwhelm the mind of every thinking creature" (*Works*, II, 231). The pain that accompanied the shaping of Jekyll's body, like that which accompanied the creation of Stevenson's fictional body, suggests that in both cases, character and creator were using the force of their wills with much the same intent.

Stevenson's illnesses not only left him bedridden for months at a time, they precipitated lifelong wanderings, from the boredom of a clinic in Switzerland to convalescence on the French Riviera, the cold of a terrible winter in Saranac, New York, and finally the peace of Samoa. Stevenson's entire life was a battle of his will to dominate his body, his twenty five volumes of published work powerful evidence of a continual struggle that finally ended at age forty four with a cerebral hemorrhage.

The body was for Stevenson what he called in "Stormy Nights," a poem about his childhood nightmares, "the cage of . . . compulsive purity" within which "my spirit beat." Jekyll, similarly, speaks of the body as "the prison house of my disposition" (85), the drug a way to throw open its gates. This desire to escape the hide bound limits that confine his spirit helps explain Stevenson's interest in the recurring motif of confinement and escape in all his fiction and, perhaps, his restless travel.

There is evidence that Stevenson may also have shared the darker side of Jekyll's relationship to his body—a desire to inflict pain on oneself or others, which expresses the need to dominate the body, to display the power of the will. However, it is always dangerous to read the author into a work of fiction, or (even worse) into the nature of his characters. Yes, *Dr. Jekyll and Mr. Hyde* had its genesis in a dream, and its author was obsessed in life with his own body's inablity to obey his will. But his novel remains a work of the creative imagination, and not a confession.

Still, there is one incident mentioned by Stevenson's wife that may suggest that the author of *Dr. Jekyll and Mr. Hyde* was also at times driven to violence, violence against a women, violence that suggests a hatred of the body and a reduction of another to object. The secret crimes of Mr. Hyde are left to our imagination. But perhaps they magnify a momentary loss of control that Fanny Osbourne recalls happened in 1880:

> When he begins to laugh, if he is not stopped in time, he goes into hysterics, and has to have his fingers bent back to bring him to himself again.... I like him very much but there are times when it is a little embarrassing to be in his company; and sometimes, I imagine, not altogether safe. Once we were going over to the other side in a cab when he began laughing, and couldn't stop, and asked me to bend his fingers back. I didn't like to do it, so he laughed harder and harder, and told me that I had better for if I didn't he would bend my fingers back and break every bone in them, which he proceeded to do, and I only saved them by suddenly biting his hand till he bled, when he immediately came to his senses and begged pardon, but I couldn't use my hands for more than a day afterward
> — Fanny Stevenson to Reardon
> [Beinecke Coll. quoted Calder *RLS* 111]

III.

Stevenson's exploration of the brutal possibilities inherent in the untrammeled exercise of the will struck a responsive chord in late Victorian England. It was the must enduring fictional treatment of a theme that reached the public that same year (1886) in Dr. Richard von Krafft-Ebbing's *Psychopathia Sexualis*, a collection of case histories of sexual deviants and psychopaths originally intended for the medical profession. However, its immediate and immense popular success meant that Krafft-Ebbing spent the rest of his life expanding the book through eleven more editions. In it, he combines gruesomely detailed descriptions of sadism and what he calls "lust murder" with expressions of moral repugnance and an attempt to find causes by chronicling the physical condition of the offender's genitals or his history of his masturbation. Krafft-Ebbing makes clear that he found his case histories revolting evidence of individual degeneracy and moral decay. However, like the story of Jekyll and Hyde and the Ripper murders, they were also riveting—real life tales of terror that fascinated and repelled at the same time, just as the gruesome details of the horror story had done for over a century.

Thus, the years surrounding the creation of Stevenson's compelling story were full of the ideas that are reflected and anticipated on its pages. It is no wonder that the story of Jack the Ripper created such public excitement, since it graphically combined all the disturbing elements Stevenson had given fictional form. The presumed motive of the murders—dissecting a woman and removing her sexual organs—is the ultimate reduction of body to thing, the exercise of an unfettered will, the end of all dehumanizing pornographic fantasy. It is clear why the Ripper was believed to be a respectable member of society, probably a doctor, and also a human monster straight from the pages of *Psychopathia Sexualis*.

At the height of the Ripper scare, in October 1888, these convictions were made explicit in the popular press. The *East London Reporter* seriously suggested that the crimes were the work of medical students experimenting on "poor friendless women," and asked the police to inquire "if any particular study or lecture of the physiologists in the neighborhood or elsewhere required a practical illustration" (Oct. 1888, 3). Florence Fenwick Miller's powerful, ironically titled article "Women Killing No Murder" in the *Daily News* argues that brutality to women was widespread and went lightly punished. She cites case after case of domestic violence, of the bodies of women

> kicked, beaten, jumped on, chopped, stabbed, seamed with vitriol, bitten and deliberately set on fire—and this sort of outrage, if a woman dies is called 'manslaughter,' if she lives, a 'common assault.' Common indeed...! Now that men's consciences and imaginations are aroused by the Whitechapel murders, I ask them *what* are they going to do to check the ever-rising flood of brutality to women, of which these murders are only the latest wave?" [2 Oct. 1888, 6].

Her comments make clear the connection between extraordinary tales of terror and the mundane horrors of daily life. Still timely, they help explain why the stories of Jekyll/Hyde and Jack the Ripper (and, as we shall see, *Dracula*) have retained their impact for nearly a century. Stevenson's private nightmare and Whitechapel's public reality were parallel events, and together foreshadowed the way the modern world has come to view human possibility. Random, purposeless violence is the ultimate horror of the city in the twentieth century, a horror made possible by urban anonymity and the loss of community. At the end of the nineteenth century, it took Jack the Ripper to raise public awareness of unrestrained brutality all around them; it took a horror story by Robert Louis Stevenson to begin to understand the reasons behind it.

*The Strange Case of Dr. Jekyll and Mr. Hyde* and the real case of Jack the Ripper show what was believed could happen when what Jekyll called the "bonds of obligation" were loosed, when the will was unchecked and bodies truly became things. Jekyll's fantasy of the perfect disguise was realized in the Ripper; he and Jekyll shared the freedom and audacity to realize the worst Victorian nightmare, to reveal the savagery behind the veneer of civilization. And both escaped detection and punishment from the guardians of law and order. Utterson could also have been speaking for the Metropolitan Police when he looks at Hyde's body and tells Poole, "This is beyond me" (71). The chief investigator in the case of Edward Hyde resigned himself to failure; Sir Charles Warren, in charge of the Ripper case, simply resigned, an event announced the day after the last of the murders.

The disappearance of both Jekyll and the Ripper have their own strange justice, however. The doctor's "Full Statement of the Case" is narrated by an "I" that purports to be Henry Jekyll. However, his account of the creation of Hyde is accompanied by an ironic touch. At that moment, he proclaims exultantly, "Think of it—I did not even exist!" (86). The narrator's triumph is undercut by the fact that he no longer inhabits either body, describing both Jekyll and Hyde with equal detachment. As has often been pointed out, the name "Jekyll" can mean both "I kill" and the "Killer of the I." The last sentences of the last document in the novel read:

> Will Hyde die upon the scaffold? or will he find courage to release himself at the last moment? God knows: I am careless; this is my true hour of death, and what is to follow concerns another than myself. Here, then, as I lay down the pen and proceed to seal up my confession, I bring the life of that unhappy Henry Jekyll to an end.

There are three characters here, as there have been throughout Jekyll's far from "Full Statement of the Case"—the doomed Hyde, the unhappy Jekyll, and whoever is writing the manuscript. That disembodied self has always created its masks; through their eyes it has seen both Jekyll and Hyde in the same mirror and with equal detachment. The puppet master of Jekyll, it has lost control of Hyde and become unable to embody itself. Utterson and Poole search the house after finding Hyde's body, but "Nowhere was there any trace of Henry Jekyll, dead or alive" (70). Schopenhauer asserts what he calls a truth that cannot be demonstrated—that the will cannot exist apart from the body. Stevenson proves it through metaphor; the triumph of the will over its "hide-bound" bodily restraints means its annihilation.

*Dr. Jekyll and Mr. Hyde* is about Utterson's failure to know as much as it is about secret knowledge. The last documents, the final two voices of the dead, are Lanyon's and Jekyll's statements, which we read after Utterson leaves Jekyll's laboratory and the fictional space of the novel. Thus the plot ends in ignorance, followed by the reading of the wills, the legacy of knowledge given directly to the reader. We, in fact, take the place of Utterson in the narrative, reading directly what he has hidden in his safe. These documents solve some of the mysteries that baffled Utterson, but like the Gothic wills from which they derive, leave us facing a future bequeathed by the dead, one that threatens to disintegrate at any minute. Both Lanyon and Jekyll testify to the pathological power of the unfettered will when it asserts its domination over the body, of the awful consequences when people become things. The unfinished tale of Jack the Ripper is more evidence of the truth of that testimony—a truth that, within a few decades, war would make inescapable.

The disappearance of the Ripper after the murder of Mary Kelly is the last mystery of that case. Recent research has gone a long way towards identifying him as Montague John Druitt, a failed barrister from a family of doctors who had his office near the murder sites, an office to which no clients came (see Cullen and Farson). His photograph reveals neither the overhanging brow ridges nor the coarse features Cesare Lombrosio and Havelock Ellis believed marked the criminal type; rather than an atavistic throwback, he seems a perfectly nondescript young man. Evidence indicates that the police were alerted to Druitt's alter ego as the Ripper by his family, but kept his identity secret out of consideration for them after he committed suicide. Thus, if these latest theories are correct, the mystery endured for a century because of the very Victorian fear of disgrace to a respectable family name.

Druitt's body was fished out of the Thames near Chiswick on December 31, 1888, more than three weeks after he had disappeared. Presumably his motives in killing himself were the same as Jekyll's; he became aware of the net closing around him, or perhaps he finally awoke to the horror of his crimes and life became insupportable. He left no suicide note, no last statement of his case. If there was a self opposed to that which wrote letters and poems exulting in evil, we have no written record of it. All that speaks to us are the pockets of his coat, which were found filled with stones, evidence of a final conflict between the will seeking self annihilation and the body struggling to survive.

*Chapter Seven*
# Dracula and the Liberation of Women (I)

> Woman's relation to man has been mixed up with the problem of pleasure: she has been sacrificed for that.... We do not ask even what woman needs, but what suits us. Those who love and honour her most are even more intent upon treating her with that utter disregard and practical cruelty (for it is so), intenser, more exquisite, than can be conceived.
> —James Hinton

The mistreatment of women exposed in journalism like Stead's series *Maiden Tribute of Modern Babylon* or in the accounts of the Ripper murders (and implied in the obscure nighttime activities of the respectable men in *Dr. Jekyll and Mr. Hyde*) was confined to the "unfortunates" of the most impoverished classes; for women of the middle and upper classes, the effects of patriarchal privilege were, as James Hinton pointed out at the time, more subtle. As society reacted to the exploitation of paupers and prostitutes, middle class women began to assert their rights in marriage and the job market, to emerge as "New Women" who engendered first ridicule, then condemnation from the men who felt threatened by their actions. Ironically, it took a man who created one of the most violently patriarchal characters in literature to provide an enduring vehicle to explore the unease that accompanied the New Woman, and, in fact, to replace the Victorian image of woman with one more suited to a new century.

In the mid 1890's, visitors to the British Museum Reading Room or guests at the Kilmarnock Inn in the small Scottish seaport town of Cruden Bay might have seen an Irishman often described as a "red haired giant" researching such subjects as Transylvanian superstitions, local folk tales, or shipwreck stories. In London, during his customary walks in Piccadilly or along the banks of the Thames, he noted the details of houses he passed. Later, he combined the notes he had jotted down on assorted scraps of paper with maps, diagrams, newspaper clippings, and typewritten extracts from his reading, which ranged from Rivington's *Theory of Dreams* (1808) to tombstone inscriptions.

All this activity came in odd moments that the writer, Bram Stoker, snatched from his extensive duties as business and stage manager to the company of the actor Henry Irving. Some six years of research resulted in a novel published in 1897. Its slow and methodical genesis stands in sharp contrast with the lightning inspiration of classic horror stories such as *The Castle of Otranto*, *The Monk*, *Frankenstein*, or *Dr. Jekyll and Mr. Hyde*. His subject, too, was quite unexceptional; as far back as 1819, Dr. John Polidori had published, as a result of the ghost story competition that produced *Frankenstein*, a tale called *The Vampyre*. Other, more popular, versions such as Thomas P. Prest's *Varney the Vampire* (1847) or Sheridan Le Fanu's *Carmilla* (1871) had kept an echo of the old middle European folk tale alive throughout the century.

Stoker's writing was in many respects also unexceptional — he tells much of his story in a conventional collection of letters and diaries rendered in voices that vary from broken English and pseudo Texan to the manly tones and womanly gush of sentimental popular fiction. Even the thrills are thinly dispersed — after an opening section in Transylvania the vampire is mostly offstage, his nocturnal habits usually described after the fact. Stoker's entire novel contains fewer scenes of horror than one chapter of *Varney the Vampire* (a book with 220 chapters)! Yet Prest's insatiable vampire is gone from the public consciousness, permanently interred on obscure library shelves.

However, like Frankenstein's Monster or Dr. Henry Jekyll, Stoker's Count Dracula lives on, the central figure in an adult fairy tale that has somehow embedded itself in modern mythology, kept alive like the others through the immense popularity of the book and of versions of the tale told in theater and on film — a nineteenth century fantasy that somehow still remains true. The elixir that gave those three creatures immortality shared the same strange recipe: an unusual individual in touch with private fears, a time when these fears were shared by the outside world, and the inspiration to use the horror tale (consciously or not) to explore the link between the two.* It was a rare brew indeed; neither Mary Shelley nor Bram Stoker ever found the formula again — their other books have all been largely forgotten.

Like both Mary Shelley and Robert Louis Stevenson, Bram Stoker suffered from a childhood that kept him preoccupied with his own isolation, with little more than his imagination as a companion. Until the age of seven

---

* *Stoker may have been aware of the connection. On May 7, 1868, he gave a talk to the Philosophical Society of Trinity College Dublin entitled "Sensationalism in Fiction and Society." Unfortunately, the college cannot find a copy.*

he was bedridden with a mysterious illness and not expected to live. During that time, a cholera epidemic swept his native Ireland; thus he absorbed at an early age the images of passivity and death that underlie *Dracula*.

Later in life Stoker managed not only to rise from his sickbed and become an athlete at Trinity College Dublin, but also, like Stevenson, to expand the boundaries of his experience to cover the world. As the devoted assistant to Henry Irving, he managed the Lyceum theater in London and traveled extensively with the troupe throughout Europe and America. His circle of friends and acquaintances was as illustrious as Stevenson's or Mary Shelley's. It included not only the actors Henry Irving and Ellen Terry, but writers such as Arthur Conan Doyle and Mark Twain, the poets Dante Gabriel Rossetti, Alfred Lord Tennyson and Walt Whitman, as well as the artist James M. Whistler and the orientalist Sir Richard Burton (whom Stoker later remembered for his long canine teeth)!

Although his descriptions of them are extensive and glowing (Stoker's longest work is entitled *Personal Reminiscences of Henry Irving* [1906], and he remembers his meeting with Whitman as one of the highlights of his life), he seems to have made little impression on them. Despite the fact that he had already published novels and short stories when he began *Dracula*, Stoker was not known as a creative artist, while we have very little information about his other career from any of his associates and acquaintances. Ellen Terry's extensive *Story of My Life*, for example, devotes only one short paragraph to him (106).

Since Stoker's first book had been *The Duties of Clerks of Petty Sessions in Ireland* and his work for Irving largely consisted of arranging the many petty details that kept a theatrical troupe in business, he was well equipped for a long process of methodical research. It encompassed not only vampire lore but such information as how surgeons treat head injuries and the ways animals at the Regent's Park Zoo express rage. In addition, he studied his locales and charted his action so well that it is possible to find many of the sites mentioned in the novel and even match the dates and phases of the moon in the book to the lunar cycle in 1893 (McNally 25). The result is a fantastic premise firmly grounded in a precise and accurate contemporary reality.

*Dracula* is, then, a landmark in the slow movement of the horror story from the vague and safely remote landscape of the Gothic novel to the sharply realized and located world of modern tales of terror, the territory of such currently popular writers as Stephen King. Stoker's use of familiar places and accurate details, like his largely pedestrian language and clerical mentality in amassing and incorporating information, creates an effect in many ways more shocking than the blood and thunder of a potboiler like *Varney the Vampire*. There, we watch while the vampire attacks a woman and "with a plunge . . . seizes her neck in his fang-like teeth — a gush of blood and a hideous sucking noise follows" (4) and we know we are in a world of Gothic imagination.

In *Dracula*, the style has the same secondhand relationship to reality as the "newspaper clippings" Stoker intersperses in the text; the reader knows of the vampire as he knows of world affairs and crimes encountered in the press—as the late Victorian reader knew, say, of Jack the Ripper. Though the public doesn't witness such events directly, the accounts of them are an intimate part of daily life. In the same way, by giving us a series of narratives about the vampire to read rather than bringing us directly in contact with him, Stoker paradoxically brings the horrors closer to the day to day experience of his audience. The novel was begun only a few years after the Ripper murders had filled those same papers; it shares with them both a style and a story of mysterious and horrible crimes committed against women in locales that the reader can find on a map, at moments he can mark on a calendar.

But Stoker's conscious efforts at blurring the line between supernatural horror and the commonplace events of diaries and newspapers, like his meticulous research and careful rewriting, account only in part for *Dracula*'s enduring popularity. Something else seeped into the mixture. Henry A. Murray describes those who create what he calls "vital myths" as people who have "experienced in their 'depths' . . . one or more of the unsolved critical situations with which humanity at large or members of their own society are confronted" (345). And at the center of both *Dracula* and the life of its creator was a paradox that poisoned the relationships between the sexes in late Victorian England.

According to his great-nephew and biographer, Daniel Farson, there is some evidence that Stoker, who married in 1878 and had a son the next year, never slept with his wife after that, and, at the time of the publication of *Dracula* in 1897, already suffered from the syphilis that may have been the cause of his death fifteen years later (233–34). Stoker, then, probably lived the dual life that popular belief has attributed to many late Victorian gentlemen. The most notorious of these was "Walter," the author of the multi-volume pornographic and autobiographical work *My Secret Life*, who lived 'respectably' with a woman he hated and pursued pleasure amid the army of prostitutes in Victorian England.

The assumption that led to the Victorian double life—that women were almost of two species—was trumpeted by such authorities as Dr. William Acton. His popular and influential treatise *The Functions and Disorders of the Reproductive Organs* (first published in 1857, but into its sixth edition by 1875) stands as the most notorious example of this attitude:

> I should say the majority of women (happily for them) are not troubled with sexual feelings of any kind. . . . Many men, and

particularly young men, form their ideas of women's feelings from what they notice early in life among loose or, at least, low and vulgar women. There is always a certain number of females who, though not ostensibly . . . prostitutes, like to attract the attention of those immediately above them. Such women, however, give a very false idea of the condition of female sexual feeling in general. . . . The best mothers, wives, and managers of households know little or nothing of sexual indulgences. Love of home, children, and domestic duties are the only passions they feel [112-113].

Acton's book goes much further than these often quoted sentiments, arguing throughout that for both sexes, too much sexual indulgence brings out our brutal biological heritage, able "literally to degrade [men] to the level of animal" (95). He is repeatedly drawn to comparisons with animals, finding counterparts for his two types of women elsewhere in nature. The sexless wives and mothers he admires are compared favorably to mares and other domestic creatures who come into heat only occasionally (113n), while wanton women are like lionesses or spiders, dangerous aggressors who dominate males, "often the smallest and weakest of the sexes" and make them their victims (96-97). Sexual restraint is for Acton the way to preserve health, insure male dominance, and help "drive out the beast." The practical consequences of such attitudes were spelled out directly by Dr. T. L. Nichols in 1873—that "married sexual indulgence" should "only take place when conception is desired" (Cominos 22). Men, believed to have an excess of "animal passion," were thus forced to look elsewhere for fulfillment.

Although Acton spoke for the majority of Victorians, he was far from the only voice on these matters. The same year, 1857, Barbara Leigh Smith Bodichon, in *Woman and Work,* responded directly to Acton, and specifically to his comparison of wanton women to lionesses and wives and mothers to domestic creatures:

> To think a woman is more feminine because she is frivolous, ignorant, weak, and sickly, is absurd; the larger-natured a woman is, the more decidedly feminine she will be; the stronger she is, the more strongly feminine. You do not call a lioness unfeminine, though she is different in size and strength from the domestic cat, or mouse [Bodichon 21]

Three years earlier, the first of many editions of the innocuously named (and anonymous) *Elements of Social Science* took an even more radically different position, one that shocked Victorian sensibilities. The author, George Drysdale, only allowed his name to be put on the 35th edition, printed in 1905 after his death. His reticence was natural, since he argued that "natural sexual feelings . . . should not be discountenanced or unduly suppressed in a girl" (174), that, for women as well as men, the "generative organs" must "in order to be vigorous and healthy, have a due amount of exercise" (78) and that "In women, as in men, physical strength is more virtuous than weakness . . . the crippling idea of chastity and female decorum binds her like an invisible chain" (167).

What has all this to do with *Dracula*? It's not hard for a reader to detect the undercurrent of sexuality in the nightmare imagery of the novel. But Stoker's real preoccupation is with the breakdown in the traditional nature of sexual relationships in his time. Clearly, since the middle of the century, the official view of the nature of women had been under attack. By the time *Dracula* was written, the unnatural divorce of goodness from sexual feeling, the division in art and literature of women into fair haired saints and dark haired temptresses, was sustained only by putting respectable women in a cage of chastity and forcing men to exploit an army of prostitutes. As the novelist Grant Allen put it in 1890, "our existing system, instead of being, as its apologists always hypocritically pretend, a pure system of marriage alone, is really a joint system of marriage and prostitution, in which the second element is a necessary corollary and safeguard of the first" (Allen 58). The real horror Stoker explores occurs when those boundaries finally are erased, when a reversion to the primitive and a reversal of sexual roles gives women a frightening new power and makes men weak and ineffectual.

Reading the novel with the film versions in mind can be unsettling. Although some of the characters and situations are similar, the focus is not on the Count who, after the opening section, appears onstage in only a handful of pages. Most of the time we see merely the horrifying evidence of the Count's power and the struggle of the other characters to understand and combat it. It is that power—sexual power—which infects the women in the book and which the men fight manfully to suppress.

An erotic and sadistic element has always been part of the vampire myth and of the Gothic tale in general. In fact, the vampire with his dark designs is just another incarnation of the traditional hero/villain, while his victims are recruits from the army of persecuted maidens. And the pattern of the vampire tale, with the infected victim recruiting others to the cause, parallels one popular plot of late Victorian pornography. In such "grateful victim" tales as *The Way of a Man with a Maid*, the rape victim becomes the enthusiastic accomplice of her seducer. Similar things are going on in *Dracula*.

One significant aspect of the way Stoker tells his tale is that most events are seen from the outside, from their effect upon a group of people who stand for civilization. They try to save the women and restore "normal" values, but Stoker uses the sexuality in the novel to call those values into question. More than the innocence of the women is in danger; threatened, too, are the naive beliefs of the men who try to save them. The method is in a way reminiscent of *Dr. Jekyll and Mr. Hyde*, where Hyde's crimes are left undefined, but the consequences on the moral certainties of the people around him are not.

This change of focus from earlier stories and the later films becomes clearest when we realize that the moment most associated with the vampire tradition, an event that appears on almost every page of *Varney the Vampire* (subtitle: The Feast of Blood)—the bite on the neck—is never viewed directly in *Dracula*. The closest we come occurs in perhaps the most horrifying scene, when the vampire hunters realize that one of the heroines, Mina Harker, is in mortal danger. After a bit of Victorian hesitation which evokes the ritual that surrounded matters of gender at the time and establishes the purity of the woman involved ("Should we disturb her?" ... "It is unusual to break into a lady's room!"), they enter to see the Count

> forcing [Mina's] face down on his bosom. Her white nightdress was smeared with blood, and a thin stream trickled down the man's bare breast which was shown by his torn-open dress. The attitude of the two had a terrible resemblance to a child forcing a kitten's nose into a saucer of milk to compel it to drink. As we burst into the room, the Count turned his face, and the hellish look I had heard described seemed to leap into it. His eyes flamed red with devilish passion; the great nostrils of the white aquiline nose opened wide and quivered [282].

The erotic content is obvious and suggests the danger posed by Dracula. He doesn't merely infect the woman by drinking her blood; he forces her to drink his. The scene is a series of reversals—of a potential wife and mother at Dracula's breast, of a vampire as a willing victim, of an obscene parody of childhood innocence used to illustrate adult violation. Dracula uses force to make the woman his slave, but also to wean her from passivity to a frightening new power.

Stoker suggests here, and throughout the book, that the depredations of Dracula have their strange echoes in the gender relationships of those combating him. Thus, immediately after this erotic, sadistic tableau, Dr. Seward tells Mina and her husband Jonathan (who had been asleep next to Mina during Dracula's visit) what happened. As they listen, they assume exactly the same pose:

> He put out his arms and folded her to his breast ... his nostrils twitched and his eyes blazed as I told how the ruthless hands of the Count had held his wife in that terrible and horrid position, with her mouth to the open wound in his breast. It interested me, even at that moment, to see, that, whilst the face of white set passion worked convulsively over the bowed head, the hands tenderly and lovingly stroked the ruffled hair [284].

Seward, who runs an insane asylum, shares our interest in the curious parallels between the violence of the vampire and the divided feelings of husband and wife. The two scenes stand clearly in counterpoint, suggesting a sexual link between the two and, perhaps, that Dracula's activities are infecting not only the women, but also the men who are trying to save them. Mina has absorbed Dracula's blood, while Jonathan combines husbandly tenderness with the twitching nostrils, blazing eyes, and bloodless pallor of the vampire. Mina's transfusion of power from the vampire is iconographically paralleled in a similar power she takes in at her husband's breast. Clearly, for both, gender relationships are no longer clear and uncomplicated.

The impact of these strangely similar moments is a clue to the power of Stoker's novel, written at a time when wider social and economic forces were shattering conventional attitudes toward men, women, and marriage. Stoker's audience responded to the real horror of *Dracula*—his vision of these attitudes at their most extreme and contradictory. The originality of the novel comes when Stoker, though a prisoner of his time, tries to escape these contradictions to find a new way for men and women to share their lives.

## II.

The opening scenes of *Dracula* are familiar to anyone who has read Gothic literature. Blissfully unaware of the mortal danger that awaits, Harker, the narrator, travels through an obscure and archaic corner of Europe to meet a sinister villain in a dark castle. Harker writes his narration in shorthand in a notebook that includes not only observations of the strange blasted countryside and superstitious inhabitants, but also a memorandum to get the recipe for the national dish, "paprika hendl." The very remoteness of the place in both space and time is suggested from the opening page, when Harker first notes how late the trains are and thinks "It seems to me the further East you go the more unpunctual are the trains" (2).

The narrator has clearly crossed the border that separates the modern world, the place where trains run on time, from a place where time has little meaning. In the castle, Harker opens the wrong doors, heads down the wrong dark corridors, and nearly suffers a fate worse than death. This is all standard stuff for the lover of Gothic tales; Walpole's *Castle of Otranto* was only the first of many such settings, places remote in space and time where the floor plan is a labyrinth and the heroine's curiosity can be dangerous, where behind every locked door hides a frightening discovery, where the owner of the castle threatens the heroine with death or violation.

But Harker is a man, despite his interest in recipes and ability at shorthand. In the first of the many role reversals in the book, his situation duplicates that of the traditional Gothic heroine; he is in danger, as she was, of losing both innocence and life to the mysterious master of a decaying medieval ruin. The "seduction scene," hinted at in the early Gothics (and consummated in the notorious novel *The Monk*), is present in *Dracula* as well, but this time it is a man whose curiosity takes him into forbidden physical and moral space.

When he cuts himself shaving, Dracula sees the blood and nearly attacks him; he is saved by the crucifix around his neck. But it is the Count himself who saves Harker when he ignores Dracula's warning and wanders in the forbidden areas of the castle. Like Catherine Morland in *Northanger Abbey*, or the traditional Gothic heroine she parodies, the protagonist lost in the castle has trouble staying put. Harker forces open a door which "seemed to be locked" and falls asleep in what "was evidently a portion of the castle occupied by ladies in bygone days." His connection with women becomes explicit here: not only does he imitate their activities, but he is drawn to the female wing, beyond the locked door that in Victorian society divided the genders. And while asleep, he dreams of three women who further disturb his confidence in his gender:

> Two were dark, and had high aquiline noses, like the Count's.... The other was fair, as fair as can be, with great, wavy masses of golden hair and eyes like pale sapphires. I seemed somehow to know her face, and to know it in connection with some dreamy fear, but I could not recollect at the moment how or where. All three had brilliant white teeth, that shone like pearls against the ruby of their voluptuous lips. There was something about them that made me uneasy, some longing and at the same time some deadly fear [37].

We never learn directly what that "dreamy fear" is, though it's clear it has something to do with his recognition that the fair haired woman is the familiar angel and innocent victim of Victorian myth, the ideal of femaleness, who has undergone a threatening transformation. She too has reversed her role, becoming the pursuer, alluring and terrifying, united with her dark haired, fallen sisters, initiating the most erotic scene in the novel:

> There was a deliberate voluptuousness which was both thrilling and repulsive, and as she arched her neck she licked her lips like an animal, till I could see in the moonlight the moisture shining on the scarlet lips and on the red tongue as it lapped the white sharp teeth. Lower and lower went her head as the lips went below the range of my mouth and seemed about to fasten on my throat. Then she paused, and I could hear the churning sound of her tongue as it licked her teeth and lips, and could feel the hot breath on my neck.

> Then the skin of my throat began to tingle as one's flesh does when the hand that is to tickle it approaches nearer—nearer. I could feel the soft, shivering touch of the lips on the super-sensitive skin of my throat and the hard dents of two sharp teeth, just touching and pausing there. I closed my eyes in languorous ecstasy and waited—waited with beating heart [38].

Any reader of the abundant pornography of the period is in familiar territory; the phony first person "erotic memoir" was a mainstay of underground literature and full of scenes like this. However, in those cases the author was usually (allegedly) a woman, so that even when Victorian proprieties were violated, the mythology of male sexual dominance remained intact. In fact, as many students of Victorian pornography have pointed out, one of the most common male fantasies is of a woman about to be raped who is both repelled and fascinated by what is sometimes called the "prodigious engine of destruction."

In Stoker's version, nearly every convention is reversed. The woman's "red tongue" and "sharp white teeth" clearly substitute for the most prominent symbol of maleness in Victorian pornography; the man plays the role of virgin victim, willing to submit to an attack that is both sexual and sadistic. What's worse, his aggressor is the Victorian archetype of innocence, made horrifying by her acknowledgement of sexual desire. Like Harker, the Victorian audience must have found this moment both sexually arousing and deeply disturbing. It not only attacked the stereotype of women, but it identified the readers, male and female, with a women's sexual perspective, confusing rape and seduction, violation and titillation, sexuality and gender.

The sexuality of this scene has another important facet: it is not focused on the genitals, but on the neck of the victim and the teeth of the attacker. Although neck biting can be seen as symbolic sexual intercourse with, in this case, the genders reversed, it also is genderless sex. Vampires can be male or female and can bite males or females. The fact that in *Dracula*, the vampires are heterosexual doesn't preclude the possibility of other couplings—heterosexuality is more a matter of choice than necessity, and sex roles more arbitrary than when shaped by organic plumbing. More importantly, either sex can be dominant, wielding the teeth the way sadists wield the whip—men on women or women on men.

And that, of course, is another connection to the secret life of Victorian England. The seduction of Harker mixes pain and passion and compares closest to the scenes of flagellation that darkened late Victorian pornography and recollections of public school life. The most famous member of this secret fraternity of flagellators, the poet Algernon Charles Swinburne, could be obsessed with his beatings by male schoolmasters (in works like *The Flogging Block* [1887] and *Charlie Collingwood's Flogging* [1879]) and could also constantly imagine being beaten by women (in such pieces as *The Whippingham Papers* [1887] [Ober 84]). Although Swinburne remained in his fantasies the passive victim, the "English vice" was a form of sexual gratification that, like neck biting, blurred gender distinctions, conferred pain with pleasure, and often turned a willing victim into one who made victims of others.

Harker's seduction is, then, kin to some dark strains in Victorian culture and introduces the deeper fear that underlies the rest of the novel. The real danger to Victorian life found in Stoker's *Dracula* lies in the breakdown of the distinctions between gender and sexuality, in the release of a destructive power and a dangerous passion among men and women at a turning point in their lives. Though the book opens in the traditional archaic setting of the haunted castle in a far off land, Stoker soon makes clear, through a progression of details that Harker notices there, that the subterranean world of the vampire also underlies English society on the brink of a new century.

Harker enters the castle through its "ancient stone doorway, much worn by time and weather." Then, while Dracula spends the nights telling of battles long past and primitive superstitions, Harker gradually sees time and distance erased. The furnishings in Harker's room, in excellent condition, remind him of those in Hampton Court, though "there they were worn and frayed and moth-eaten." In the library, he finds a vast number of English books and magazines "though none of them were of very recent date" (19). But when Harker sees the Count later that night, he is lying on the sofa "reading, of all things, an English Bradshaw's Guide" (22).

This collection of British railway timetables may seem odd reading matter, but it connects to Harker's opening notation of the exact time he had left Munich and his subsequent observation about the lack of punctuality of Transylvanian trains. In mastering Bradshaw's Guide, Dracula reveals his intention to enter the ordered world of late 19th century England. Trains were to the Victorians the clearest evidence of their modernity and technological mastery; the building of the railroads, and the tunnels, bridges, and viaducts they required, was a huge project, "a feat of construction never previously equaled nor, perhaps, since surpassed" (Reader 2). It also made possible a new mobility which allowed for the vast social changes of the period. Just as Dracula leaves his ancient home for a London teeming with new possibilities, the sons and daughters of families that had lived in one place in rural England for centuries used the webwork of railways to enter the cities. The enormous shift in population that resulted was a change in the real Victorian world as radical as the fictional threat posed by Dracula. In the opening scenes of his novel, Stoker records in wild Gothic exaggeration a familiar nineteenth century scene—the abandonment of the worn out land of the family farm for the crimson tinted lure of the city.

Harker's journal, which ends when the novel leaves Transylvania, is only the first of many vehicles Stoker uses to move his story along. *Dracula* is told by a series of narrators who record their observations in newspapers, diaries, letters, and even on wax phonographic cylinders. *Dracula* is, in fact, constructed more as a collection of evidence than a novel. This technique enables Stoker not only to simulate contemporary reality, but also to manipulate various voices and points of view (between men and women, the experienced and naive, those close to the danger and those farther away) and avoid one final answer to the problems he poses.

After Dracula leaves for England, Harker escapes (the last line in his journal tells of his climb down from the castle, a fantasy space where gender is blurred, to a place where sexual identity seems clear again: "Where man may sleep—as a man" [53]). Thus, Harker has simultaneously played two roles in Gothic fiction—the persecuted heroine and the young hero—by saving himself. Dracula, whom he cannot bring to destroy in the castle when he has a chance, is the symbolic father of both. Like Manfred in *The Castle of Otranto* or, more aptly, General Tilney in *Northanger Abbey*, his absolute control of his home is tempered by his obsession with time—the movement of history as well as the daily cycles of night and day. For Stoker, the "king vampire" embodies all the dead forces of patriarchy and tradition that refuse to remain in their graves.

After Harker's escape, the scene shifts from Transylvania and the Gothic landscape to the major focus of the novel, the small band of men and women who wait in England. For as Harker confronts his sexual dilemma, they are confronting theirs; all six main characters (including Harker) are at the same crucial point in their lives as Gothic heroines like Catherine Morland—on the brink of marriage. And, in the last decades of the nineteenth century, that stage in life was a particularly precarious one.

For many men and women in late Victorian England, marriage was one of the more terrifying moments in life. Although many marriages developed into happy and sexually healthy relationships, a lack of accurate sexual knowledge often led to anxiety in both parties as the date approached. The culture defined womanly "purity" to include sexual ignorance. (A brief example: a few days before her marriage, Edith Wharton pleaded with her mother, "I'm afraid, Mamma—I want to know what will happen to me!" Her mother's reply, accompanied, as Wharton remembered, by the "expression of a person whose nostrils are assailed by a disagreeable smell," was to suggest Edith remember what nude statues look like and stop asking "any more silly questions" [Gay 401].) Women feared what Victorians toward the end of the century called the "brute in the bedroom." The wedding night was sometimes seen as little more than sanctioned rape, the scene reversed in

Harker's account of his near violation by vampires. This same standard of "manliness" often made men fearful that they might not be able to perform the prodigious duties popular belief (and pornographic fantasy) said were required of them (Gay 290).

The need to make a "good" marriage went beyond the individuals involved; it was seen as the linchpin which held society together. The commitment to marry often came at the end of a long courtship, arranged as a union between families and designed to improve the financial and social prospects of one or another of the partners. Most importantly, marriage reinforced the traditional relationship between the sexes. On all levels — sexual, social, and economic — it meant a transfer of power.

Until 1870 and the Married Women's Property Act, a woman lost all rights to her property to her husband upon marriage and could not even make out a will. The new law was decried in some quarters (the *Saturday Review* commented, "There is besides a smack of selfish independence about it which jars with poetical notions of wedlock" [Pearsall 181]). These concerns were in a sense borne out; the Act and the subsequent gradual liberalizing of the divorce laws were the first steps in a movement which culminated, after the First World War, in women's suffrage.

With the reform of the marriage laws women began to redefine their place in society. In the last quarter of the century, during what was known as the debate on the "marriage question," it became clear that men and women would have to discard some of the 'poetical notions' which condemned many Victorian women to a life of boredom, drudgery and powerlessness. For middle and upper-class women at least, recognition of marriage rights meant the possibility of some autonomy. Many men reacted strongly to what they believed constituted a threat to traditional male prerogatives, to the gender defined notions that seemed essential to social stability. Some wondered if marriage itself would survive.

These issues of power and marriage are raised early in *Dracula*. While Harker plays the persecuted maiden in Dracula's castle, besieged by three women, a similar situation is echoed and reversed back in England. Stoker's two heroines, Lucy Westenra and Mina Murray, exchange a series of letters; Lucy's news is of three fellows, all manly adventurers, who, in a single day, have each asked for her hand in marriage. Thus, Harker is sexually assaulted by three women as Lucy is matrimonially assaulted by three men. In both cases, what's at stake is power.

Lucy seems the traditional heroine, what has been referred to as the Victorian ideal of the "enchanting ignoramus"; her letters gush in the syrupy style of popular romances and confirm the image Victorian men would like to have of their women ("My dear Mina, why are men so noble when we women are so little worthy of them?" [59]). After rejecting the polite advances of Dr. John Seward and Quincey Morris, she accepts the hand of

Arthur Holmwood, soon to be Lord Godalming, a friend since childhood. He's the only one who doesn't even seem to ask her; in her confused recollection, "it seemed only a moment from his coming into the room till both his arms were around me, and he was kissing me" (60). (Her description has the same lack of detail and compressed sense of time that Lucy will later employ in describing the depredations of Dracula.)

Lucy follows the well worn path of Victorian womanhood, for her power ends after she rejects her first two suitors and is swept off her feet by her future husband. From then on, while she's alive, the only strong feeling associated with her is weakness. She acts out, in the exaggeration of Gothic fantasy, the Victorian ideal of woman — languid, listless, and inert. At this time in history, many women suffered from diseases diagnosed as neurasthenia, anorexia, or hysteria. They all shared this same life threatening exaggeration of the feminine ideal, as a description of hysteria by a doctor, S. Weir Mitchell, in 1877 shows:

> The woman grows pale and thin, eats little, or if she eats does not profit by it. Everything wearies her . . . and by and by the sofa or the bed is her only comfort. Every effort is paid for dearly, and she describes herself as . . . needing constant stimulus and endless tonics [qtd. Pearsall, *Worm* 521].

The first victim of Dracula in England, Lucy spends most of her time languishing in bed, drained of blood, and, in the opinion of the men who are singularly unsuccessful in restoring her to health, at her most beautiful. As Peter Cominos points out, "so deep rooted was dependence in their character, that it is no exaggeration to say that the 'womanly woman' was markedly masochistic in her character-orientation" (245).

Lucy, in fact, becomes the temporary reservoir for the blood of the men who wish to marry her. They keep giving her transfusions to revive her, and Dracula keeps removing her blood. It's obvious that this exchange has sexual overtones, since the rejected suitors are eager to make the donation, yet careful to keep their nocturnal transfers secret from Lucy's fiancée. But it also is a transfer of a vital force, as if the male blood carries with it the power of men. (As Ernest Jones has pointed out, "In the unconscious mind, blood is commonly an equivalent for semen" [119].) When Lucy gets stronger, the men weaken. One of them remarks, "No man knows, till he experiences it, what it is to feel his own life-blood drawn away into the veins of the woman he loves" (128).

The horror of *Dracula* is the horror of extremes, and Lucy, even before she takes up her dual role as languishing maiden and emerging vampire, embodies the two extremes of Victorian womanhood. At the time Dracula reaches the English seaport of Whitby, Lucy and her friend Mina are

# 7. Dracula *and the Liberation of Women (I)*

Whitby Harbor at the time of *Dracula*, photographed by Frank Meadow Sutcliffe: "It turns out that the schooner is a Russian from Varna, and is called the *Demeter*. She is ... with only a small amount of cargo—a number of great wooden boxes filled with mould." *Dracula* (1896). Reproduced by permission of W. Eglon Shaw, The Sutcliffe Gallery, 1 Flowergate, Whitby, Yorkshire England.

vacationing there together; even before he arrives, Lucy resumes her "old habit of walking in her sleep" (72). Dr. Seward, the suitor who also runs a lunatic asylum, has called Lucy a "curious psychological study" (55); her sleepwalking would seem to indicate that she has always had another side which emerges only at night. Her restlessness is an indication of the larger restlessness of the Victorian woman; Seward's conclusion that the reason is psychological rather than social was unfortunately the usual diagnosis, and one reason the asylums of England at this time contained a preponderance of women (see Showalter). And, as we shall see, Lucy's extraordinary encounter with a vampire led to results that were far from uncommon.

Dracula's arrival on the ship "Demeter" (the goddess who lost her daughter to the forces of darkness) brings out in full force what had been present all along and all around her. Lucy's sleepwalking intensifies; she

The Gothic ruin of St. Mary's Church, Whitby in the 1890s, photographed by Frank Meadow Sutcliffe. Bram Stoker used this place for the meeting of Lucy Westernra and Dracula — an image of horror that existed in reality. Reproduced by permission of W. Eglon Shaw, The Sutcliffe Gallery, 1 Flowergate, Whitby, Yorkshire England.

restlessly wanders the cliffs of Whitby and sits on the "suicide's seat," where Mina sees a "long and black" figure, with a "white face and red, gleaming eyes" bending over her.

The seat spans a tombstone which is inscribed, in part, "Sacred to the memory of George Canon, who died ... falling from the rocks at Kettleness. This tomb is erected by his sorrowing mother to her dearly beloved son" (67). Mina and Lucy learn from a local fisherman that these maternal sentiments are a lie. Actually the son and mother hated each other; he "blew the top of his head off with an old musket," committing suicide and putting his soul in peril so that his mother wouldn't collect on the insurance that she had put on his life.

Thus, Lucy and Dracula meet where sentimental illusion meets grim reality. She too, will come to reflect two aspects of a woman — an idealized lie and a dangerous truth. At her most passive, as she lies on her deathbed, she conforms to the fair haired stereotype; her hair "lay on the pillow in its usual shiny ripples" (160). Yet she awakens one last time to summon Arthur to her "in a soft, voluptuous voice" which lures him (as a similar voice did to Harker) precariously close to submitting and in the words of the vampire hunter Van Helsing, "losing your living soul!"(148).

But the message of the suicide seat is more than a reminder that appearances can deceive. It also shatters the most cherished myth about Victorian women, the belief that, in historian Walter Houghton's words, "of all women in the world, the most pure ... was Mother." She was the highest rank in the pantheon of women as angels, "an image wonderfully calculated not only to dissociate love from sex, but to turn love into worship, and worship of purity" (355). (This cult of "mommism" is evident in the title of the enormously popular poem published by Coventry Patmore in 1854, *The Angel in the House*.) And, after Lucy dies and becomes a full fledged vampire, her corruption is presented in terms of the perversion of her maternal qualities.

The first evidence that she is indeed among the Undead comes in the reports of a lady who lures children to dark places and leaves them with two small marks on their necks. The vampire hunters wait near Lucy's tomb and are horrified by what they see:

> far down the avenue of yews we saw a white figure advance—a dim white figure, which held something dark at its breast ... a ray of moonlight ... showed ... a dark haired woman, dressed in the cerements of the grave. We could not see the face, for it was bent down over what we saw to be a fair-haired child ... then as we looked the white figure moved forward again.... We recognized the features of Lucy Westenra ... the sweetness was turned to adamantine, heartless cruelty, and the purity to voluptuous wantonness [211].

The reversal is complete; even her hair color changes from light to dark, though the color of the child's hair reminds us of the innocence she is corrupting. But worse is to come. Dr. Seward, one of her would-be husbands, responds in terror and anger:

> At that moment the remnant of my love passed into hate and loathing; had she then to be killed, I could have done it with savage delight.... With a careless motion, she flung to the ground, callous as a devil, the child that up to now she had clutched strenuously to her breast, growling over it as a dog growls over a bone. There was a cold-bloodedness in the act which wrung a groan from Arthur.... She still advanced, however, and with a languorous, voluptuous grace, said:—"Come to me Arthur.... My arms are hungry for you. Come, and we can rest together. Come, my husband, come!" [211]

Lucy's claim to Arthur as a husband makes all that goes before even more hideous. Most of Stoker's contemporaries believed that a woman's main reason for existence was to be wife and mother. To reject motherhood and assert sexuality invited visions too horrible to contemplate. The reader is reminded of the opening scenes in Transylvania. There, Harker faints when he glimpses the three vampire women begin to feed on a child Dracula has brought them; later he watches the child's mother pleading at the gates of the castle, then torn to pieces by wolves, and responds, "I could not pity her, for I knew now what had become of her child, and she was better dead" (45).

Even at this time, however, there were some who questioned the elevation of wives and mothers to a powerless sainthood. Many Victorians must have been incredibly shocked when, for example, they read in the June 8, 1895, edition of the *Saturday Review* that "The only woman at the present time who is willing to be regarded as a mere breeding machine is she who lacks the wit to adopt any other role" or, in Grant Allen's novel *The Woman Who Did* (1895), that "In a free society, was it not obvious that each woman would live her own life apart, would preserve her independence.... Then only could she be free." An article in the *Westminster Review* in May of 1894 provoked outraged reaction because it argued that Victorian marriage was itself unnatural. It concludes: "So long as society refuses to recognize all other forms of sexual union than those of 'life long monogamy, tempered by divorce' so long will the existence of [prostitutes] be necessary."

The argument that an underclass of "fallen women" was necessary to perpetuate the myth of the sexless wife and mother had been powerfully made by the feminist writer Mona Caird in 1888. Her article, which produced some twenty seven thousand letters in response and set off a two month controversy, ended with a frightening image:

> Prostitution is as inseparable from our present marriage customs as the shadow from the substance. They are two sides of the same shield, and not the deepest gulf that ever held human beings asunder can prevent the burning vapours of the woman's inferno, which is raging beneath our feet, from penetrating into the upper regions of respectability and poisoning the very atmosphere ["Ideal Marriage," *Westminster Review*, Nov. 1888].

When Lucy, the Victorian heroine destined for matrimony, lets Dracula transform her restless sleepwalking into the nocturnal horrors of vampirism, Mona Caird's prediction comes true. Like her counterparts in Dracula's castle, Lucy as vampire surely also suggests Lucy as prostitute — she appears at night, both attracts and disgusts men with her "voluptuousness" and carries a debilitating, ultimately fatal, disease (see Fry 21).

Her crime, then, is to acknowledge sexual desire and thus destroy the false dichotomy that divides and defeats Victorian women. In the shape of the vampire legend, Bram Stoker gives form to the greatest horror hidden in the Victorian system of sexual relations—not merely that respectable women could become prostitutes, but that they did indeed partake of the passions that were believed reserved only to men.

The myth of feminine purity had been crumbling since as early as 1862, when Henry Mayhew wrote about London houses of assignation, where married women could meet other men for sexual purposes (*London Labour* IV 258). Five years earlier, Dr. George R. Drysdale had argued in *The Elements of Social Science* that sexuality was "the natural right of every person, male and female" and even that female hysteria like Lucy's was caused by the lack of a sexual outlet. One of the most discussed and often reprinted magazine articles of the 1860's, Mrs. E. Lynn Linton's "The Girl of the Period," condemned fashionable woman for imitating the language, dress, and manners of the prostitute because "Men are afraid of her; and with reason" (Linton 7). That fear is realized thirty years later in *Dracula;* Lucy's transformation shatters the edifice of Respectability that defined men, women, and marriage. It is little wonder that she is seen as the victim of a foreign infection, her blood tainted by a new and mysterious illness.

Lucy's pathology, from her first restless moments to her final disintegration, resembles a real disease first identified at that time. Dr. William Gull defined anorexia nervosa in 1873, listing its major symptoms as extreme emaciation, loss of appetite, amenorrhea (absence of menstruation) and restless activity, and arguing that the sufferer is "not ill pleased with her condition, notwithstanding the unpleasantness it is attended with" (Showalter 127). The constellation of symptoms (including an inexplicable lack of blood) is associated with Lucy, as is the feeling that her condition is a self-punishing protest against the unreasonable demands of the outside world.

Lucy, like many women of her time, was caught in the middle of an unresolvable conflict, between her natural needs and human feelings and the artificial demands placed upon her gender by Victorian society. As Elaine Showalter has shown, mental breakdown came for women who "defied their 'nature,' attempted to compete with men instead of serving them, or sought alternatives or even additions to their maternal functions" (123). In the most extreme cases, called at the time "puerperal insanity," sufferers used obscene language, flaunted their sexual feelings, and even resorted to infanticide. We are reminded of Lucy at her most frightening in one contemporary description of a sufferer who shows "a total negligence of, and often very strong aversion to, her child . . . explosions of anger occur, with vociferations and violent gesticulations; and, although the patient may have been remarkable previously for her correct, modest demeanor

... most awful oaths and imprecations are now uttered, and language used which astonishes her friends" (58). Interestingly, the widely known literary model for such a madwoman was taken from Sir Walter Scott's *The Bride of Lammermoor* (1819) and subsequent nineteenth century plays based on the story—a woman, named Lucy, who kills a man she cannot marry and is discovered in his bedchamber with her nightgown covered in blood.

The males who treated such forms of insanity reacted much the way the paternalistic and ineffectual men of Stoker's novel do to Dracula's infection of Lucy. Doctors also tried to prevent blood loss, since they attributed women's diseases to excessive menstruation, which they tried to delay as long as possible by cold showers and a meatless diet. They also believed that the monthly lunar cycles (carefully noted in *Dracula*), resulted, like pregnancy and childbirth, in a weakening of the female mind and a predisposition to madness. And they felt such diseases (like Lucy's vampirism), were caused by hereditary taint in the blood. But stronger than any of these opinions was the conviction that "uncontrolled sexuality seemed to be the major, almost defining symptom of insanity in women" (Showalter 74). (It led to the most brutal of treatments: the surgical mutilation of the sexual organs, performed on hundreds of women, including five whose "madness" consisted of wishing to divorce their husbands (Showalter [76]).)

As late as 1894, the widely respected medical authority Dr. von Kraft-Ebing, in the ninth edition of *Psychopathia Sexualis*, intoned of woman: "If she is normally developed mentally and well brought up, her sensual desire is small. Were it not so, the whole world would be a bordello, and marriage and the family unthinkable." It's no wonder that the sexuality which the reborn Lucy exudes is so frightening to the men and provokes such anger and brutality. Her transformation portrays, in the extremes of nightmare, the fear that the acknowledgement of sexual feelings in respectable women would mean the end of marriage and motherhood. There may have seemed to be no acceptable alternative to the repression of sexuality in Victorian life and literature.

Stoker himself confessed his sympathy with this view when, in 1908, he argued in favor of censorship by declaring "a close analysis will show that the only emotions which in the long run harm are those arising from sex impulses" (Farson 209). His greatest novel uses the power of the horror story to give form to that conviction, presenting the sexual awakening of a woman symbolizing Victorian purity as a disease process, a metamorphosis that takes Lucy from angel to whore. Dracula, in fact, liberates the sleepwalking self that has always stood in her shadow. By doing so he spreads the infection from his native land to England and threatens to become, in the words of vampire hunter Abraham Van Helsing, the "father and furtherer of a new order of beings" (302), the mid-European Fuhrer of a master race of women.

As John Allen Stevenson has pointed out, Dracula is defined by his foreignness, just as those who believed they encountered Jack the Ripper could only agree on one thing—that he came from outside England. The danger the outsider poses is one that Imperial Britain found real and immediate—that foreign blood would taint British racial purity, as foreign men and ideas attracted British women. The Count is an extreme example of Continental decadence; French novelists such as Balzac, Sand, Gautier, Zola, and Baudelaire were violently condemned as dangerous to chastity, creators of the "literature of prostitution." F. W. H. Myers, writing in 1885, said of George Sand, who wrote of free love and sexual equality, that her name was "for many years a 'word of fear' in British households" (Houghton 359, 364). In 1898, a small organization called the Legitimation League, dedicated to the replacement of conventional marriage with "a union between free and equal partners" was broken up by the police. Its publications were seized as obscene and its purpose declared to be anarchist. Many believed that the first stirrings of women's desire for equality were proof of foreign forces working, like Dracula, to destroy the family and hasten the destruction of civilization—identified, of course, as a culture dominated by white British males.

This attitude of fear and anger is presented most starkly when the men dispatch Lucy the vampire in the graveyard. At the time of her apparent death, the father of her fiancé, Arthur Holmwood, dies, and Arthur is elevated to the peerage. As Lord Godalming, he gains the authority to act as the counterpart to the infamous Count, a representative of the British nobility confronting the perverted foreign social order Dracula dominates.

And in that role, he enables Lucy to "take her place with the other Angels" (215). Just as Dracula (as Stoker well knew) means "devil," Arthur's new name is "Lord God—" and suggests that his mission has divine blessing. The impression is confirmed by the consecrated Host Van Helsing brings along to seal up the tomb. In the end, however, the men depend upon a more pagan source of power.

In the notes to his edition of *Dracula,* Leonard Wolf points out (60) that each of Lucy's suitors is clearly connected to a "masculine" weapon. When Dr. Seward proposed to Lucy, she writes that "he kept playing with a lancet in a way that made me nearly scream" (56). Quincey Morris, Stoker's idea of a Texan (who proposed by asking, "Won't you just hitch up alongside of me and let us go down the road together, driving in double harness?" [58]), carries a bowie knife. Even Harker, Mina's suitor, is armed with a kukri knife. But, in the graveyard, Lord Godalming is given the most formidable weapon of all: "a round wooden stake, some two and a half or three inches thick and about three feet long. One end of it was hardened by charring in the fire, and was sharpened to a fine point. With this stake came a heavy hammer..." (214). Using these tools, he stakes Lucy's body to the coffin, as she writhes and screams. The scene, as described by Seward, can only be called bracing for the assembled gentlemen:

> But Arthur never faltered. He looked like a figure of Thor as his untrembling arm rose and fell, driving deeper and deeper the mercy bearing stake, whilst the blood from the pierced heart welled and spurted up around it. His face was set, and high duty seemed to shine through it; the sight of it gave us courage, so that our voices seemed to ring through the little vault [216].

When he is finished dispatching Lucy, her face returns to the "unequaled sweetness and purity" it had before her first death, and, as they leave the tomb, Professor Van Helsing, vampire fighter and father figure, gives the key to Arthur. This last act has special significance, since at that time possession of the latch key was a masculine privilege women were only beginning to demand. The reformer Grant Allen wrote in 1890 that "when you begin to give your women a latch-key, trust me, you may feel sure that the moral order . . . is tottering, all benown, to its rotting foundations" (60). To preserve that order, the men in *Dracula* are driven to desperate remedies; the "Angel in the House" has become the body in the tomb. This last tableau, with Arthur pocketing the key to Lucy's new home while she, blankly smiling for eternity, lies transfixed by a three foot stake, is the Victorian ideal of marriage presented as Gothic nightmare.

As late as 1905, a group of Oxford undergraduates who asked if women enjoyed sex were told that "nine out of ten women are indifferent to or actively dislike it; the tenth, who enjoys it, will always be a harlot" (Gay 289). The response to Lucy's transformation included, then, not only pity, but rage. Lord Godalming's desperate remedy makes clear that once women have been exposed to the "infection" of new ideas and the awareness of their own sexuality, they can never return to their former state of pristine powerlessness and, to many, were better off dead.

The destruction of Lucy is a display of the desperate power of gender, exemplified by the latch key and stake that keep Lucy confined and supine for eternity. But the implications go beyond the echoes of pre–Freudian symbolism or the equation of women's autonomy and sexuality with a fatal disease. The stake itself was the primary symbol in a much earlier ritual, one that also involved searching the subject for a hidden mark that signified possession by the devil, accusations of child stealing and cannibalism, of secret nocturnal lives, of supernatural powers and the stealing of souls. Those accusations also led to violence against women by men with the sanction of theology and society, men who believed they were extirpating a secret society that threatened to destroy their culture. For clearly Lucy is also identified with witches, and the men around her with witchhunters.

## 7. Dracula and the Liberation of Women (I)

The witchhunting craze, which condemned thousands of women to torture and death, began around 1550 and ended in the early 1700s. According to Joseph Klaits, the reason for that outbreak of misogynic mania is similar to the hidden dynamic in *Dracula:* reaction by men to changing sexual roles of women. He argues that witch hunting "rose upward on a tide of popular anxieties" (50). The gender of the victims, the sexual fantasies of the witches sabbath (complete with cannibalism of children—similar to the activities in Dracula's castle) and the nature of the process of accusation and trial, are all presented as evidence of the nature of those anxieties. In short, Klaits sees the witch mania as a reaction to the changing role of women in Reformation Europe, a way for men to express fear and hatred of female power and assert the prerogatives of gender in the most violent way.

The connection between this dynamic and that behind the infection and destruction of Lucy is obvious, widening the circle of significance of Stoker's novel. What happens to Lucy—whether defined as disease, fall from purity to prostitution, or demonic possession—has echoes that resound beyond individual lives or specific moments in history. The struggle between genders, and between culture and the forces that seem to threaten culture, underlie all lives and all history. Drawing from that well of images, *Dracula* also draws upon their primeval power.

The anthropologist Mary Douglas, in *Natural Symbols,* makes clear the connection between witchcraft symbolism generally and the vampire myth used by Stoker when she defines the witch as one who stands outside the group, the body politic, one whose "real inner self has escaped from social restraint" (139). She argues that the symbolism of witchcraft "shows the dominance of symbols of inside and outside" of witches who harm victims by getting "access to their inner bodily fluids," destroying the body politic by appropriating the substances inside the body (160).

The body itself, the battleground of the vampire, connects all these manifestations of social disorder—the physicality of gender, the bodily imperatives of sexual desire, social discontent defined as disease, the contrast between internal rebellion and outward conformity. The body becomes, in *Dracula* as in *Dr. Jekyll and Mr. Hyde,* the body politic in microcosm. In "curing" Lucy's strange condition by destroying her, the men who protect an outmoded set of social values manifest their own maladies. Dividing men from women and women from each other, they have become unwitting accomplices to Dracula's assault on the fabric of Victorian culture.

From Harker's confrontation with the three women in Dracula's castle to the final blow from Arthur's hammer, the same point has been driven home: the light haired saint and dark haired whore are sisters under the skin. The final destruction of Lucy takes the Victorian cult of the invalid as feminine ideal beyond the usual fictional climax of a romantic death to the realm of nightmare. It foretells the end of what Abba Gould Woolson called in 1873 "the familiar heroines of our books, particularly if they are described by masculine pens ... a little too spiritual for this world and little too material for the next, and who, therefore, seem always hovering between the two" (Dijkstra 29); it also marks the failure of the traditional popular heroes to cure an infection destined to reach half the population. A shocking moment for Stoker's readers, it implied that their much cherished myths would soon have to give way to new realities.

*Chapter Eight*
# *Dracula* and the Liberation of Women (II)

> Man for the field and woman for the hearth;
> Man for the sword and for the needle she;
> Man with the head and woman with the heart;
> Man to command, and woman to obey;
> All else confusion.
> — Alfred, Lord Tennyson

> In women, exactly as in man, superior bodily strength, physical daring, and nervous power are indisputably requisite to form a fine character.... The crippling idea of chastity and female decorum binds her like an invisible chain wherever she moves, and prevents her from daring to think, feel, or act impulsively.
> — George Drysdale

Along with the new, limited rights of married women came new social realities which, at the turn of the twentieth century, threatened to revolutionize the relationships between the sexes. Because Stoker reacted to those changes, Lucy is not the only heroine of his novel. His second heroine, Mina Murray Harker, takes over after Lucy's death as the focus of the battle between Dracula and the band of men. But she is nothing like Lucy Westenra. Mina stands somewhere between the stereotyped extremes — exalted angel and fallen devil. She, too, is infected by the mania carried by the vampire, but in a different way and with different results. The war between the vampire hunters and Dracula for the soul of Mina ends in her salvation, but also in an uneasy truce. The woman who survives at the end of the novel is indeed a new woman and a new heroine, one who reconciles the battle between sexual stereotypes and gender confusion which marks the novel from the first moments Jonathan Harker sets out on his journey to Transylvania. Although hampered by the prejudices of his time, Bram Stoker tries through her character to define a new way for the sexes to come closer to sharing power.

We see the contrast between Lucy and Mina from their first exchange of letters, early in the novel. Mina's first words are about her job as assistant schoolmistress, "overwhelmed with work." She discusses the perfection of her typing skills and the fact that she and Jonathan Harker exchange letters in shorthand. Her style, unlike Lucy's girlish gush, is, as she says, modeled on that of another group of Victorian career women: "I shall try to do what I see lady journalists do: interviewing and writing descriptions and trying to remember conversations" (54).

Later, much is made of her talent with the typewriter and stenography. She possesses an almost superhuman ability to turn reams of handwritten notes and recorded journals into typed copy overnight. In fact, Mina becomes the author of *Dracula,* since she assembles the collected evidence into a coherent narrative. This also means that she is not protected from hearing of the horrors the men have experienced, as Lucy is. Like the men, she is shocked by the depredations of Dracula. But, also like them, she is able to declare, "Fortunately, I am not of the fainting disposition" (223). Her secretarial abilities make her more than just a secretary, however, since she knows as much or more than any one of the others, both about the strengths of the vampire and the weaknesses of her would-be protectors. When she transcribes Dr. Seward's phonographic cylinders she deduces his anguish from the tone of his words, but reassures him that "I have copied out the words on my typewriter, and none other need now hear your heart beat, as I did" (222). After Lord Godalming cries on her shoulder, she comments, "I suppose there is something in a woman's nature that makes a man feel free to break down before her and express his feelings on the tender or emotional side without feeling it derogatory to his manhood" (229).

Confidences like this lead to Mina's playing mother; in her case as well as Lucy's the distortion of that role suggests something is wrong in the relationship between the sexes. When comforting Lord Godalming after Lucy's death, she felt, "this big, sorrowing man's head on me, as though it were that of the baby that some day may lie on my bosom, and I stroked his hair as though he were my own child. I never thought at the time how strange it all was" (230). The men, as well, seem confused as to how Mina should be stereotyped, as for instance when Van Helsing follows his pronouncement that Mina "...has man's brain—a brain that man should have were he much gifted—and woman's heart" (234), by declaring that she is to have nothing to do with destroying Dracula ("it is no part for a woman"). Just as Harker opens *Dracula* playing the part of Gothic heroine, Mina will close the book playing the hero. In a novel where a man collects recipes and a women knows more than anyone, no one seems able to link personal qualities to gender in the traditional way.

At one point Mina reveals her true feelings about the strange relationships between men and women, goaded by another irritating male assumption about women's deficiencies. As part of his investigation, Van Helsing asks Mina about Lucy's sleepwalking at Whitby; she replies,

> "I can tell you, I think, Dr. Van Helsing, all about it."
> "Ah, then you have a good memory for facts, for details? It is not always so with young ladies"
> "No, Doctor, but I wrote it all down at the time. I can show it to you if you like."
> "Oh, Madam Mina, I will be grateful; you will do me much favour." I could not resist the temptation of mystifying him a bit—I suppose it is some of the taste of the original apple that remains still in our mouths—so I handed him the shorthand diary. He took it with a grateful bow and said:
> "May I read it?"
> "If you wish," I answered as demurely as I could. He opened it, and for an instant his face fell. Then he stood up and bowed.
> "Oh, you so clever woman"....
> "Forgive me," I said: "I could not help it; but . . . I have written it out on the typewriter for you" [182-3].

Mina scores her point with Van Helsing by contrasting her demure behavior with a sharp reminder of the superior skills associated with her from her introduction, suggesting as well that she communicates in a different language, one a man like Van Helsing can never understand. But including shorthand and the typewriter in the book, like Seward's use of a phonograph diary, doesn't only connect the tale to the technology of England in 1897 and add to its immediacy. The invention of the typewriter, like that of the telephone, became instrumental in changing the role of women in late Victorian England.

With few exceptions, the only jobs available outside the home for respectable women until the 1880s were as governess or schoolmistress. With the invention of the telephone, women's voices became a salable commodity, so that, by the end of the century, forty percent of the employees in the field were female. But the typewriter caused even more dramatic changes. Clerks had been male because a masculine hand was preferred; before the eighties ". . . the idea of a woman employed in an office was practically unheard of. The number of women clerks returned at the 1881 census was negligible. By 1891, nearly 18,000 were returned, by 1901, 55,784" (Reader 159). At the same time, the phenomenal growth of the popular press at the end of the century provided opportunities for journalists, many of them women. Thus Mina, schoolmistress and typist, modeling her style on "lady journalists," becomes all the "new women" who were changing society as they discovered their own independence. Her command of the word in *Dracula*, like the neutering of the word brought about by the typewriter, was emblematic of the sweeping changes that would come about when ability was decoupled from gender.

The advent of the "New Woman" was much debated at the time; the term stood for all the changes in economic, social, educational, and marital status which women were beginning to achieve. "New Woman" writers were the precursors of the suffragettes. By advocating, among other things, birth control, women in the professions, less restrictive dress, and freedom to travel unescorted, they threatened to realign the relationship between the sexes. Here, too, we see Mina as an example.

Early in the book, she mentions the "New Woman," curiously enough while she and Lucy are walking the cliffs of Whitby, "with our hearts full of a constant dread of wild bulls" (88). (Cattle *were* permitted to roam the cliffs, so the fear is justified, but one might argue that the connection between the two events reminds us of the scalpels, knives, and stakes carried by the men — contemplating equality has its dangers.) In any case, Mina comes dangerously close to proposing sexual liberation when she thinks, "Some of the 'New Woman' writers will some day start an idea that men and women should be allowed to see each other asleep before proposing or accepting. But I suppose the New Woman won't condescend in the future to accept; she will do the proposing herself" (89). This line of discussion is initiated after she and Lucy have a prodigious meal and Mina comments, "I believe we should have shocked the 'New Woman' with our appetites" (88). In fact, the entire episode and the fears that surround it hint at women's new appetites — their appeal and their danger.

Although Mina is somewhat ambivalent about her attitudes toward the New Woman, it is clear that her relationship with Jonathan Harker is very different from Lucy's with Lord Godalming. As Dracula's attacks on Lucy begin, Mina travels to Budapest where Harker is recovering from a 'brain fever' caused by his experiences at Dracula's castle. There she marries him. The scene reverses what's happening back in England: like the passive Lucy drained of blood and resembling a victim of neurasthenia or hysteria, Jonathan is lying in bed, "thin and pale and weak looking" and in danger of going mad (103). Having temporarily forgotten what is recorded in his journal of his visit to the castle, he gives the book to Mina, telling her to "Take it and keep it, read it if you will, but never let me know" (104). Again, Mina is the guardian of knowledge. By trusting her with what he himself is afraid to be told, Harker recognizes the balance of power in their relationship.

That journal, written in a private language none of the other men can read, represents the new, private understanding that underlies their marriage. Throughout the novel, since everyone (including the reader) learns of events through the medium of print — newspapers, journals, Mina's typewritten transcriptions — the act of writing itself becomes a source of power as well as a medium of communication. By controlling that source, Mina gains control over the events and the men around her. She reads everything except Harker's journal; instead, at his request Mina ties it up and seals it with her wedding ring, as an "outward and visible sign for us all our lives that we trusted each other" (105). Later, when Harker sees the Count and seems to be on the verge of a relapse, she breaks the seal without telling him. This doesn't destroy the pact, however, because she reads the journal for his good (and later tells him what's in it). In other words, the exchange of words between Jonathan Harker and Mina Murray goes beyond their marriage vows; it encompasses an exchange of the power coded language can have (power she withholds from Van Helsing, the ostensible leader), and suggests that their relationship at least approaches a concept of male and female equality.

Stoker may well owe this suggestion of sexual equality to his mother Charlotte, who is remembered as a social worker and writer as well as the mother of seven children. She reportedly once proposed in a newspaper article to "equalize the sexes, both here and in our colonies, by encouraging emigration. In new countries there is a dignity in labor, and a self-supporting woman is alike respected and respectable" (Ludlam 14). It is interesting that Charlotte Stoker's belief that only in other countries could women find equality is echoed in the fact that Mina's pact with her husband is made in Budapest and that, later, she is at her strongest when the troupe of vampire hunters leaves England. And certainly Stoker knew what it meant for a woman to be self supporting, since he toured the world with a theater company that employed both actors and actresses.

Mina Harker and Bram Stoker are even more closely connected. Stoker was actually the secretary for Irving's company, keeping the records and conducting Irving's correspondence, which at times amounted to several hundred letters per week (Farson 25). An imposing figure (the "red haired giant"), Stoker nevertheless performed essentially the same motherly role that Mina did, recognized in actress Ellen Terry's nickname for him — "Mama." Thus, Stoker was both the man noted for his athletic prowess (and cited for attempting to save a man who jumped off a steamer in 1882) and the secretary who did for the acting company what Mina did for the little band of vampire hunters. There even has been some speculation about his relationship with Irving, whom Stoker served for twenty-seven years with all the dedication of a wife.

The intensity of their association is suggested by Stoker's account of their introduction. After a dinner in Dublin, the assembled guests listened to Irving's passionate reading of a melodramatic poem by Thomas Hood. Stoker recalled that, "after the climax of horror. . . . [Irving] collapsed, half fainting." Stoker's reaction was no less dramatic; by his own admission, he "burst into something like hysterics." Not to be outdone, Irving composed himself, ". . . went into his room and, after a couple of minutes brought me out his photograph with an inscription on it, the ink still wet (another private gift of language): 'My dear friend Stoker. God bless you! God bless you!! Henry Irving. Dublin, December 3, 1876'" (Stoker *Reminiscences* 1 30–33).

All this means that Stoker could see how male and female roles might be combined in one person. (And in a later book, *The Man* [1906] he does just that; his heroine, named Stephen, questions conventional sex roles [Roth 38–51].) Mina Harker is, in part, a female counterpart of Bram Stoker—a secretary who keeps a company of adults together by playing both dutiful subordinate and surrogate mother. And, as we have seen, both Mina and Stoker wrote *Dracula*. Stoker's notes in the Rosenbach collection show that the novel evolved over six years, created out of his reading, interviews, and observations, and recorded on such scraps of paper as hotel stationary. Parts of the notes are verbatim transcriptions from his reading, allusions to maps and timetables, and even newspaper clippings. Mina's efforts are described in much the same way. Her transcription and ordering of the varied data she collects constitute the novel which, on the last page, is called "nothing but a mass of type-writing" (378).

Stoker's life in the theater, traveling the world, made it easier for him to escape the gender linked demands of Victorian convention as well as to see women playing all their contradictory roles. Among the theater audience prostitutes congregated, while on stage the most popular heroine was a woman like Lucy, what one writer called the "lovely imbecile of Victorian melodrama" (Dalziel 84). But these were not the only heroines. In comedy, especially, witty and able women were common, while the popular art of burlesque involved women dressed as men and acting in stereotypical male fashion for comic effect (Davies 55–58).

This confusion of sexual identities in women of the theater was reflected in the social ferment in the wider world. For example, a group of working class women was an ongoing source of scandal throughout this period. Their pictures were sold surreptitiously like pornography, and attempts were made to restrict their activities. One man, Arthur Munby, was obsessed with visiting, talking to, and photographing these women at work and in their working clothes. Yet they weren't prostitutes, but laborers at the pit openings of the Wigan mines who, out of necessity, wore men's trousers. Evidence at a committee hearing on the "problem" stated it succinctly: "It is rather a man's dress that they wear ... and it drowns all sense of decency betwixt men and women, they resemble one another so much" (Hiley 48).

The "pit brow workers" (they shoveled coal at the mouth of mines) were physically strong, economically independent, and dressed like men. The attempt to restrict their dress or ban them from the mines entirely was seen at the time for what it was, a response by men who felt threatened by women who resembled men in more than their clothes. They became one focus for the equal rights movement at the end of the century; in May 1887 a deputation from the mines wearing trousers, clogs, and topcoats, marched to the Home Office at the head of a demonstration to demand their right to work dressed "like men"—and won (Hiley 60).

Mina Harker, clearly more intelligent and able than the men who set out to save her, is still no crusader for women's rights. She fears not only the powers of Dracula, but the threat her own ability seems to pose for the structure of society. Like many women of the period, Mina is caught between wanting to assert her new social and economic power, yet fearing being stigmatized as a threat to male security and superiority. In fact, after she is forced into an act of vampirism, her stigmata actually appear. When Van Helsing touches the Sacred Host to her forehead, it leaves a scar, reminiscent of the scar Harker put on Dracula's forehead in a vain attempt to destroy him in his castle. Thus, Dracula and Mina share the mark of Cain, binding them as social outcasts and tainting her with the stain of impurity [her response is to shout "Unclean" and vow not to "touch or kiss" her husband again until the mark is gone (297).]

The rest of the book details the pursuit of Dracula by Mina and the men who need to destroy him to return her to purity. They would like to leave her out of it, but she has gained the ability to unite with Dracula's mind under hypnosis and thus give them some idea of where he is. While they race across Europe and make all the wrong guesses, she busily composes memoranda on her "Traveller's Typewriter," assessing the situation and suggesting a course of action. Even Van Helsing, the supposed leader of the expedition, is forced to declare, "Our dear madam Mina is once more our teacher" (353).

At the same time Mina becomes "one of the boys" and outdoes them at their own game, she observes the Victorian proprieties, asking them to kill her if she seems in danger of becoming the ultimate "fallen woman"—a lady vampire. She even has them read the Burial Service over her, perhaps recognizing that something in her has already died. For her, as for Lucy, Dracula has initiated a disease process, though it fills her with a new strength rather than an enervating weakness. The reversal in the scene where she drinks his blood suggests the reason; instead of losing her vitality to an outside force, she has taken on some of Dracula's male power with his blood.

With the "infection" of Mina, Dracula's invasion of England ends; from then on, as he tries to escape, he cuts a somewhat pathetic figure, slipping aboard ship in a straw hat, deprived by the vampire hunters of his last few possessions—a clothes brush, hair brush and comb, and some papers: "all were covered up in thin wrapping paper to keep them from the dust" (301). Mina feels pity for him, possibly because she has a window into his mind, possibly because she senses he is ultimately helpless and anachronistic, like the men who surround and try to save her.

In the guise of freeing women, both Dracula and his adversaries try to dominate them. Dracula wants to release them to share his nocturnal passions, but as his possessions. He exults to the vampire hunters, "Your girls that you all love are mine already" (306). The men believe they are freeing Lucy from a horrible fate, but use brutal force to return her to passivity and dependence. Both even use the same patronizing term: Mina happily reports that Lord Godalming once calls her "little girl" — "the very words he had used to Lucy" (231). Yet Dracula and the men trying to destroy him are identified as the real children; Van Helsing pontificates on Dracula's "child brain," while Mina notes how the other men act like little boys.

The men around Mina certainly make a strange group of heroes. Dr. William Acton, in *Functions and Disorders*, wrote that men "approach more or less the standard of human perfection" (115). But not in *Dracula*. Van Helsing, the fatherly vampire expert, is sometimes thoughtlessly cruel and once frightens everyone by breaking into hysterics. Dr. Seward at one point even suspects him of madness (194). Seward himself, the head of an insane asylum, is presented as depressed and suicidal ("I am too miserable, too low-spirited, too sick of the world and all in it, including life itself, that I would not care if I heard this moment the flapping of the wings of the angel of death" [158]). He often takes drugs to sleep and fears becoming addicted. Jonathan Harker, unnerved by his experience at Dracula's castle, is always in danger of a relapse of "brain fever"; Quincey Morris, a minor figure in the group, once stands near a house where the company is assembled and recklessly blasts away at a bat with his gun. (Renfield, Seward's patient and Dracula's reluctant disciple, who dies fighting to save Mina, is, of course, a certified lunatic.) Even the stalwart Lord Godalming seems a bit dense. Not only does he break down on Mina's bosom, at one point he reads her narrative and confesses he "doesn't quite see the drift of it" (229). Like the women, the men seem to find it difficult to play the roles popular mythology assigns to them. It's not hard for Mina to be the most competent in the group.

The last part of *Dracula* is, then, a jumble of contradictory emotions. It would be wrong to say Mina is a liberated woman; she loves the role of secretary/helpmeet and abhors the stain to her purity represented by the mark on her forehead. Her abilities are defined as masculine, while she cherishes her submissive "woman's heart." She takes charge, nonetheless, while appearing not to, deferring only enough to keep all the men comfortable.

Victorian women who wished to be independent yet avoid society's censure sometimes displayed an attitude quite similar to Mina's. The same year *Dracula* was published, a remarkable woman named Mary Henrietta Kingsley published *Travels in West Africa* (1897), chronicling her adventures in what was then dark and dangerous territory. Niece of the crusading novelist Charles Kingsley, she was a woman who sincerely believed she had no sexual urges yet kept fighting cocks because she "loved their beautiful ferocity" (Longford 205). When her parents died, she went to West Africa alone and spent years traveling through the jungles, encountering various wild animals, enduring incredible hardships, and finally writing a massive book about her experiences.

Mary Kingsley, like Mina Harker, confronted danger and discomfort fearlessly, yet was always careful to avoid being too "masculine." She told everyone she was looking for her (nonexistent) husband, refused to wear men's clothes in the jungle, and because she did "not think it ladylike to go shooting things with a gun" (545) carried only a Bowie knife. Still, as Mina says of herself, Mary Kingsley was "not of the fainting disposition." Immediately after we learn of her curious gender induced choice of weapons, she tells us of her encounter with a leopard:

> The leopard crouched, I think to spring on me. I can see its great, lambent eyes still and I seized an earthen water cooler and flung it straight at them. It was a noble shot; it burst on the leopard's head like a shell and the leopard went in the bush [546].

She also claims she once struck an attacking crocodile on the snout, was saved at the last moment from a charging gorilla, and spent hours up to her neck in the "stinking slime" of a swamp looking for a passage out. Yet she took on the prudish attitudes of a Victorian matron as soon as she returned to civilization, even if civilization was defined as an isolated outpost in the bush. Once, returning to such a place, "mud caked and with blood on her face and hands" she was offered an "instant hot bath" but declined, since the arrangements didn't allow for quite enough privacy (Longford 216).

Catherine Stevenson, writing about Mary Kingsley, notices how her narrative keeps switching between two voices; when she recounts acts of bravery, her voice takes on a confident, even aggressive "masculine" tone. However, whenever she seems to be deviating too much from the conventional female role, she is careful to insert self deprecating, socially acceptable comments about her helplessness before the superior power of men. At these moments, a new voice takes over, that of the "lady traveler, the amusing spinster prone to 'feminine nervousness' which makes her flee from wild animals" (Stevenson 138). In private life she was careful to disassociate herself from suffragettes, whom she called "shrieking females and androgins" and announced "I do not relish being called a New Woman" (Longford 223).

Mary Henrietta Kingsley and Mina Murray Harker were alike in that they were most free to exercise their power when far from England. In a social as well as a geographical sense, they ventured into largely unexplored foreign territory; even there they needed to remind themselves to act as if the old rules applied and probably believed that they did. Both were caught in the dilemma that faced women at the turn of the century—social and sexual identity seemed inextricably bound.

*Dracula* is, of course, more than a book about the feelings engendered by the changing status of women. It ranges from religious allegory to Freudian psychodrama. (At the time the events recorded in *Dracula* were supposedly happening, Freud was studying the sexual origins of female hysteria and beginning to expound the theories that underlie modern psychology.) And some of the characters not germane to this discussion, like the madman Renfield and his morose keeper Seward, are worth an exploration in themselves. But it is clear that the horror that underlies the novel is a close relative to what's been called the "unmistakable note of horror and fear" (Houghton 359) that accompanied the changes in the status of women at the turn of the century. Bram Stoker was no crusader for equal rights—his picture of the ideal relationship between men and women would be shared by few women today and few "New Women" at the time. But he does show, whether he was aware of it or not, that the contradictory images of woman as angel or whore are irreconcilable and self destructive, that some new model for women would have to take their place.

That his picture of Mina, his new heroine, contains another artificial distinction—between what he calls a "man's brain and a woman's heart"—simply shows that Stoker was a creature of his time. For, like Mary Kingsley and Mina herself, most Victorians saw qualities like independence, courage, and tenderness linked to gender. When Lord Godalming cries, he deserts the role society assigns him; in Stoker's words, he is "unmanned," a condition Stoker himself confessed to having undergone when he met Henry Irving (Stoker, *Reminiscences* I, 33). Women writers often used male pseudonyms so that they would be taken seriously. In 1887, Victoria Benedictsson wrote in her diary, "Damnation! That I should be a woman with the brain of a man! A woman is nothing for herself and by herself, and I am only a woman" (Gay 113).

Mina Murray Harker, like Jonathan Harker, did not fit into the gender stereotypes that, at the end of the nineteenth century, still determined personality, occupation and power. But they were not the only men and women who didn't; as we've seen, Bram Stoker may have been another. Some other writers at the time tried to find a way out of this contradiction by expanding the definition of gender. Edward Carpenter, in an article called "An Unknown People" published the same year as *Dracula* (1897) begins by stating "In late years (and since the arrival of the New Woman among us) many things in the relation of men and women have altered" (1). He goes on, here and in a later book, to propose an "intermediate sex"—men and women who "belong physically to one sex, and mentally and emotionally to the other" (8).

The intermediate ("normal homogenic") woman he describes is remarkably like Mina, "thoroughly feminine and gracious" but with an "inner nature [that] is to a great extent masculine; a temperament active, brave and originative, somewhat decisive, not too emotional . . . good at organization, and well pleased with positions of responsibility . . . making an excellent and generous leader" (36). Carpenter's attempt to account for the new woman (and the new man) by literally proposing new genders encountered an extremely hostile contemporary public reaction, in part because he was linked to the Uranian movement. This group argued that homosexuality was a legitimate third gender at a time when, as Oscar Wilde put it, he was jailed for the crime of "gender failure."

Whether Stoker knew of Carpenter's writings is uncertain, though the controversy they generated shows that the questions of gender and personality raised by the nascent women's movement worried many, and not only women. The memoirs of Daniel Paul Schreber, begun in 1893, (which, since they were not published until 1902, Stoker definitely did not see before writing *Dracula*) demonstrate how this conflict, which brought the fictional men of *Dracula* close to insanity, drove one actual man to madness. Schreber was institutionalized because he became convinced that his "body was gradually being transformed into a female body" a process he, like Stoker, called "unmanning" (5). The analysis of his case was that, "under the impact of a threatening reality which imperiously demanded of him an active masculine role, his latent passive feminine tendencies broke into consciousness"(370). In other words, unable to face living as what he defined as a man with a woman's brain, he believed his body and personality were slowly resolving the discrepancy. As Stoker did in *Dracula,* Schreber translated the conflict between male and female into the fiction of a strange, metamorphosing disease. Just as the men following Mina in pursuit of the vampire keep checking her to see if her teeth are any sharper, poor Daniel Schreber's memoirs often refer to the moments he feels "the gradual filling of my body with nerves of voluptuousness (female nerves)" (99).

*Dracula* is, then, the story of both infection and cure, invasion and retreat, waged in the human body and the body politic of England; the final pages of the book recount a pursuit across Europe and the destruction of the vampire, which simultaneously erases the stain on Mina's forehead and blunts the points on her slowly sharpening teeth, while ending the uncertainty about her loyalties. However, though everyone in the novel fears what Dracula represents — a threat to the stable relationships between the sexes, to the hierarchy of marriage and the social order, to the certainty of the link between personality and gender — no one quite wants to return to the way things were.

In one sense, the foreign ideas represented by Dracula are destroyed; it's significant that the only man to die at the end is the American Quincey Morris, who also has represented a foreign way of thinking and an implicit threat to the society England was fighting so desperately to preserve. But, though the mark of the vampire disappears when Dracula dies, his blood still runs in Mina's veins. And for all of them, the lure remains strong. In a final note, we learn that in the seven years since the events of the novel the group has already returned once to Transylvania and continues "talking of the old time." Quincey is even reincarnated in Mina's child, born on the anniversary of his death and given his name.

The child's birth, like the news we receive that "Godalming and Seward are both happily married" (378) make clear the real task of the vampire hunters. At the beginning of the book all were poised on the brink of marriage at a time when the conventional ideal of marriage was threatened by the awakening economic, social, and sexual power of women. By the end they have fought off the alien and catastrophic threat represented by Dracula at the cost of Lucy, who embodied the two extreme and unreal Victorian female stereotypes. An outmoded and illogical set of social values, the mainstay of Victorian popular fiction, melodrama and myth, has been replaced by an uneasy ambivalence.

It was clear to many of the "New Woman" writers that the marriage question would begin to be solved when women could define themselves as competent, free, and feminine. An article from the *Westminster Review* of June 1895 states the problem most clearly:

> A girl requires an occupation for her energies and deserves a lover for herself. Too often, the kindest of parents will give her money without an occupation and will hurry her blindfold into marriage at any price. Too late she learns her incapacity for useful work and too late and with more bitterness she discovers that her marriage has shut her out from love for the whole of her life.... The independence and usefulness of gentlewomen is the first step toward remedying our social evils [A. L. Lee, "The 'Impasse' of Women" 568].

As Barbara Leigh Smith Bodichon argued many years earlier, in *Women and Work* (1857), "Activity of brain, heart, and limb, gives health and beauty, and makes women fit to be the mothers of children. A listless, idle, empty-brained, empty-hearted woman has no right to bear children" (Bodicohn 21). Lucy, enervated by the sanguinary demands of patriarchy, dies childless; Mina, energized by drinking the blood of the vampire, engenders new life and power.

All of the distortions of the maternal role — in the gruesome tastes of Dracula's women, Lucy's nocturnal activities, Mina's nursing of grown men, and even Dracula's opening a vein in his chest and forcing Mina to drink his blood—are answered by the birth of Mina's child. Mina becomes a wife and mother who is useful, competent, and independent. Her other child, the book she amasses from experiences around her, is the only testimony to the reality of their struggle, and proof that the power of the word lies with her. The "heroes," more fallible than the paragons of popular fiction, prepare for the next generation. All have come close to mental breakdown as the culture around them faces the destabilizing forces of social change. Though they set out to save her, at the end of the book it is Mina who leads the reluctant band of men into the twentieth century.

# Part Four
# Shaping the Darkness (1900–18)

*Chapter Nine*
# The Fantasy of Reality

> The love of victory and conquest is still strong within us, and the lust for the war by the great nations of the world at the present time is only curbed by the fear of the dreadful and lasting consequences that might follow defeat
> —H. S. Alford and W. D. Sword

> The drama of terror has the irresistible power of converting its audience into its victims.
> —Charles Maturin

The birth of the new century and the death of Queen Victoria soon afterwards were seen at the time as dual portents of great change. But familiar problems remained: industrial strife, population upheaval, the plight of the poor, the threat of crime and social disruption, the demands of women for greater rights. There was one great difference — many of these fears were magnified in an atmosphere which, much more often than before, turned from suffering and indignation to violence. The total breakdown in society that had been feared a century before as a result of the French and Industrial revolutions seemed to many to be finally about to arrive. The terrors of fiction, as well, had gone from distant and unreal fantasies to contemporary and cataclysmic possibilities. History and horror were about to converge, as an entire generation learned from popular literature how to read meaning into their lives.

The agitation against vivisection is one minor example of the heightened social instability of the new century. Instead of merely provoking another Royal Commission like the one in 1875, the suffering of a brown mongrel terrier at the hands of vivisectionists led, in 1902, to two years of street riots in London. Two women medical students had witnessed and published a record of two cruel demonstrations on the dog by a lecturer at University College London, and a statue was put up in Battersea Park in honor of the unfortunate canine. When medical students attempted to destroy it, crowds of up to 3,000 defended it, often leading to pitched battles. The poor dog suffered a second indignity when, in 1907, the statue was taken down and turned into scrap (only to be re-erected seventy-seven years later by the still vigilant Anti-Vivisection Society).

Agitation for women's rights also turned violent. Birth control information was disseminated by Margaret Sanger, Marie Stopes and others, amid harassment and the usual responses from men in power that it would lead to "free love, amateur prostitution, and other evils of that sort" (Pearsall, *Edwardian* 154). But the strongest attack on male complacency and female subjugation came from the suffragettes, headed by Mrs. Emmeline Pankhurst and her three daughters. They didn't content themselves with the mild protests of the "New Woman" movement; instead, they organized heckling from the Strangers' Gallery in Parliament and led marches, demonstrations, window smashing sprees, and other forms of violent protest. Many were imprisoned; some responded with hunger strikes and were brutally force fed.

The feeling that vast changes in the social structure were imminent was enhanced by the friction between classes. As in earlier decades, the urban poor constituted a vast segment of society, swelled since the 1880's by an exodus of agricultural workers from the impoverished countryside and an influx of immigrants from Eastern Europe (about 200,000 between 1881 and 1914). Workhouses were still largely the only provision for the poor, and they remained for many a worse alternative than suicide. Exposes continued to be written, most notably Jack London's *People of the Abyss* (1903) which, like their mid–Victorian predecessors, conveyed wrenching anecdotes of ghastly living conditions in a manner designed to increase the horror.

The difference was that the downtrodden, too, were no longer suffering in silence. The trade union movement had grown, along with socialist organizations including the Labour Party, which gained a small representation in Parliament. Immediate results were a modest old age pension scheme and a wave of strikes, riots, and other industrial violence. Miners, dockworkers, seamen, and others met police and, at times, troops, who opened fire on more than one occasion. Calls by union organizers for a general strike were met by hysterical denunciations of "anarchists" and repressive legislation. In 1912, H. G. Wells announced "we are in the opening phase of a real and irreparable class war" (Pearsall, *Edwardian* 103), a conflict prophesied by Jack London in *War of the Classes* (1905).

The widespread fear of collapse from within was heightened by the terrorism of those already at war with order itself—the anarchists. In the twenty years before a political murder set off the cataclysm of the First World War, five monarchs and one U. S. president had been assassinated by assorted anarchist fanatics, all convinced that such a deed would trigger worldwide revolt. Although anarchists by definition shunned any organization, it was commonly believed that huge conspiracies were behind each act. G. K. Chesterton's best seller *The Man Who Was Thursday* (1908) depicted the headquarters of such an organization hidden beneath a seedy beershop in London, complete with a steel chamber hung with rows of bombs. Although Chesterton labeled his story "a nightmare" (and filled it with absurd touches including the hero's reaction to the bomb filled room—he lights a cigar), for many the anarchist panic was real.

Chesterton's book ends with the comic revelation that each of the supposed anarchists is really a police spy, implying that the fear of anarchism, in England at least, was a form of mass hysteria. The facts seem to bear him out, since, despite the conviction that anarchists were everywhere, only one person was killed by an anarchist weapon in Britain, a French anarchist destroyed in 1894 by his own bomb (Shpayer-Makov 490). The anarchist scare reached epidemic proportions because it focused familiar fears of the parallel breakdown of self and society exploited in horror fiction like *Dr. Jekyll and Mr. Hyde* and *Dracula*. The word "anarchy" had been applied since the 1870's to mean social disorder, not just a political movement, while, throughout the popular press in the 1890's, the anarchist was depicted as suffering from "a deep and incurable inner disease and not the effects of social circumstances" (Shpayer-Makov 499–500). Anarchists were supposed to be degenerates (Cesare Lombrosio classified anarchists as yet another type of atavistic throwback, recognizable on sight) and foreign (anarchists were invariably identified with immigrants, usually Jews).

A foreign underworld marked another popular fantasy, which followed the pattern of *Dracula:* millions believed the English way of life was threatened by a secret invasion from the Continent. In many versions of this story, the invaders, like Dracula and the legions of the labyrinth that had been a part of the Gothic universe since its inception, were literally supposed to come from underground. In 1882–83 and 1887–8, speculative fictions depicted a secret Channel tunnel as the highway for an infiltration of troops disguised as tourists, while in 1901 Max Pemberton's extremely popular novel *Pro Patria* had the French secretly tunneling their way to Dover, planning to emerge in a farmhouse where the tunneling was disguised as the building of an ornamental lake!

But, by the start of the twentieth century, the French had been supplanted as the main villains in fantasies of invasion. Their defeat by the Germans in 1871, which led to German troops marching into Paris, helped influence the British to focus their fears on another potential enemy. Sir George Chesney's *The Battle of Dorking*, first published the same year in *Blackwoods Magazine* and later as a sixpenny pamphlet, was indeed a contemporary "shilling shocker." It sold over 80,000 copies in the first month and inspired countless newspaper discussions and imitations, frightening the populace with visions of fierce Prussians overcoming feeble British defenses.

Six years into the new century the scare returned with William Le Queux's *The Invasion of 1910* (1906), which had an even greater impact. Translated into 27 languages (including German) and selling over a million copies, it depicted another fictional German invasion using the scrapbook apparatus of *Dracula,* complete with maps, plans, facsimiles of official documents by the occupation forces, and defiant proclamations by the British War Office and "League of Defenders." It also included hairraising accounts of barbaric Uhlan cavalry terrorizing London during the bombardment of the city, as the populace cowered in the darkness of the Underground, "caught like rats in a hole" (346). In retrospect, it may have seemed prophetic that the man who placed Queen Victoria, symbol of the British Empire, into her coffin on the evening of January 22, 1901, had been none other than her nephew, Kaiser Wilhelm of Germany.

Although traditional Gothic fiction continued to appear in these years — some of it quite good — the familiar ghosts and haunted castles didn't have the popular impact of this new form of horror. The underground world that undermined the Gothic city and the Victorian landscape had greater potential for disturbing the public consciousness than insubstantial spectres in remote castles. Tunnels under England disgorging foreign invaders or rooms beneath the streets harboring anarchists and lined with bombs seemed potent evidence that what Charles Kingsley had feared at the middle of the century ("I see our civilization as a thin film lying over a volcanic pit. Some day the pit will break through and devour us all") was apparently about to come to pass. The horror stories that captured the largest audience were no longer set in the medieval past or the Edwardian present; they were histories of the near future, destined to be revealed in a few years as fantasy or prophecy. At the time of publication, either seemed possible. This new type of terror not only played upon fears of mass destruction, but also blurred the line between what never was and what well might be.

Fiction that purported to report the coming horrors was matched by other forms of popular entertainment that kept the panic simmering. In 1909 an invasion by "the Emperor of the North" was depicted in Guy du Maurier's play *An Englishman's Home.* A spectacle entitled *Invasion* and organized by John M. East played regularly at the reconstructed Crystal Palace in Sydenham early in the century. At least 25,000 spectators at a time gathered on the grounds to see actors in a reconstructed village play out an attack by a Zeppelin disgorging parachutists, complete with bomb bursts, a spy signaling the (obviously German) invaders, and a last minute rescue by a company of British soldiers. The mock village was actually destroyed each time and had to be rebuilt for the next performance. If that weren't enough, every Thursday huge fireworks displays, using thousands of rockets and tons of high explosives and often purporting to reenact famous battles, were set off at Sydenham and visible all over London.

These two complementary fears—of anarchy and invasion—were brought together in the almost universal belief that England was ridden with an underworld of spies just waiting for the word to take out the hidden arms, unveil their disguised gun emplacements, and help the invaders subdue the hub of the Empire. Until "Der Tag" they were supposedly busy setting bombs or fomenting strikes and other forms of unrest. Estimates in the popular press and such books as *The Invasion of 1910* or *The Enemy in Our Midst* (1906) of their number ran as high as 300,000 (Clarke 158). The story, retold in both newspapers and fiction, was a product of the mythmaking power of the public, further evidence that reality could be altered to fit a narrative that fulfilled deep seated needs. Real places in Stevenson's novella, the mass of manufactured evidence that comprised Stoker's, were supplanted by horror fantasies that nearly everyone was convinced were true. Unfortunately, the actual results were many unwarranted arrests of alleged spies and anarchists and a growing wave of anti–German and anti–Semitic agitation.

Some believed the future held more than simply invasion or war; the preacher Stopford Brooke predicted in 1908 that the new technology of aeroplanes and poison gas would mean "the whole fabric of civilization will be expunged, and Europe will go back to savage conditions. It will need no God's interference to put an end to our vile society. It will destroy itself, and the destruction will be the work of modern science" (Jacks, II, 653). H. G. Wells' books such as *The War of the Worlds* (1898) or *The War in the Air* (1908) visualized these fears, combining fantasy and prophecy in different proportions. Even though the first pitted Englishmen against invaders from Mars, both books shared one very real concern: that new weapons in the hands (or tentacles) of barbaric invaders could bring the world as Wells knew it to a cataclysmic end. Sir Arthur Conan Doyle (who was later to aid recruitment with a pamphlet entitled *To Arms*) came closest to seeing what would actually soon occur when he predicted (again in the guise of fiction) unrestricted submarine warfare in an story in the *Strand Magazine* in July 1914 entitled "Danger!"

However, the predictions and prophecies that comprised this new form of horror fiction were also akin to the earlier fantasies of Gothic literature in that they expressed the secret fears of the populace, not what the official culture wanted to believe. Outwardly, many saw an impending war with Germany as an heroic adventure, a ritual cleansing of society and revitalization of the individual, settling the uncertainties and insecurities of the time in brief and glorious combat. A group of Naval officers responded to Conan Doyle's story in an appendix entitled "What the Naval Experts Think," asserting confidently that submarines were overrated weapons and that, since an attack on a merchant ship would be "unsporting," it would not be allowed: "any officer who did it would be shot" (21).

Erskine Chalders, who wrote another "future history," *The Riddle of the Sands*, in 1903, created Carruthers, a hero in the best schoolboy tradition who discovers Germany preparing for a war to take place in 1913 and thwarts their plans. His method of dealing with the twin dangers of invasion and subversion begins on the first page with what he calls his "ritual of discipline," a distillation of colonial British values that would soon seem laughably archaic and inadequate in facing a grim reality:

> I have read of men who, when forced by their calling to live for long periods of utter solitude — save for a few black faces — have made it a rule to dress regularly for dinner in order to maintain their self respect and prevent a relapse into barbarism [1].

Though, as we shall see, many believed in "playing the game" and keeping up appearances until well beyond the bitter end, when the war actually came it neither ended civilization nor revivified it. Nor were the fictive prophecies directly fulfilled. British civilians, who had fantasized suffering from the cruelty of invaders and the treachery of turncoats, were left largely untouched (the only slight danger to them came, not from underground or from within, but from the Zeppelins in the air); romantics, who had seen the war as an opportunity to revive British public school virtues in a quick and bracing conflict, were soon disillusioned. Instead, some eight million soldiers suffered and died in a long, savage, and ultimately purposeless war of entrenchments fought in a featureless wasteland. It became, as Max Beerbohm predicted, "not so much purge as additional poison" (Pearsall, *Edwardian* 281).

Some of the problems many hoped the war would solve were indeed resolved, but in ironic ways. Women, whose violence could not secure them the vote, were enfranchised after the war as payment for ninety-five hour weeks many spent in munitions factories so that men could engage in greater violence. The "submerged classes" who threatened revolution emerged to be recruited into "Pals' Battalions," shipped off to the front, and slaughtered wholesale. Public horror over the barbarism of murderers like Jack the Ripper or the threat of unnamed anarchists throwing bombs seemed strange indeed when compared to casualty figures from the Front — thousands died or were mutilated each day between battles from what was called "wastage," while on the worst day of all, Saturday, July 1, 1916, the start of the Battle of the Somme, 993 officers and 18,247 men were killed and over 35,000 wounded.

Even the agitation against cruelty to animals had its ironic echo in the War, reflected in what many called the "pathetic sight" of thousands of horses killed and wounded in the fighting. Their uncomprehending fear and senseless sacrifice seemed a stark contrast to the parallel and deliberate slaughter of supposedly rational creatures. The suffering of animals sometimes became harder for men to take than the death of fellow human beings. Submarine commander Freiherr von Spiegel, who torpedoed a steamer in 1916, coldly watched the struggles of the crew through his periscope, but "could not bear the sight any longer" when he saw the horses being transported on the decks leaping in panic into the sea (Chapman 239).

In time and space only a short distance separated archaic forms of battle from the grim and modern business war became. Millions of soldiers traversed an equally short semantic distance between patterning the war in boyhood tales of chivalry or frightening tales of terror. When the war began, the generals believed it would be decided by cavalry—in the first skirmishes of August, 1914, many of the wounds were administered by sword and lance. The British Commander Sir Douglas Haig continued to proclaim the superiority of the horse to the machine gun for years; in 1916, he kept troops of cavalry in readiness to exploit the "breakthrough" on the Somme that never came. When horsemen did go into battle, it was only to replay the Charge of the Light Brigade against Russian cannon more than half a century earlier, but with even more disastrous results.

An artilleryman, William Pressey, recalls an incident early in the war when the vision of battle as beautiful, heroic, and sporting, shared in this instance by spectators, soldiers, and staff, came to an abrupt end. In this case it inspired no poetry, but was nearly forgotten in the far greater slaughter:

> Coming towards us were a troop of French cavalry, I should say one hundred and fifty to two hundred strong. Gosh, but they looked splendid.... They laughed and waved their lances at us, shouting "Le Bosch fini." What a picture they made with sunlight gleaming on their lances....
>
> Over the top of the hill they charged, lances at the ready.... Then, only a few seconds after they disappeared, the hellish noise of machine guns broke out.... Not one man came back....
>
> Who had sent that splendid troop to certain death? Surely all conditions should have been known before sending lances against machine guns ... did anyone think the Germans would leave their machine guns and fight evenly, lance to lance? [Moynihan, *People* 150-1].

As late as 1917, Edwin Campion Vaughan watched a troop of horses stopped by a "few thin strands of wire" and decimated by machine gun fire (78). It was soon clear to those actually doing the fighting that what had begun as a replay of the Crimean War had quickly turned into a battle of tanks, airplanes, massive bombardments and poison gas—the technological apparatus of modern mass destruction.

The physical distance between the ideal and actual, between heroic fantasy and what became Gothic reality, was equally short. Because of rigorous censorship and a reluctance of returning troops to tell those at home what the war was really like, it remained a glorious crusade for those back in England almost until the end, even though the sounds of artillery barrages and mine explosions could clearly be heard in the South-east. Troops embarking across the Channel to France for the first time continued to echo the sentiments of Private W. T. Colyer:

> The romance of it . . . the glowing enthusiasm and lofty idealism of it: of our own free will we were embarked on this glorious enterprise, ready to endure any hardship and make any sacrifice, inspired by a patriotism newly awakened by the challenge to our country's honour [Brown 43].

As Paul Fussell has shown in his marvelous book *The Great War and Modern Memory* (1975), words such as "idealism," "glorious," "sacrifice" and "honor," ceased to have any meaning for those exposed to the horrors of the Western Front. Soldiers were forced to find a new way of looking at the world, a new set of beliefs, a new pattern for existence. In his examination of war poetry and memoirs such as Robert Graves' *Goodbye to All That* (1929), Fussell explores what he calls "the simultaneous and reciprocal process by which life feeds materials to literature while literature returns the favor by conferring forms upon life" (ix). Fussell deals, among other things, with pastoral, mythological, and artistic patterns that were adopted and transformed by the men who left records of their experience. However, one crucial component in that process needs to be considered.

The mass audience that had read Gothic literature and its offshoots for over a century became the mass army fed into the jaws of battle. From the medieval fantasies of such tales as *The Castle of Otranto* or *The Mysteries of Udolpho*, through the use of horror motifs in fiction and non-fiction later in the Victorian period, they had participated vicariously in literature that enabled them to confront their fears in a safely disguised form. Horror stories slowly came to pattern their readers' responses to reality. In 1820, Charles Maturin, in *Melmoth the Wanderer*, made an observation that, over a century, finally proved accurate in a way he never intended: "The drama of terror has the irresistible power of converting its audience into its victims" (II, 149).

In the end, the language and imagery of the horror story became much more than a metaphor for the horrors lived in World War I. To the participants, it became the only way to 'read' events for which nothing else prepared them. As Peter Medawar has argued in his essay "Science and Literature" (46), we cannot make any sense of experience unless we have a theoretical model in which to place it; even scientific understanding begins by creating a fictional construct, an "imagined world" which is then tested against what we perceive. Examining the diaries, letters, and memoirs of a small but representative sample of the soldiers who suddenly found themselves in the surreal landscape of the Great War, we hear echoes of imaginative literature that helped the participants give form to otherwise unimaginable fears.

Over the previous century, as horror stories moved closer to daily life, readers came closer to defining the world around them in terms set by the creators of the tale of terror. When, finally, the fears echoed for a century culminated in a cataclysmic truth, nothing else could provide a model. Horror stories prepared their audience for a universe of darkness and despair dominated by the dead, with the living perpetually underground, constantly in danger and ruled by irrational and uncontrollable forces. Millions read their experience on the Western Front as the most profound of horror fictions, when they realized that what had begun as an heroic dream had quickly turned into a Gothic nightmare.

II.

*The Journey Into Darkness*

Horror stories almost always begin with movement from the safe and familiar world of the present to a "sublime," archaic, and terrifying landscape, a setting for the dreamlike fears that are then given form. In the first Gothic tale, that journey is made through the fictional device of a modern "translator," who, in *The Castle of Otranto*, comments in a preface on the strange nature of the ensuing story, allegedly "found in the library of an ancient Catholic family in the north of England" (3). Thus the first action in the story, the finding of the manuscript, occurs in the present and presumably by the "translator." He disappears before the narrative begins, but not before making the prophetic remark that "though the machinery is invention ... the groundwork of the story is founded on truth" (5). Catherine Morland in *Northanger Abbey* similarly moves in stages from familiar surroundings to the town of Bath, to the mysterious abbey—from the world of her readers to a locus for fantasy.

Later in the century, the mediators between present and past, the day and night worlds of reader and romance, continue to take us step by step between the two realities. We hear the incredible story of Frankenstein and his Monster through the intermediary Robert Walton, stuck on the featureless plain of the Arctic ice, writing letters whose only reader is the reader of the novel. Henry Mayhew in *London Labour and the London Poor* is, like the other purveyors of sociological horror, more than a detached observer of their terrors—his exploration into the subterranean depths of the city becomes part of each of the tales he brings back to his readers, while he remains a participant through his continuing dialogue with the poor. Similarly, Utterson, the purveyor of the tale of Jekyll and Hyde, is a mediator between the commonplace and the miraculous, a decidedly mundane lawyer who leads us into a nightmare landscape when he hears a story told by his friend while taking a Sunday stroll.

This sense of a journey through barriers that divide the reader's world from the Gothic universe is most effectively conveyed at the start of *Dracula*. The narrator, Jonathan Harker, begins his journal in the distant but actual town of Bistritz, while commenting in the first sentence on the more familiar cities of Munich and Vienna and on the modern preoccupation with the railroad and leaving on time. He then passes through a series of ominous portals—across the Danube "leaving the West and entering the East," into the midst of the Carpathian Mountains, past a town that still bears the scars of a seventeenth century war, through the Borgo Pass ("it seemed as though the mountain range had separated into two atmospheres, and that we had got into the thunderous one" [12]), and finally through the "great round arches" of the medieval Castle Dracula.

Along the way he keeps encountering unsettling events, including peasants meeting him with warnings or charms and gifts to ward off evil, and the constant sight of prayers muttered at roadside shrines. His mode of transport also keeps changing—from train to coach to caleche—as he moves further and further back in time into a primitive, sublime, and horrifying setting, trapped in the terror of the castle, day and night reversed, death and danger always near. This repeated pattern is echoed in the many accounts of young and naïve soldiers on their way to the Front for the first time. Many of the similarities may seem coincidental, but the response of those who traversed this road was not; they came to see their experience as paralleling the Gothic journey from modern certainty to an archaic and irrational landscape.

Although the actual distance from England to Flanders was short, the trip was long, consisting of many stages and modes of transport, a slow transition from one reality to another, one set of attitudes to its opposite. As the soldiers moved from fantasies of war to its actuality, they recast the literary pattern into which they molded their experiences. Both patterns were medieval in design; the first, of war as an exercise in chivalry and heroism, had been laid out in the popular fiction of boyhood adventure. It soon became as useless as the cavalry, and just as outmoded. The second became, curiously enough, a way of seeing a new and frightening world. If we follow a typical group of soldiers down that path, we see from their language what they soon realized: that proximity in space can conceal a vast gulf of awareness and experience, that the fantasies of Romanticism and Gothicism were as far apart as myth and reality.

At first the feeling of the typical English soldier such as Captain Francis Grenfell was excitement and anticipation; he believed himself to be "the luckiest man alive" (Chapman 106). The train that led to the Channel ports became the last link with the safe and ordered world they were about to leave, a world that opens *Dracula*, where the trains run on time for the last time. Ford Madox Ford, in his series of novels about the war, *Parade's End* (1924-28), recognizes the importance of this symbol of security and modernity with his opening image: The two young men . . . sat in the perfectly appointed railway carriage. The leather straps to the windows were of virgin newness; the mirrors beneath the new luggage racks immaculate as if they had reflected very little . . . the train ran as smoothly . . . as British gilt edged securities (11). Edwin Campion Vaughan, recalling his trip from Waterloo Station to the Western Front, remembers both the "long triple row of happy, excited faces protruding from the carriage windows" and how his fellow passengers quickly settled down to reading the newspapers, heading for war as if to the office (1).

The first barrier was the Channel, where many soldiers encountered the first small taste of what was to come. Not only did they, like Harker, have to deal with unpunctuality, but also, like him many saw the first portents of horror. Private C. W. Mason, waiting to embark, watched a huge hospital ship filled with wounded pull in: "From the upper deck a voice shouted, 'Are you down-hearted?' to which we replied to a man, 'No-o-o!' Back came the voice, 'Then you bloody soon will be!'" A Captain, R. S. Cockburn, also waiting for hours in Southhampton, encountered a returning Belgian officer, and remembered it as his first moment of Gothic terror: "I almost started with fright when I looked at him. He had the face of a ghost" (Brown 41).

Once across the Channel, and often after a training period at Etaples, the soldier headed for the Front. The trains he took in France were jammed, slow, often inexplicably delayed, and dehumanizing; one private described them as "plain cattle-trucks with a little straw on the floor," and an officer declared there was "nothing worse for the morale of an officer or man . . . than his railway journey up to the front" (Chapman 54). The train trips alternated with long forced marches with little rest, the last from the railhead through the increasingly wild and devastated landscape and past the bombed out ruins of Albert or Ypres.

As in the Gothic journey, time became less precise, the present itself receded, and the traveler entered a medieval world. Thus the soldier was slowly transported to a landscape more familiar from his reading than from his past. Ypres had been especially noted before the war for its beautifully preserved Cloth Hall, Cathedral and Town Hall—Augustus Pugin, who headed the Gothic Revival in nineteenth century architecture, actually chose to illustrate the Town Hall in his book *Contrasts* (1836). At the center of the notorious Salient (a bulge in the British Front subject to constant bombardment from three sides), Ypres presented the arriving soldiers with a stereotypical scene from the horror story—in the center of desolation, strewn with debris and mangled bodies, slowly pounded to rubble, "and leaning miserably over all, the gaunt, maimed cathedral tower and Cloth Hall" (Brown 247). [See illustration, page 93.]

The poet Edmund Blunden, in a dreamlike moment, first sees the ruins "glimmering whitely, life in death," as a "sepulchered, catacombed city" (167):

> ...the staring pallor of the streets in that daybreak was unlike anything I had ever known. The Middle Ages had here contrived to lurk, and this was their torture at last. We all felt this, as the tattered picture swung by like accidents of vision ... we scarcely seemed awake and aware [156].

Like Harker's first vision of Dracula's castle "whose broken battlements showed a jagged line against the moonlit sky" (17), Ypres fulfilled the requirements of Archibald Alison, the theorist of the aesthetics of horror, who had declared in 1790 that "The Gothic castle is still more sublime, because besides the desolation of time, it seems to have withstood the assaults of war" (227). Harker, like Blunden, feels he "must have been asleep" (19); he, too, sees the sublime architecture belonging to a nightmare world.

The battlefields themselves were littered with ruined farmhouses, villages, and churches, a veritable Gothic universe. Soldiers who wandered among them used language Alison would find fitting. Siegfried Sassoon found himself with a platoon on patrol among "some ruined buildings on the outskirts of a village. I have dim remembrance of the strangeness of the place and our uneasy dawdling in its midnight desolation" (58).

Medievalism also meant Catholic imagery, and the tale of terror is replete with monks and nuns, prayer and curses, chapels and tombs, and the perverted spirituality of the Inquisition. Mindless belief in the face of overwhelming evil became in many such stories the signature of the Middle Ages. Even Jonathan Harker saw in the desolate Transylvanian wilderness many roadside crosses, evidence of a hopeless search for salvation in a land cursed by war; soldiers like Edwin Campion Vaughan traveled through similarly deserted landscapes:

> Away from the villages, and even in them, I rarely saw a human being. It quite impressed me on these bare windswept roads, to come across the rough wayside cross, or calvary: behind the figure of Christ radiated metal stars, in the forked points of which the villagers are wont to insert their petitions for the prayers of passersby [10].

The journey from crowded and punctual trains to timeless ruins and empty landscapes served, as it did in novels like *Frankenstein* or *Dracula*, to erase a sense of security and order, a belief in rationality and the certainty of time itself. Every Gothic traveler from Gabriel Utterson and Henry Mayhew to Robert Walton and Jonathan Harker entered a changed and desolate world and was in turn profoundly changed. Like all Gothic heroes and heroines, like the poor who fell into the urban abyss, on arriving at the Front the soldier became in some sense an orphan, cast out from familiar surroundings, transformed from potential hero to anonymous victim. The world he encountered, though populated by millions of men, is described again and again as empty of any life except his own.

Each soldier, like his Gothic predecessors, felt abandoned, pursued by a nameless fear, constantly in danger of destruction, lost in a labyrinth and forced to survive by discarding the values with which he entered that world. Like the travelers to earlier Gothic universes, his most difficult task when he returned was to convince those still safe at home of the reality of the horrors he had witnessed—many soldiers didn't even try. Like the supernatural events of the tale of terror, the incredible suffering of the Victorian poor, the indescribable crimes of Dr. Jekyll and Jack the Ripper, or the frightening contradictions hinted at in *Dracula*, the day to day events in the Great War were literally beyond what people wanted to believe. To continue to function, the soldier had to redefine himself; to comprehend or communicate his experience, he had to use another language. That is why in the accounts of survival on the Western Front we see the apparatus of the horror story brought to life again.

*The Sublime Universe*

As soldiers approached the trenches, their descriptions echoed the notions of the sublime—the eighteenth century aesthetic that underlay Gothicism. Edmund Burke and his followers saw the sublime in any scenes that could evoke awe, astonishment, above all terror in the viewer. Sights such as vast and desolate landscapes and ruins, sounds like "vast cataracts, raging storms, thunder or artillery," (Burke 194), even smells like "excessive bitters and intolerable stenches" (198); all possessed "sublime" qualities, qualities which also included darkness, power, danger, and difficulty. Burke concludes that "the sublime is an idea belonging to self-preservation; that it is therefore one of the most affecting we have; that its strongest emotion is the emotion of distress" (174).

Wilfred Owen described his first view of the Front much as Robert Walton did when he first met Frankenstein on the Arctic ice (or, indeed, as Frankenstein himself did when he met his Monster on the glacier field near Mt. Blanc), as a vast and desolate landscape, a "frozen desert" with "not a sign of life on the horizon" (Brown 11). In fact, many soldiers were, like

Robert Case, "astounded" by "miles of trenches, populated by scores of thousands of men, and yet one cannot see a living soul" (Moynihan, *Greater* 128). Since the sublime depends upon the individual reaction to the outer world, it's significant that the trenches for many enhanced their feeling of being alone and abandoned, lost in a "stark and shattered scene . . . [with] not a sign of life anywhere—but an obsession of human eyes, watching" (Brown 246).

The sheer magnitude of the Western Front—a huge network of trenches running right across Europe—was invisible to the millions confined to their minute sectors, but its sublimity was evident in the awe expressed by airman Duncan Grinnell-Milne:

> Turning South, I stared down intently at the battlefield. And my first impression was of its immensity. It was incredibly vast. It did not seem possible that men had made all this mess within one short year. From the North Sea to the Alps! But surely if this gigantic network, this labyrinth had been constructed by men in uniform, there could have been no one left to fight while the digging was going on [66].

This observation adds to the qualities of sheer size and grandeur two other aspects of the sublime, what Burke called "rudeness" and difficulty: "when any work seems to have required immense force and labour to effect it, the idea is grand . . . the rudeness of the work increases this cause of grandeur, for it excludes the idea of art and contrivance" (187).

The Western Front was, then, a catalog of the elements of the sublime Burke enumerated, including among the sights, sounds, and smells, "the natural inarticulate voices of men, or any animals in pain or danger" (197), and what he calls the general privations of vacuity, darkness, and solitude (177). The difference, of course, was that for Burke the sublime was an aesthetic construct, a theory of taste for the Gothic; the reaction of awe, astonishment, danger, and terror that signaled the success of the sublime was carefully distanced from real experience. He himself recognized that "when danger and pain press too nearly, they are incapable of giving any delight and are simply terrible; but at certain distances and with certain modifications, they may be, and they are delightful" (134).

Proximity, then, destroyed the sublime, and indeed, such was often the case in the war. For those at home, the war retained its grandeur, the true suffering lost in a haze of lofty language telling tales of stirring deeds. Although the bloody battles that marked the war gained, if anything, little more than a few hundred yards at a time, the large scale maps printed in the newspapers made each advance seem immense. Even retreats were turned into moments of heroic splendor, with headlines after one huge setback announcing: "Thrilling Dispatch from Sir John French: Glorious Stand of British Troops" (*Evening News*, 10 Sept. 1914). With few exceptions, the heavily censored press depicted the mindless slaughter as what was called a "crusade," its horrors transformed by language and distance into a sublime spectacle, a source of vicarious terror and strange delight.

Despite the mounting casualty lists, the newspapers continued to give the impression that a somewhat different delight was shared by the troops, who were always depicted as carefree, prone to whistling or singing in the face of danger, or going into battle with "a completely careless laugh, as of a holiday maker" (*The Times* 3 July 1916, 9). This last lie was told of the soldiers about to go over the top at the Battle of the Somme, the bloodiest disaster in British history, which the papers depicted as a victory. It's no wonder that many survivors of the Great War never again believed what they read in the newspapers.

To the men living in the nightmare world of the war, the newspapers had become works of fiction that turned horrifying events into adventures from *The Boys' Own Paper*. The irony of Edwin Vaughan's memory of starting for the war among officers reading the newspapers is heightened when we realize they were entering a realm that was left unreported. The newspaper is our daily anchor to a wider reality, confirmation that our individual experiences fit in the mosaic of the contemporary world. When millions of soldiers could no longer connect what they lived with what they read in the papers, what they knew with what civilians at home believed was true, that anchor was cast overboard. Journalism had become fantasy, and fantasy became real.

It's therefore not surprising that papers like *The Bradford Daily Telegraph* could report on that terrible day in which over 50,000 men were killed, wounded, or missing in action, that "our casualties have not been heavy" (1 July 1916, 1). But staff officers closer to the battle were almost as well insulated from reality as those at home; for example, Major Charles Lionel Atkins Ward-Jackson, writing from the headquarters of VII corps, echoed the papers: "I believe our casualties have not been very heavy" (Moynihan, *Greater* 108). Before the battle he anticipated safely witnessing a sublime scene by climbing a tree "so that I can see something of what is happening" and predicted, using the language of the newspapers, that "It will all be wonderfully thrilling and the noise will be tremendous" (100).

Even fighting men could experience the detachment that allowed for the sublime when they spent time behind the lines or in a quiet sector. Edmund Blunden recalls a moment where he is acutely aware of the strange appeal of the scene of horror, a scene he describes in language and imagery strongly reminiscent of the sublime fascination religious gloom had for the creators of both Gothic landscape architecture and the tale of terror. His battalion was posted behind the lines in a district of shrines and keeps.... The large church, and the almost rococo churchyard, astonished everybody: they had been bombarded into that state of demi-ruin which discovers the strongest fascination.... Men went to ... stare into the very popular tombs all around, whose vaults gaped unroofed, nor could protect their charges any longer from the eye of life. Greenish water stood in some of these pits; bones and skulls and decayed cerements there attracted frequent soldiers past the "No Loitering" notice board [56].

Thus, the soldiers of the Great War felt themselves in an archaic universe that had been mapped out in the fantasies of an earlier century; in the moments they could become audience and not victims, they could experience the peculiar delight in terror labeled the sublime. Sometimes even conditions in the trenches briefly made that possible. Siegfried Sassoon recalls one moment when, significantly, he "was looking westward, away from the war" at "the shell-pitted ground sloped somberly into the dusk; the distances were blue and solemn, with a few trees grouped on a ridge, dark against the deep glowing embers of another day endured.... Guns were grumbling miles away." At that moment he recalls an "incomplete impression of a strange, intense, and unique experience." Its kinship to the pleasures Burke and his followers found in the tale of terror is evident in the language Sassoon uses to describe his feelings: "if ghosts can traverse time and choose their ground, I would return to the Bois Francais sector as it was then." He also calls it a "spectral presence" and a "haunting" experience "saturated by the external senses" (33).

The scene is also reminiscent in its language and effect of such moments as Emily St. Aubert's approach to Montoni's castle in Mrs. Radcliffe's *The Mysteries of Udolpho* (1794); she travels through a desolate landscape "where no vestige of humanity, or even of vegetation, appeared," past pine trees that "crowned the ridgy precipice" to view the battlements lit by "a melancholy purple tint" and "invested with the solemn duskiness of evening" (225–27). Sassoon's version of what Mrs. Radcliffe calls "this sublime scene" is leavened by the true horror of his experiences; he feels not merely the astonishment of the pilot over the immense battlefield or the spectator anticipating a safe thrill. He is a participant, distanced momentarily from the immediacy of pain and danger and the grim business of survival, glimpsing in a world of horror Edmund Burke's vision of a terrible beauty.

*Inside the Labyrinth*

Once the Gothic traveler reached his destination, the universe contracted to the surrounding walls. All places became echoes of "that long labyrinth of darkness" Isabella wandered under the castle of Otranto. We find it again in the corridors of uncounted castles, the dark warrens of Victorian slums, sewers, and mines, the fog shrouded streets of Jekyll's or Jack the Ripper's London, and the labyrinth that leads to Dracula's castle — roads that were "hemmed in with trees, which in places arched right over the roadway till we passed as through a tunnel" (14). In all these places, the way is intricate and cluttered with the bits and pieces of past lives; the dim light of a sputtering candle or a momentary flash of lightning discloses gruesome sights; even the sounds, smells, and very atmosphere are frightening, murky or murderous. The wanderer in that black maze becomes a model for the individual caught in an irrational world and a metaphor for the state of mind that occurs in a nightmare. The constant feeling is of danger and pursuit in a universe where the miraculous and supernatural have become almost commonplace.

Over the century, the labyrinth and its elements evolved by expanding to fill every crevice of the abyss that underlay an entire culture. The foul blackness of Otranto, the "unwholesome dews and the vapours, that crept along the ground" in Udolpho (345), became the mud and smoke of *Bleak House,* the "great chocolate-colored pall" of fog, the "embattled vapours" (29) that pervaded Jekyll's London, the "malodorous air" that permeated the lairs of Dracula (222). And the horrors evolved as well, from the ludicrous apparitions of *Otranto* and its many imitators to the elaborate hoaxes of *Udolpho* (parodied in *Northanger Abbey*), from the chronicles of medieval torture to the catalog of commonplace suffering that darkened the pages of mid–Victorian realism. Finally, in the stories of Dr. Jekyll and Jack the Ripper, the horrors became literally unspeakable. As the castle grew larger, its tenants became familiar and its gruesome secrets more openly acknowledged. The furniture and fears of the labyrinth became metaphor, a way to embody the frightening realities hidden in Victorian culture and the constant struggle between concealment and illumination.

This familiar image of the labyrinth is constantly used by soldiers in the Great War to describe the incredible earthworks that comprised the Front. There were communication and support trenches as well as those on the Front line, an estimated 12,000 miles worth on the Allied side alone (Fussell 37). Many were marked by names and signposts taken from London streets, creating a vast underground equivalent of the capital and a dark parody of the unknowing and safe city left behind. G. Nightingale called the trenches "an absolute maze" (Moynihan, *Greater* 95); Major Frank Isherwood, like the airman Duncan Grinnell-Milne, saw it as a "labyrinth," adding, "you can't get out of them and walk about the country or see anything at all but two muddy walls on each side of you" (Fussell 51). In fact, soldiers described their experiences in the trenches using the language and imagery of the Gothic labyrinth — it was eerily appropriate to the reality, which no longer needed the mask of metaphor.

The trenches of the Western Front thus uncannily connected the familiar nomenclature of London streets with elements of the Gothic labyrinth, from isolation and horror to confusion and death. At times the conjunction of reality and fiction was uncanny. For the "unwholesome vapours that crept along the ground" in *Udolpho* and its descendants, read poison gas, the most lethal of the fogs pervading the Gothic landscape, which arrived in "greenish-yellow clouds" or a "bluish-white mist," then hugged the bottom of the trenches. In the Battle of Loos, large numbers of shell shocked and wounded suffocated at the bottom of the trenches, while the surviving infantry wandered aimlessly, some "coughing up quantities of blood and pus," others looking in vain for the firing line, everyone lost "in this evil smelling maze" (Clarke 79, 155).

Though the fictional Gothic maze is often full of lost souls, the heroine, and the reader, is never really lost. There is always a guide, someone who knows the pattern of survival and can lead the protagonist to at least momentary safety. Thus, in *The Castle of Otranto*, Isabella tells Theodore, "follow me; dark and dismal as it is, we cannot miss our way" (27); in *The Mysteries of Udolpho*, Emily follows Barnadine's dim torch which barely illuminates the "high black walls around them" as he walks through long and intricate passages (345); Catherine Morland is led through Northanger Abbey by her spiritual guide, Henry Tilney; Victor Frankenstein, in pursuit of his creature across the world, is guided by food and messages left by the Monster; *Bleak House* has Inspector Bucket, who leads Esther "with great rapidity, through such a labyrinth of streets that I soon lost all of idea of where we were" (827); the men in *Dracula* are guided by Mina's mental powers through England and halfway across Europe. And, in the explorations of Victorian poverty and crime, the reader is brought along by a traveler who, like Henry Mayhew or Inspector Field, has been there and returned to tell of it.

On the Western Front, to become separated from one's unit and lost in the maze could mean unexpected horror, while the millions who lived in the labyrinth saw no way out (one popular belief was that signing up for "the duration" meant a life sentence). Almost all recollections of frontline experience include stories of wandering in the twistings and turnings of the trenches and encountering unpleasant surprises; a Captain Meluish once wandered for hours until he came to what he thought were his men, slithered down the side of the trench "only to find himself sitting, staring into the faces of a group of Germans" (Vaughan 124). Edmund Blunden once "no longer knew which was the German line, which was our own. I almost joined a German working party . . . after such a careless circuit" (74). Every trench seemed identical, every turning the same, while looking over the edge to get one's bearings could mean a sniper's bullet in the head.

The problem was compounded because the dangers of daylight meant life was reversed. Like an army of vampires, the soldiers slept by day in dugouts scratched from the soil and emerged only at night to tend to the trench or venture on patrol into the dark and tangled waste of No Man's Land. Edmund Blunden estimates that "Not one man in thirty had seen the line by daylight—and it was a maze even when seen so, map in hand" (96). In the Gothic tale and its offshoots, a guide implied hope for the future and the possibility of understanding the present; the aimless wandering in the vast tangle of the Great War became a metaphor for a hopeless, meaningless and seemingly unending struggle.

In the horror stories of Victorian social reformers, the dark labyrinth of the city slum and the gloomy wasteland of the Black Country each concealed yet another maze—the network of sewers in London and the mines that underlay the countryside, visual analogues for the buried truths that threatened to erupt and destroy the facade of social order. And the microcosm of Gothic England on the Western Front had its own dangerous underworld. One tactic of both sides was to mine under the opponents' trenches and set off huge explosions entombing those above, a death feared more than any other. In some sectors, everyone constantly strained to hear the sound of digging or, worse, the clicking of the timer that preceded a detonation. Like the dark corridors left unexplored in the Gothic castle, the deeper labyrinths that underlay Victorian prosperity, or the prewar fantasy of invasion from a secret under Channel tunnel, the lower depths beneath the Western Front reminded the soldiers of the unplumbed darkness in both society and the self that threatened to undermine everything.

Soldiers wandering the maze of trenches, like the lost souls in earlier labyrinths, found their confusion mirrored in both the chaotic external forces threatening social collapse and the constant private fear of mental disintegration. Shell shock became, like so much else the soldiers experienced, a heightened version of the depression and madness which haunted so many Victorians living through the quieter conflicts of their lives. As Elaine Showalter makes clear, shell shock was actually hysteria, a mental ailment that had led to the confinement in asylums of legions of women in the previous decades (167-94). She argues that men fell victim in unprecedented numbers for the same reasons women had—they could not reconcile their feelings with what the culture told them they must feel. Women had been forced into passivity while wanting sexual and social freedom; men were told to be heroes when all they felt was terror. These same contradictions made life so difficult for the women and men in *Dracula*, bringing them all close to or beyond the borders of madness. In the shock of battle and the stress of survival, a generation of men lived constantly with emotions believed emblematic of women; it drove many of them insane.

Daily life in the trenches differed little from what were called battles by those at a distance—in both cases the ordinary soldier felt the same confusion, disorientation, and fear of sudden death. One such soldier, private Ernest Atkins, later recalled that he found out he had been in a battle only when he read letters and newspapers. He and his mates

> could not describe battles. We did not know one was taking place.... We marched here, we marched there, we heard the thunder of the guns, we went into action, we came out and went somewhere else [Moynihan, *People* 219].

Like the women in Gothic stories trapped by a nobleman's dark designs or the poor caught in the web of their despair, the Great War soldiers lost in the physical maze of the trenches were powerless prisoners in a world whose pattern they could not know, but which nevertheless determined the shape of their lives. The contradictions of their troglodyte world was reflected in the state of their minds, so that many hovered on the edge of breakdown.

*Mud and Darkness*

The Western Front obliged those who saw in it the pattern of the horror story by providing appropriate weather. It seems from all accounts to have been constantly raining or snowing, adding to the suffering of troops ill equipped to live in partly flooded trenches built to last only until the 'imminent' great breakthrough that didn't come for four long years. One private, coming up to the line for the first time, was greeted by what he remembers as a classic Gothic thunderstorm:

> The sky was very angry, black as ink.... Lightning and thunder and torrents of rain came on—I have never seen such lightning, zig-zag flashes that looked as if they would blow up the whole world [Moynihan, *Greater* 20].

The usual thunderstorm was man-made, the sound a continuous rumble from the greatest artillery barrages in history, the sky "continually lit up by their flashes" (Vaughan 17). And also always in the background was another "sublime" sound transformed into a chorus of horror:

> From the darkness on all sides came the groans and wails of wounded men; faint, long, sobbing moans of agony, and despairing shrieks. It was too horribly obvious that dozens of men with serious wounds must have crawled for safety into new shell-holes, and now the water was rising about them and, powerless to move, they were slowly drowning.... And we could do nothing to help them [Vaughan 228].

Such deaths were not uncommon — in the Ypres area alone it was estimated that during some periods up to 900 men a month drowned in slime. In the Battle of Passchaendale, literally thousands of men and horses were sucked down to their deaths in what Winston Churchill called a "sea of choking, fetid mud." For many, the most horrible and vivid memory of the war was of the mud that was everywhere, thickly coating their bodies, making every movement slow and agonizing, and turning every shell hole into a trap that could make a misstep fatal. Some men in one battalion, caught in mud up to the armpits, could not be pulled out and were left to die (Blunden 131). A typical vignette, reported by Second Lieutenant Blake O'Sullivan, was of his company, led by a guide who had lost his way, wandering into a trench "half full of liquid mud" where they "waded slowly through the cold sludge, tripping and tangling in the wire and stumbled over a dead man . . . actually half afloat in the mud [who] nodded his head solemnly as each man passed by" (Brown 203).

The mud had particular significance for the majority of the men, who came from what was called the "respectable" working class. Mud and dirt had been identified with the poor, and especially the urban poor — not only in the reports of Victorian reformers, but in the minds of an entire class struggling to free itself from the downward pull of poverty. The women in such homes saw a preoccupation with cleanliness as the feature "marking them off from what were often regard as feckless, dirty, uncaring and undeserving poor"; they "struggled unceasingly against the smoke and grime of industrial towns or the mud and excrement of country lanes." Even their doorsteps were scoured weekly, the room that faced the street was kept spotless (and often unoccupied), and on wash days "the streets were festooned with lines of washing . . . and there was fierce competition to have the cleanest washing in the street" (Burnett, *Destiny* 218-9). In the mud of Flanders, then, many children of the respectable poor saw their parents' worst fears become literally, gruesomely, real.

Mud and darkness became the most famous metaphors used by those who tried to find meaning in the outbreak of the Great War. Turning back nearly three quarters of a century to the opening pages of *Bleak House*, we find dogs "undistinguishable in mire" and "horses scarcely better" and "tens of thousands of foot passengers . . . slipping and sliding . . . adding new deposits to the crust upon crust of mud," while darkness from smoke and fog wins out over the "haggard light" of the gas lamps, lit before their time, heralding "the death of the sun" (1). Dickens saw this scene as symbolic of a corrupt and anachronistic system, of a culture that had literally lost its way. A few years later, in *Hard Times*, Stephen Blackpool's refrain "It's all a muddle" carries forth the association of mud with confusion and injustice. David Lloyd George, who, when the Great War began was Chancellor of the Exchequer, and then became Prime Minister, recalled Blackpool's words in his famous admission, "We muddled into war," while the Foreign Secretary, Sir Edward Grey, is remembered for one statement uttered as the war began: "The lamps are going out all over Europe; we shall not see them lit again in our lifetime."

Officers, too, functioned in an almost perpetual Gothic gloom illuminated in true Gothic style. Siegfried Sassoon described "the main characteristics" of his dugout as "mud and smoke. Mud was everywhere ... after dark we sat and shivered ... reading, playing cards, and writing letters with watering eyes by the feeble glimmer of guttering candles" (132). At another time the he turns the scene into a perfect Gothic set piece:

> Rain was falling steadily. Everything felt fateful and final. A solitary candle stood on the table in its own grease ... [the next morning] Larks were shrilling in the drizzling sky.... Behind me were the horror and the darkness [23, 29].

A private, Peter MacGregor, stumbled into a German dugout, and described it as follows:

> I am sure that we are more than twelve feet underground. The place is dark, dirty, the supports of the roof black with smoke of ages, the floors filthy, large stones all over the place ... rats as big as cats wander up and down, eat your grub [Moynihan, *Greater* 27].

He could well have fallen into the cellar of the castle of Otranto, the dungeons of the Inquisition in *The Monk*, or the chapel of Carfax abbey in *Dracula*, places actually rather than apparently ancient and also "alive with rats" (223).

To see the trenches and dugouts as relics is to connect them with a primitive Gothic world of individual barbarity and social decay. The various villains of the tale of terror live in atavistic surroundings that echo their own debased natures: Dickens' dark London is a fit home for dinosaurs, while both Mr. Hyde and Dracula survive as throwbacks to ancient man and to a time when, it was believed, the darkness was that of the soul. Thus, Edmund Blunden enters the war at the "Old British Line at Festubert" and immediately sees it, not as an earthworks less than two years old, but as a place that

> had the appearance of great age and perpetuity; its weather-beaten sandbag wall was already venerable. It shared the past with the defences of Troy. The skulls which spades disturbed were in a manner coeval with those of the most distant wars [25–26].

Midnight gloom and echoes of a barbaric past made the war a nightmare world, so described by many who lived through it. Major Robert

Campbell tried to make sense of it by concluding, "Possibly I was dreaming; all these events had the absurdity of a dream" (26); an unnamed member of the "Other Ranks" declared that, during a battle, "from this time my thoughts were really more like a nightmare than thoughts of a wide awake being" (Chapman 277). The pilot Cecil Lewis described the nocturnal activity on the roads of France as a "noisy nightmare." Like the others, he was drawn to Gothic imagery, struck by the contrast between the "sinister ghosts" of the nocturnal army and the strange desolation of daytime, evidence of a time "when night contradicted day" (Lewis 77).

Gothic tales are often connected to nightmare, and it would be obvious to say war was for many a bad dream. However, the many correspondences between the setting and events of the horror story and the experiences of the soldier in the First World War go much further than either simple coincidence or trite metaphor. They indicate that the war made real the cultural contradictions and nightmare fears that had found an outlet only in forms of fantasy. Soldiers who read their lives, from the moment they arrived at the gaunt medieval ruins of Ypres, as a horror story, were instinctively returning to a pattern which had enlivened their solitary nights of reading while shaping the obverse side of an optimistic Victorian facade. The elements of horror fiction had always been mirrored in the lives around its readers; until the mass trauma of the war, that mirror had been clouded in supernatural fantasy and sublime speculation. On the Western Front, the mirror became a window on day to day experience, etched with the imagery and words of Gothic terror.

The most important connection between horror fantasy and daily life in the Great War was the omnipresence of death—dead places, primitive emotions, the dead themselves, who at times were indistinguishable from the living. Siegfried Sassoon, for example, once notices what he calls the "almost spectral appearance" of his men returning from battle, framing the picture he creates in the Gothic language of the sublime. Day and night are reversed, and the "ordinariness" of the scene contrasted with the remarkable way he reads it. Sassoon realizes, as did so many of his contemporaries, that in the war he is living the same terror and fascination he had once experienced vicariously, that all around him is the text of an imaginative reality once known as the horror story:

> Soon [our company] had dispersed and settled down on the hillside, and were asleep in the daylight which made everything seem ordinary. None the less I had seen something that night which overawed me. It was all in the day's work—an exhausted Division returning from the Somme Offensive—but to me it was as though I watched an army of ghosts [84].

*Chapter Ten*
# The Transformation of the Dead

> In former days we used to look at life, and sometimes from a distance, at death, and still further removed from us, at eternity. Today it is from afar that we look at life, death is near us, and perhaps nearer still is eternity.
> —Jean Bouvier, February 1916

*The Dead Return*

The landscape of the Western Front was distinguished by the pall of death that hung over it, the fear of death that was felt by everyone on the front line, and the dead themselves, who were everywhere. Millions were forced to face not only their own mortality, but the power of death itself in the workings of the natural world and the working out of history. In this modern recreation of a medieval hell on earth, a generation of lost souls found that a century of imaginative visions of death evolving from the horror story provided a model for their senseless and surreal universe. For in the landscape of the tale of terror, the dead also define reality and determine the future, refusing to remain powerless or out of sight. Death itself, resurgent and omnipresent, stands behind all the other images of fear, casting a shadow that covers the characters in the text and the audience compelled to read it.

In Gothic fantasy, the dead often return as ghosts, without material substance but with the power to affect the material world, cursing those who wronged them and aiding those who need help—apparitions from the past who change the future. Realistic fiction brought back Gothic ghosts in such guises as the tangible memory of the dead Mrs. Tilney, which poisons her husband's thoughts in *Northanger Abbey*, and, in *Bleak House*, the written traces of the law scrivener Nemo, which haunt his lover Lady Dedlock, luring her to her death from beyond the grave. The papers of Dr. Jekyll are another example of disembodied language as a voice from the dead, both curse and warning. Whether as ghosts or simply ghostly messages, these dead remain visions and voices from another plane of reality, dead hands shaping a living world.

Another way the dead return is in bad dreams, commonplace events in the night world of the Gothic story. Sometimes the dreamers in such tales, from Victor Frankenstein to Jonathan Harker, are not sure if they are awake or asleep when they encounter apparitions. Thus the authors can keep the supernatural in the realm of possibility while blurring the line that separates the internal and external worlds. Ghosts in these cases may be subjective, but they are no less powerful in their ability both to frighten those to whom they appear and to predict and control the future of the flesh and blood characters they haunt. The return of the dead in the Gothic imagination determined how death would be characterized both in realistic fiction and when a generation entered a place where death dominated everything.

The most famous story of the Great War invoking actual ghosts is unambiguously miraculous, though it didn't originate anywhere near the battlefield. On page three of the September 29, 1914, edition of *The Evening News* appeared a column by Arthur Machen entitled "The Bowmen." It purports to tell of an incident during the British retreat at Mons when a soldier, absentmindedly muttering a Latin prayer he had seen on a dinner plate, conjures up St. George and a Heavenly Host of bowmen, who slaughter German regiments wholesale yet leave no marks on their bodies. Machen's depiction of the British Tommies is no less absurd than the ghosts, as they supposedly react to a "terrific cannonade" like this: "The men joked at the shells and found funny names for them and had bets about them and greeted them with scraps of music hall songs." Many civilians believed the entire story nonetheless; similar tales circulated after every British setback (and there were many). The troops themselves, under the incredible stress of trench life, sometimes saw visions of crosses, swords, or angels in clouds or the smoke of battle, or encountered what they believed to be spectres of dead comrades, but there was no Heavenly intervention.

Soldiers in the nightmare world of the war were much more likely to be haunted by their dreams. Siegfried Sassoon, convalescing in hospital with a "cushy wound," and momentarily believing he has escaped the war, recalls that

> awake or asleep, shapes of mutilated soldiers came crawling across the floor; the floor seemed to be littered with fragments of mangled flesh. Faces glared upward; hands clutched at neck or belly ... some ... looked at me reproachfully, as though envying me the warm safety of life which they'd longed for [176].

A gunner, William Carr, wondered after the war about the sleep of a staff officer who sent men to die in a hopeless attack: "Do the ghosts of those officers and men, unnecessarily dead, disturb his rest o' nights, or is he proudly wearing another ribbon for distinguished service" (Carr 130)?

## 10. The Transformation of the Dead

Just as in horror stories, where ghosts torment the sleeper in revenge for injustice or to deliver a curse, in both these instances hauntings become punishment to officers for escaping the suffering of their men. Merely to survive is to be guilt-ridden and somehow responsible for those who did not. Dreams of ghosts were a psychologically valid way to disinter the dead, to give form to the anxieties and guilt of survival. And such dreams did become curses, disturbing the sleep of veterans in many cases for years after the war, a constant reminder of the collective evil that created so many ghosts.

In horror stories, the dead had returned in another way, through a pattern of imagery that evolved from its introduction in the early tales of terror to its gruesome culmination in the Great War. As early as *The Castle of Otranto*, Walpole used the convention of the Gothic discovery to bring back actual corpses — a character opens the door of a great chamber to disclose the leg and foot of a giant, first indications of the return of the true heir to the castle. Mrs. Radcliffe refined the technique into the pattern of the lifted veil — her heroines constantly draw aside curtains to find gruesome tableaux. In *The Mysteries of Udolpho* Emily imprudently lifts a veil on a picture, a bedcurtain, and a curtain over a doorway. Typical is the last, which conceals, "a corpse, stretched on a kind of low couch, which was crimsoned with human blood, as was the floor beneath. The features, deformed by death, were ghastly and horrible, and more than one livid wound appeared on the face" (348). The body behind the veil soon became the most common weapon in the Gothic arsenal, so often repeated that one would think horror story heroines would learn to mind their own business. But, of course, fascination with death and what it meant was part of their business — they served as stand-ins for their readers and acted out for them the dangerous urge to draw aside what they knew concealed their deepest fears.

We can see echoes of this pattern when Frankenstein's bed curtain is drawn back to reveal the grinning face of the living dead Monster, in *Bleak House* when a sputtering candle reveals the body of Nemo stretched out on a similar couch, in *Jekyll/Hyde* when Utterson breaks down the door of Jekyll's study to encounter Hyde's distorted and still twitching corpse, in *Dracula* when the men burst into Mina's bedroom to see her nursing a living corpse with her blood. In non-fiction horror as well, investigators like Henry Mayhew constantly make gruesome discoveries of living corpses when they penetrate the darkness, while George Walker's expose of London burial grounds repeatedly tells how lifting the thin veil of earth almost anywhere in the city disinters a subterranean population of the dead.

In the Great War the dead are beneath every shovelful of earth, constantly appearing as trenches are dug or dark corners rounded. The discovery of corpses became, in fact, so commonplace that Captain Edwin Vaughan could dig a few inches in his dugout to level a rickety table and find a body he treats as still alive: "we struck an old blue tunic, and when we gave it a tug ... an unpleasant smell warned us that we had a guest, so we apologized and patted the earth back" (34). Sometimes it wasn't even necessary to dig; the bodies of soldiers who drowned in shell holes could "lie concealed for days until their bodies, porous from decomposition, would rise once again to the surface" (Clarke 40). Only when the moment was in any way unusual did the return of the dead seem worthy of note for a generation that lived and worked in a charnel house.

But Mrs. Radcliffe and those who followed her also went beyond using simply the dead themselves as a source of horror. Behind the veil was often either a corpse (like Nemo or the vampires) that at first seems to be alive, or a person (like the skeletal Madame Montoni) who first appears to be a corpse. Throughout the Gothic tradition, (most memorably in *Frankenstein* and *Dracula*) the horror of the discovery is compounded by uncertainty — life and death seem at times indistinguishable.

Similarly shocking misidentifications recorded in the memoirs of the Great War combine both terror and a strange irony. Thus, Siegfried Sassoon remembers kicking a soldier, apparently asleep, to ask "God blast you, where's Battalion headquarters?" and then letting his torch beam settle "on the livid face of a dead German whose fingers clutched the blackened gash on his neck" (159). Robert Graves once called "Stand-to, there" to a boy who had already committed suicide (90); Edwin Vaughan once heard a voice screaming and stopped to raise the head of a body he had stumbled over in the darkness, "but my hand sunk down into the open skull and I recoiled in horror" (191). A gunner even remembered shelling what he thought was a mass of Germans only to discover he was mutilating an enormous pile of corpses (Chapman 234). The most horrific of these discoveries comes from the journal of Lieutenant William St. Leger, where he turns an incident into a Gothic tableaux reminiscent of the groaning and sighing portraits in *The Castle of Otranto*; as he records it, a corpse seemingly returns to life to reproach those who disturb his rest:

> ...a little further on we came upon a great broad chested man of the Irish Guards lying on his back in a part of the trench half blown in.... He was dead, and as each man passed he had to tread on his chest. The weight compressed the corpse's lungs and the dead Irishman groaned and gasped.... [Moynihan, *People* 47–8].

These incidents became common set pieces in the memoirs of the Great War because the familiar horror story formula gave form to the widespread belief that all those in this graveyard landscape, though still with the attributes of life, had been given up for dead. The point was made less frequently but with greater force when those still living were mistaken for corpses. Captain Vaughan clearly constructs a Gothic discovery scene out of one such encounter, complete with a candlelit, subterranean setting, a protagonist somewhere between sleep and wakefulness, the language of the tale of terror, and a lifted veil:

> After coming off duty, I was lying alone in the straw, and just dozing off, when I heard some one stop outside the cellar. Sitting up, I saw the blanket slowly lifted and a head appeared in the dim light of the candle. I hardly repressed a scream of horror, and an icy numbness gripped me as I scanned — a blackened face, thick lips, and aquiline nose, big eyes that stared at me, and a cap comforter drawn down almost to the eyebrows. It was the face of the dead man that I had buried [43].

The face turns out to belong to Corporal Harrison, a "dead ringer" for the deceased. But Vaughan's relief is only momentary since the implication of the encounter is clear. It has been estimated that out of every ninety soldiers sent to the front line, only about fifteen survived; even the living were in a sense walking dead from the start. And they knew it. Every memoir is full of moments when death is escaped by sheer chance, when a sudden explosion instantly transforms comrades into corpses. Vaughan's use of this Gothic tradition echoes the message in these patterns of horror. Even before the Great War made the inevitability of death immediate and real to every soldier, the secret behind the Gothic veil still lurked in fiction; in those moments of shocking discovery, the heroine and each of the readers of the tale of terror saw their future reflected in the face of the living corpse.

*The Dead Transformed*

Mrs. Radcliffe would sometimes explain away her gruesome visions by revealing them to be not human at all, but elaborate stage sets designed to frighten the heroine for some nefarious purpose. Thus, the corpse behind the veil Emily uncovers in *The Mysteries of Udolpho* is, we discover some two hundred pages later, actually a wax dummy "designed to reprove the pride" of the Marquis of Udolpho (662). (Jane Austen, in *Northanger Abbey*, parodies such disappointing denouements when her heroine stays awake all night waiting to read a mysterious manuscript that turns out to be a laundry list!)

In the Great War as well, people sometimes encountered corpses that turned out to be something else. Edward Vaughan was once "sickened by the sight of a body impaled upon iron spikes." Like Mrs. Radcliffe's heroine, who is compelled to gaze at the waxworks corpse "for a moment, with an eager, frenzied, eye" (348), he is "impelled by curiosity" and peers into the face to discover a realistic dummy: "Nevertheless, in the eerie half-light, with the flicker of flames on that scene of devastation, it was a gruesome spectacle" (60). Edmund Blunden also consciously evokes a Gothic atmosphere when he recalls being terrified by "what looked like a rising shroud over a wooden cross in the clustering mist. Horror! but on closer study I realized the apparition was only a flannel gas helmet spread out over the memorial" (34).

Identifying things as corpses had a more sinister side than these vignettes suggest. Throughout the Victorian period, we have traced a continuing fascination with living things becoming objects—in the construction of Frankenstein's Monster from organic components, in the gruesome revelations of George Walker about the dead of London pervading the earth, water and air, in the obscure crimes of Dr. Jekyll and gruesome mutilations of Jack the Ripper, in the agitation about vivisection and the popularity of pornography, and even in the transformation of women in *Dracula* to sources of food and walking blood banks. For Mrs. Radcliffe, making bodies from objects was largely a device to create suspense; for those who followed in the next century, equating people with things became a metaphor for the growing dehumanization of modern society.

In the war, when millions became little more than cannon fodder, their deaths defined as "wastage," the repeated imagery of dehumanization took on grotesque dimensions. For to die in the trenches often meant literally to become less than a corpse, to be transformed into a thing. Since relatively few of those killed could be properly buried, No-Man's-Land and the trenches themselves were littered with bodies, bodies that soon became part of the architecture of the front. A private, Archie Surfleet, records in his diary how he came across "more than one poor soul buried in sandbagging and forming part of the trench side.... Poor devils: used even after death" (Brown 71). Edmund Blunden describes the Schwaben Redoubt, where "a corpse had apparently been thrust in to stop up a doorway's dangerous displacement, and an arm swung stupidly" (131). A German counterpart remembers how, on the "fearful battlefield"

> One is overcome by a peculiar, sour, heavy and penetrating smell of corpses. Rising over a plank bridge you find that its middle is supported only by the body of a long dead horse. Men that were killed last October lie half in swamp and half in the yellow-sprouting beet fields. The legs of an Englishman, still encased in puttees, stick out into a trench, the corpse being built into the parapet; a soldier hangs his rifle on them.... Nobody minds the pale Englishman who is rotting away a few steps farther up [Chapman 147].

The horror of such scenes is, of course, compounded by the matter-of-fact language with which they are described. Yet the attitude is a culmination of a movement toward the domestication of horror that we have seen throughout the Victorian era. When early Gothic writers attempted to shock their audiences, they used overwrought language as well as gruesome imagery. The most notorious moment in Charles Maturin's *Melmoth the Wanderer* (1820) is also about a man turned into a thing, torn to pieces by a crowd:

> Dragged from the mud and stones, they dashed a mangled lump of flesh right against the door of the house where I was. With his tongue hanging from his lacerated mouth, like that of a baited bull, with a fracture in every limb, with one eye torn from the socket and dangling on his bloody cheek, and a wound in every pore, he still howled for "life—life—life—mercy!" till a stone, aimed by some pitying hand, struck him down. He fell, trodden in one moment into sanguine and discolored mud by a thousand feet. The cavalry came on, charging with fury... [II, 147].

Between Maturin's fevered vision of the individual obliterated and the greater, but parallel, horror of a landscape one soldier described as "cancerous with torn bodies" in which "mud, death and life were much the same thing" (Blunden 131) stood a century in which mass suffering and anonymous death had become part of daily experience. We see its reflections in the symbol of Krook's store in *Bleak House,* a place full of rags, paper, bones and hair—the litter of countless obliterated lives. We see it as well in descriptions of the London streets and back alleys—filthy, malodorous, crammed with debris and the anonymous, suffering poor—and in the churchyards filled to overflowing with their bodies. On the Western Front, an enormous dump overflowing with munitions, discarded supplies, barbed wire and lumber as well as corpses, the individual alive or dead was lost in a world of objects that came to have equivalent value.

Henri Barbusse, in his autobiographical novel *Under Fire* (1917), describes a section of the front some months after a battle as a gigantic Krook's store, a place where organic and inert objects are equated, reduced to one standard of uselessness:

> Some thigh-bones protrude from the heaps of rags stuck together with reddish mud; and from the holes filled with clothes shredded and daubed with a sort of tar, a spinal fragment emerges. Some ribs are scattered on the soil like old cages, broken, and close by, blackened leathers are afloat, with water bottles and drinking cups pierced and flattened. About a cloven knapsack on the top of some bones and a cluster of bits of cloth and accouterments, some white points are evenly scattered; by stooping one can see the finger and toe of what was once a corpse [264].

There is, perhaps, greater horror than in all of *Melmoth the Wanderer* in one typical and understated moment of discovery in the Great War when language and circumstance emptied of emotion unite useless junk and human life: "Near by was a pit, the result of much sandbag filling; among its broken spades and empty tins I found a pair of boots, still containing someone's feet" (Blunden 71).

Beyond the reduction of man to thing, the horror story sometimes depicted human beings as food for animals. The dark castles and dungeons of the tale of terror teem with rats; like the rat that is seen at Nemo's grave in *Bleak House*, we assume that they feed upon the dead—an assumption made explicit in some of the more gruesome shilling shockers, as well as in the accounts by Henry Mayhew of Victorian sewers and by George A. Walker of London graveyards. The rat was, from the start, a symbol of horror because it represented rapaciousness, inverted the biological order by consuming corpses, and reminded the reader of our ultimate fate and organic nature. Writers like Stoker and Stevenson created people who, like rats, used human bodies to serve their perverted tastes (Bram Stoker makes the connection explicit in *Dracula*, when one gift of the vampire to his disciple Renfield is "millions of rats"), while the crimes of Jack the Ripper were clearly more than a horror story fantasy—dismembered bodies satisfied an inexplicable craving.

One variation of this theme developed in the most popular series of Victorian penny dreadfuls, G. A. Sala's tales of *Sweeney Todd, the Demon Barber of Fleet Street* (1878), who processed his unfortunate customers into "savoury, delightful" meat pies. The story had been around since the 1840's in a periodical series called *A String of Pearls* by W. P. Prest of *Varney the Vampire* fame, and continued to resurface for the next quarter century in slightly altered versions such as *The Link Boy of Old London* (1883) and *The Boys of London and New York* (1893). (Charles Dickens retells a similar tale from his childhood of a Captain Murder who ate meat pies made of his wives, in his "Nurses Tales," published in his magazine *All the Year Round* and collected in 1860 in *The Uncommercial Traveler*.) The readers of all such stories—from childhood fantasies to newspaper realities—found terror in the vulnerability of the victims as well as in the subhuman quality of their predators.

The battlefields of the Great War were, as one might expect, also infested with rats, some allegedly as big as rabbits, which tormented both the living and the dead. Aggressive and unafraid, the rats wandered about in daylight feeding openly on corpses. A gunner remembered one: "He was enormous, with ferocious and venomous eyes, and I freely admit I flattened myself against the trench wall and let him go past, which he did without turning his head" (Brown 89). This might simply be another of the assorted horrors of trench warfare, if it didn't reinforce another metaphor used by the soldiers—they constantly referred to themselves as food. The war itself was called the "sausage machine," while soldiers described particularly devastating attacks as "like a butcher's shop" and called themselves "sheep" (during mutinous disturbances in the French armies in 1917, soldiers marched off to the front bleating loudly).

One of the most persistent myths of the war, perpetuated by newspapers like *The Times* in 1917, was that the Germans had a "Corpse Exploitation Establishment"—a series of factories where bodies were rendered into lubricating oil, tallow, and food for pigs. In the final British advance of 1918, C. E. Montague entered one place reputed to be part of the system, recalling the experience with full Gothic paraphernalia:

> At Bellincourt the St. Quentin Canal goes into a long tunnel. Some little way in from its mouth you could find, with a flash-lamp, a small doorway cut in the tunnel's brick wall, on the tow-path side of the canal. The doorway led to the foot of a narrow staircase that wound up through the earth till it came to an end in a room about twenty feet long. It, too, was subterranean.... Loaves, bits of meat, and articles of German equipment lay scattered about, and two big dixies or cauldrons, like those in which we stewed our tea, hung over two heaps of cold charcoal. Eight or ten bodies, lying pell-mell, nearly covered half the floor.... Another body, disemboweled and blown almost to rags, lay across one of the dixies and mixed with the puddle of coffee it contained.... A quite simple case. Shells had gone into cook-houses of ours, long before then, and messed up the cooks with the stew [74].

Montague and his men find the scene "disappointing," as what began as a Gothic myth is revealed to be what he calls a "hopelessly normal" event: "Life had failed to yield one of its advertised marvels." His description begins with a literary evocation of the marvelous in the journey to an underground world and ends in what, for the soldiers of the Great War, was a domestic scene. It summarizes an entire century of the tale of terror— moving from fabulous and remote events conveyed in equally romantic language to the matter-of-fact recording of commonplace horrors.*

Here again, as throughout the war, dead and living have been united, both victims of real and imagined terrors. The dead were eaten by rats or chewed up by high explosives, the living consumed by the war and those who kept it going. Like the coffee in the cauldron, all the food the soldiers ate was contaminated with a bitter and ironic taste of what they were and would become: "One needed no occult gift to notice the shadow of death on the bread and cheese in one's hand, the discoloured tepid water in one's bottle" (Blunden 194).

---

*One truly horrible outcome of this piece of propaganda was that a quarter century later memories of the "Corpse Factory" hoax caused many (including government officials) to disbelieve similar reports of Nazi concentration camps.*

One way to go on living in such a world was to develop attitudes that those isolated from such a reality would call callous. Edwin Vaughan remembers a fellow officer laughing at him when, as he was sucked down into a muddy shell hole, he saw "the leg of a corpse sticking out of the side, and frantically I grabbed it; it wrenched off" (223). What one soldier calls a "charming incident" occurred south of Ypres where "a French soldier lies buried in the side of a trench with one hand sticking out from the side" and everyone who passes shakes the hand for luck (Moynihan *A Place* 122). Siegfried Sassoon recalls "a pair of hands (nationality unknown) which protruded from the soaked ashen soil like roots of a tree turned upside down." His response is to "laugh hysterically" and conclude:

> And the dead were the dead; this was no time to be pitying them or asking silly questions about their outraged lives. Such sights must be taken for granted, I thought, as I gasped and slithered and stumbled with my disconsolate crew. Floating on the surface of the flooded trench was the mask of a human face which had detached itself from the skull [157].

With memories like these, it's clear to see why soldiers who traversed the short distance back to England for leave or convalescence were reluctant to communicate their experiences. As in late Victorian horror stories, the proximity of conventional lives to extraordinary events tainted the idea of normality itself. When Jekyll became Hyde, he went out another door into a different, darker London; when the criminal who was the Ripper left his presumably middle class home, he entered an adjoining but utterly different universe. Even Lucy Westernra in *Dracula* moves easily from one place to another, from where she is an angel in the home to where she becomes a monster who feeds off children.

Heroes at home, the soldiers in the Great War were ghouls at the front, lost in a vast charnel house, reminded daily of their own vulnerability and complicity in mass slaughter, forced to respond with callous disregard to the horrors around them. Gothic fantasy depends upon the readers' desire to imagine scenes of terror and to delight in their gruesome details; thus it assumes from the start that its audience can enter another universe of the imagination. But for the generation that lived the double life of the front line soldier in the Great War, both worlds were horribly real and terribly close.

*Self and Other*

In part because Gothic fiction requires the reader to enter a radically different life in his imagination, the theme of the double, the divided self, became one of its distinguishing characteristics (see Miyoshi). The horror story villain from Manfred and Montoni to Jekyll and Dracula is never wholly evil—his torment is a product of what Stevenson called "the war in the members," the battle within the individual. From the start, he is by turns vengeful and remorseful, without pity and pitiful, either two beings alternatively in control, or one self bitterly divided. That conflict pits noble against barbaric impulses, what came to be seen as the civilized and primitive parts of man, staged on both the level of the individual fighting madness and of the society struggling against contradiction and collapse.

Outside the world of fiction, this same image dominated the iconography of woman divided between light and dark angel, the blueprint of the city shadowed by the underworld of the black slums, and even the understanding of history, matching the progress of civilization with the parallel survival of a hidden subculture of barbarism. Everywhere there was the other—as prostitutes, brutes, the mobs of the oppressed—threatening to upset the uneasy balance. As Fredric Harrison points out,

> The idea of one mind splitting into its component parts, good and bad, with the originally sinful part threatening to overpower and destroy the virtuous one, formed the basis of an obsession that consistently recurred throughout the nineteenth century [18].

The reasons for this obsession are fairly obvious. In the century before Freud articulated a vocabulary for discussing the complexities of the subconscious, the idea of the other was a convenient shorthand for all that seemed to stand in the way of both personal and social stability. At the same time, the proximity of both sides or, often, their physical likeness, made clear that the forces of order and chaos in culture and the individual were two faces of the same coin.

Like the familiar Victorian fictional figure of the orphan, the double was an outcast who sought acceptance. However, although orphans often found a place in the human family, it was widely believed that to accept what the double signified—often the barbaric component of man or the sexual component of woman—would mean madness or anarchy. Still, because the other was an abstraction of an integral part of the self, it needed expression and found it in imaginative literature. There, the hidden and hated side of man could be projected on to another being threatening to invade and conquer, or man himself could divide into twins, each fighting for supremacy over one body.

Karl Miller has recently remarked that in the fiction of the double, "Hostile actions are ascribed to some further or to some foreign self, are performed by proxy" (25). And, in the hostile atmosphere of the war, the Germans were clearly the other for many, the incarnation of evil, the dark double of Gothic imagination. Homefront propaganda compared the Huns to barbarians, savages, animals, vermin, even microbes. They became in popular fantasy a nation of Jack the Rippers led by a bloodthirsty madman, one writer defining "lust murder" and "girl-stabbing" as "a Teutonic species of crime" (Haste 189). In a widely quoted and praised speech, Rudyard Kipling argued that a German victory meant "robbery, rape of women, starvation as prelude to slavery," and went on to say that "however the world pretends to divide itself, there are only two divisions in the world today—human beings and Germans" (*Morning Post* 22 June, 1915, 9).

In an eerie foretaste of a later German outbreak of this madness, a campaign arose to "Destroy the Blond Beast"—which meant not only internment for all Germans, but serious calls by the newspaper magnate Lord Northcliffe and rabble rouser and publisher of *John Bull* Horatio Bottomley first, for all naturalized Germans to "wear a distinctive badge and not be allowed out after dark" (Haste 127), and, finally, for "a vendetta—a vendetta against every German in Britain—whether naturalized or not.... You cannot naturalize an unnatural abortion, a hellish freak. But you can exterminate him" (126). Lest one think that these attitudes were confined to a few hotheads or only developed late in the war, we need only quote the Prime Minister, Lord Asquith, two months after the war began calling Germans "hordes who leave behind them at every stage of their progress a dismal trail of savagery, of devastation, and desecration, worthy of the blackest annals in the history of barbarism" (*The Times* 3 October 1914, 10).

The very savagery of this campaign hints at its reasons. Germans became the ultimate, concrete and visible embodiment of the other that plagued British society. The role they fulfilled as they marched through Belgium had been prepared for them in over a century of imaginative literature, in the Monster, Hyde, Dracula, and the other embodiments of evil and barbarism. For those on the home front and for the staff behind the lines who urged their men to "Kill the Germans! Kill them ALL! Spike them! Stab them! Stick your bayonets in them!" (Moynihan *Greater* 101), they were trying to kill, as well, the primitive forces that lay within.

The patriots far behind the front lines attacked the Huns with such ferocity because they were portrayed as acting out the unspeakable deeds which the British themselves practiced. Thus, much was made of the execution by the Germans of Nurse Edith Cavell (an acknowledged spy) and of many other alleged summary executions. Yet the Germans shot few civilians and almost never their own soldiers. In the British army, on the other hand, more than three hundred men were shot for cowardice, often "for some momentary failing after facing lead and high explosive for months and years on end or, again, for refusing some minor order when well distant from the front" (Dallas 43). Non-white civilians from the British colonies were kept segregated behind the lines to labor as virtual prisoners. On September 6, 1917, a group of Egyptian laborers, frightened by air raids and suffering from cold and hunger, refused to go to work; though unarmed, twenty three were shot dead and twenty four wounded by the guards (Dallas 86).

In addition, as Paul Fussell points out (117–120), the well known story of the "crucified Canadian," whom the Germans supposedly displayed across the lines, had no basis in fact but did have a curious parallel: British soldiers were given "Field Punishment No. 1" for minor infractions. A private, Archie Surfleet, described it and the reaction of those who witnessed it: "At first, I could not believe my eyes, but as we came quite close to the guns, I saw that one of the artillery men was lashed with rope to the wheel . . . cruciform-fashion, his arms and legs wide apart. . . . I don't think I have ever seen anything which so disgusted me in my life, and I know the feelings amongst our boys was very near to mutiny at such inhuman punishment" (Brown 235).

To the British soldier on the front line, Germans were not hellish incarnations of the other or projections of their own evil; they were accepted as a curious kind of twin, encountered on a stage peculiarly suited to the iconography of the double. The Western Front consisted of two parallel sets of trenches, almost mirror images of each other, divided by the narrow wilderness of No Mans' Land. The pattern of daily existence for each side was identical, and their jobs the same — to lob explosives over the intervening distance, to shoot at anything that appeared over the opposite parapet, or to venture out on patrol in the darkness. From the air, the dualistic nature of the battlefield was obvious, sometimes absurdly so:

> Flying low over a quiet sector of the Western Front one Sunday in 1915, a French pilot descried two religious services in progress on either side of No Mans' Land. The two altars, the two padres, the two groups of soldier worshipers, seemed reflections of each other — 'so exactly alike that it looked silly' [Moynihan *God* 11].

Those who actually lived in the curious double world of the front didn't, therefore, agree with those they left behind that the Huns were the locus of all evil. The war was for them not a battle against an external other, but a form of self murder as two mirror armies of soldiers committed mass suicide. Graham Greenwell recalls one time in No Mans' Land when a fellow officer on night patrol encountered some "Germans," then engaged in furious hand to hand combat until one surrendered. Only then did the officer discover that he had been fighting, and had nearly killed, one of his own men (46). Moments when, as Edmund Blunden recalls (74), two patrols from one battalion decimated each other, each thinking the other to be the enemy, only pointed out how alike the two sides were and acted out in microcosm the self destruction constantly going on within the larger brotherhood of victims to which both British and Germans belonged.

The ghostly image also haunted the Western Front in World War I: "It was all in the day's work—an exhausted Division returning from the Somme Offensive—but for me it was as though I had watched an army of ghosts."—Siegfried Sassoon.

*Sniper in Camouflaged Suit with Camouflaged Rifle* (1918). Reproduced by permission of the Imperial War Museum, London.

10. *The Transformation of the Dead* 209

*World War One Soldiers in Gas Masks.* Reproduced by permission of the Imperial War Museum, London.

At the same time, real Germans were not often seen, at least clearly. Instead, they were a series of noises in the night, or sometimes a brief glimpse of a face through a rifle's sights. Siegfried Sassoon, after taking part in raids and witnessing the death of his men, commented "Curiously enough, I hadn't yet seen a German. I had seen dim figures on my dark patrols, but no human faces (29). The enemy, then, shared the mysterious twilight existence of the British soldier, transformed by distance into something quite unreal. To those in England, the fighting forces across the Channel were mystical heroes; to their comrades they were the walking dead. The soldiers themselves saw Germans at a distance as spectres, while in comradeship or close combat, they became the most intimate echo of the self.

For many, the real enemy was the staff, which stayed well back from the fighting, yet sent troops into hopeless battles or besieged them with useless requests and impossible demands that only added to the already appalling casualties. The order, for example, that each soldier fire across the lines a certain number of minutes per day (to "keep up the fighting spirit") merely called forth an answering bombardment that increased the senseless loss of life. In a very real sense, the Staff was more of an enemy to the British than the Germans, who remained fellow sufferers caught in a strange suicidal symphony, orchestrated by madmen behind the lines and marked by the percussion of exploding shells and the rhythm of rifle and machine gun fire.

The contrast between the ranting of civilians and staff and the attitude of those actually doing the fighting was striking. In the sky over France, the comradeship of British and German soldier was made most explicit, cast in the chivalrous imagery of single combat. In their memoirs, pilots invariably refer to what Cecil Lewis called "the strong magnetic attraction" between adversaries in aerial combat, and echo his respect for those he calls "our friends the enemy" (31). Long after the war, the airman Duncan Grinnell-Milne remarked, "I have to-day no warmer feeling of friendship, no greater a respect or admiration, no deeper an understanding, of the men of the German Flying Corps than I had on the day of my capture" (182).

On the ground, during the famous Christmas truce of 1914, soldiers from both sides met in No Mans' Land, showing family photos, exchanging gifts and addresses, "fraternizing in the most genuine manner" and even singing carols together (Chapman 100–102). Edmund Blunden reports that a German officer and about twenty of his men once appeared above their trench and shouted "Good morning, Tommy, have you any biscuits?" After some shouted pleasantries, both sides returned to their trenches and the business of mutual destruction (81). Though these moments were rarely repeated (in both cases British soldiers were disciplined for not shooting immediately), troops on both sides retained respect for each other. When a private, Daniel J. Sweeney, was able for once to see the man he killed, he describes the event as almost the murder of his twin:

> The German that I shot who died afterwards was a fine looking man. I was there when he died poor chap. I did feel sorry but it was my life or his ... to tell you the truth I had a tear myself, I thought to myself perhaps he has Mother or Dad or sweetheart. ... I was really sorry I did it but God knows I could not help myself [Moynihan *Greater* 85].

By accepting the double reviled on the homefront — the bestial Hun — as one's twin, a brother in despair and fellow sufferer, the soldier on the Western Front came to accept what the culture had been fighting within itself. From early in the evolution of the horror story, these same two visions of the double contended, for they expressed the conflict between denying and integrating the darker sides of our nature and our culture. We see both sides in Frankenstein's ambiguous relationship to his Creature, which he sees both as a hideous fiend and as his abandoned child. Later, the embodiments of evil from Hyde to Dracula share in the minds of the audience the role of double and orphan, accepted and rejected at the same time, as the reader is simultaneously drawn to, and horrified by them. This tension between the two aspects of the double is one of the most powerful components of the literature of fear, for it raises the most frightening questions. To want to read tales of terror is to admit a need to participate vicariously in the life of the double, to accept that the evil other is a projection of our divided selves. Like Private Sweeney, who killed his double and suffered for it, each member of the audience for such literature sees the other destroyed, but not before recognizing that it is echoed in a part of himself.

*The Survivors*

At the end of *The Castle of Otranto*, the usurper, Manfred, has abdicated his throne, while Theodore, the rightful heir, has replaced him. But it is a Pyhrric victory. The castle itself is in ruins, while Theodore is in mourning, only reluctantly persuaded to marry "one with whom he could forever indulge the melancholy that had taken possession of his soul" (110). Later horror story heroes fare little better. After Victor Frankenstein dies and the Monster disappears, the narrator Robert Walton returns to civilization, his own dreams shattered, mourning the loss of the only friend he ever had. At the end of *Bleak House*, Ada, Miss Flite, and the other would-be heirs ruined by the Jarndyce suit must rebuild their own lives, while Gabriel Utterson, the reluctant detective in *Jekyll/Hyde*, must live with the knowledge of man's dual nature that has killed his friend Lanyon. Even the band of vampire killers in *Dracula* is aware that the taint of the vampire remains in their veins, that the culture he tried violently to overthrow was changing irrevocably in his absence.

In every case, the survivors have glimpsed the mad forces that run their universe and, in trying to overcome them, have learned instead to live with them. The Gothic villains merely acted out latent tendencies of the Gothic heroes. In the crumbling of certainty that accompanies the end of each of these stories, the survivors recognize the darker side of themselves while they look into and accept an absurd universe.

The metaphor throughout is blackness—the melancholy mourning of Theodore in the ruins of Otranto, Frankenstein's Monster "lost in darkness and distance," the "black buttoned up unwholesome figure (924)" of Mr. Vholes announcing the end of the Jarndyce suit, the dark and deserted streets where "scud had banked over the moon" on the night Utterson discovers Jekyll's secret (59), the black night that arrives as Dracula dies. Edwin Vaughan concludes his war memoirs with the same image; after the near annihilation of his "happy little band.... Feeling sick and lonely I returned to my tent to write out my casualty report; but instead I sat on the

Over the course of century, the "long labyrinth of darkness," complete with scenes of horor, gradually left the pages of the Gothic novel and defined the geography of daily life, a place of dark and muddy mazes, blighted nature, and death. See next six photos.

A typical late Victorian slum street — New Way Ghaut in Whitby in the late 1800s, photographed by Frank Meadow Sutcliffe. Reproduced by permission of W. Eglon Shaw, The Sutcliffe Gallery, 1 Flowergate, Whitby, Yorkshire, England.

Like the collection of human relics in Krook's store in *Bleak House* (1852), the organic and inert, the profound and trivial remnants of life were jumbled together on the battlefield, all reduced to one standard of uselessness. *Top:* A dead soldier in a trench (n.d.). Reproduced by permission of the Imperial War Museum, London. *Bottom:* A dead German soldier outside his dugout, 1916. Reproduced by permission of the Imperial War Museum, London.

**Gird Trench: An officer wading through the mud (1916). Reproduced by permission of the Imperial War Museum, London.**

10. *The Transformation of the Dead* 215

"Dogs, undistinguishable in mire. Horses scarcely better, splashed to their very blinkers ... adding new deposits to the crust upon crust of mud"—Dickens, *Bleak House* 1852. *Above:* Mule team in difficulties in a muddy area (1917). Reproduced by permission of the Imperial War Museum, London.

floor and drank whiskey after whiskey as I gazed into a black and empty future" (232).

But all is not gloom in the Gothic tale or even in the memoirs of the survivors of the Great War. For horror stories contain in them the seeds of modern thought, of not only the recognition of inescapable madness in the universe, but also of the means to accept it. Throughout the century and more of the horror story, authors and audience faced in fantasy the contradictions of their world. The popularity of the aesthetic of the sublime that underlay tales of terror—fictional or factual—is evidence that the audience was prepared to learn to live with fear, to expose the secret shapes of horror rather than to deny them. At first, those horrors were clothed in the language and imagery of the fantastic and resided in a remote universe. But they were brought closer through the mediation of characters (from sociologists like Mayhew to fictional narrators like Utterson) who resembled their audience. And the stories themselves moved from the wild metaphor of Gothic romance to the narrative of the daily newspaper.

Finally, in the experience of the Great War, millions raised on adolescent fantasies of fear had to learn to live in just such a fantasy made real.

And that, of course, is the point of all these remarkable connections between the evolution of Gothic imagery and the atavistic landscape of Great War reality. It isn't all a coincidence, but a clue to the reason horror stories continue to wield such imaginative power. In one sense they were prophetic, creating a textual landscape that later took form on the torn fields of France. But that happened because they had always expressed, in a disguise that slowly melted over the century, the tendencies in man and society that created the Great War and kept it going. At the same time, those who fought the War used that imagery to shape their response to it, creating memoirs and memories that followed the only textual pattern that, finally, seemed to make sense of their lives. By giving the soldiers who had lived vicariously with fear in the tale of terror something to use to make an otherwise lunatic landscape comprehensible, the pattern of horror provided a way, paradoxically, to remain sane.

That most soldiers did retain their sanity is fantastic in itself. But they did more than that; they accepted their world and sometimes found comradeship, purpose, even a kind of happiness in it. Thus, Edwin Vaughan can record a conversation with one of his men returning to the line from hospital about whether either would like a "blighty" (a wound that sends them home):

> "Would you really like a blighty?" I asked. "I think it's much more fun out here." "No, I wouldn't really," he replied. . . . "this is the only country where a bloke can feel really at ease" [151].

For Vaughan, England itself became unreal; though he records with incredible honesty every detail on the line, his trip home is noted with one word: "August 1–7: Leave" (188). The horrors of war can have a grotesque reality, yet still be familiar enough to become just another Gothic text:

> Sinking back into my mud chair I looked into the face of the body behind me. He had a diamond-shaped hole in his forehead through which a little pouch of brains was hanging down; he was very horrible but I soon got used to him [201].

Edmund Blunden also learned to live with death, to accept the madness of his existence. His memoirs are full of Gothic description, of

*Opposite:* A scene of desolation in a wood (1917). Reproduced by permission of the Imperial War Museum, London.

"ruins grimacing in the dark day" (90), of a lifeless landscape, strewn with the dead, with "many spots mouldering on, like those legendary bloodstains in castle floors which will not be washed away" (49). He also recalls how he kept a copy of a book of Gothic poems, Edward Young's *Night Thoughts*, in his pocket, always finding appropriate lines (176). But at the same time he speaks of the pleasant nature of his duties, of his enjoyment in tidying up his quarters or weeding a patch of garden when recuperating in a billet behind the lines.

Like Cecil Lewis, who saw the war as a "grotesque comedy—a prodigious and complex effort, cunningly contrived, and carried out with deadly seriousness, in order to achieve just nothing at all" (82), Blunden saw the humor in the absurd requests of the staff, the bureaucratic bungling, and the "bright ideas" that made no sense to anyone actually doing the fighting. Horror and happiness coexisted for him throughout, frozen in his last image of Buire-sur-Ancre, a beautiful landscape behind the lines where he recalls that he was "filled with simple joy," and then mentions that, a few weeks later, it was overrun by the war and destroyed. Despite learning the "depth of ironic cruelty" in the world, Blunden can still see himself as a "harmless young shepherd in a soldier's coat" (242).

To learn to live with fear, to accept the certainty of death, to laugh at the madmen running the universe, to find joy in the midst of despair became the formula for survival. It differed radically from the moral certainties of official Victorian culture, attitudes still trumpeted on the home front. There, God was fighting with the Allies, the war was fought to preserve Christian civilization, the General Staff were brilliant strategists, military catastrophes were great victories, and those who died, died fighting evil. But the soldiers knew better. The tradition of the tale of terror had prepared them for a world run by the hidden hand of the dead or the inexplicable machinations of a remote and irrational system, where culture was always sliding into anarchy and men into madness, where the darkest horrors were projections of parts of the self.

One soldier who missed surviving the war by only one week was Wilfred Owen, the greatest of the war poets. His work ranges from evocations of bitterness and despair to scenes of horror and mutilation. But one poem that sums up his feelings, that contains what he calls "the pity of war distilled" has a quite different mood. In "Strange Meeting" the narrator escapes battle "Down some profound dull tunnel" to a "sullen hall" where "encumbered sleepers groaned." The hall is Hell, and in that Gothic setting one of the dead rises and recognizes him:

> I am the enemy you killed, my friend. I knew you in this dark: for so you frowned. Yesterday through me as you jabbed and killed. I parried; but my hands were loath and cold. Let us sleep now . . . .'

In this subterranean dungeon, at the end of the long Gothic labyrinth, the darkness contains one final revelation. The corpse that rises is that other self that for more than a century was feared more than any other horror, the figure that attracted and repelled an entire culture. It is not only part of the self and society that had been so ineffectively interred; it is Death itself. For the ultimate horror of all horror stories, the corpse that will not stay buried, is our own dead future, the body we bury and disinter with every retelling of the tale of terror. A century of horror stories, in versions from the ridiculous to the realistic, all have one underlying secret—they draw their power from our fascination with repeatedly confronting our fear of our own mortality. In the final moment of "Strange Meeting," the narrator and the dark double he had fought for so long find peace when they accept their commonality in death. And Wilfred Owen reveals their true nature—as old friends.

# Bibliography

Acton, William. *The Functions and Disorders of the Reproductive Organs in Childhood, Youth, Adult Age and Advanced Life, Considered in Their Physiological, Social, and Moral Relations.* 4th ed. London: John Churchill & Sons, 1865.
──────. *Prostitution* (1857), ed. Peter Fryer. London: MacGibbon and Kee, 1968.
Alison, Archibald. *Essays on the Nature and Principles of Taste.* Dublin: Byrne, Moore, et al., 1790.
──────. "Of the Nature of the Emotions of Sublimity and Beauty," *Eighteenth Century Critical Essays,* ed. Scott Elledge. Ithaca, New York: Cornell University Press, 1961.
Allen, Grant. "The Girl of the Future." *The Universal Review* 7 (1890): 49–64.
Altick, Richard D. *Victorian People and Ideas.* London: J. M. Dent, 1973.
Annan, Noel G. *Leslie Stephen: His Thought and Character in Relation to His Time.* London: Macgibbon & Kee, 1951.
Appleyard, Bryan. "In the Empire of the Birds: Penguin Books." *London Times,* 5 September 1985, 8.
Auerbach, Nina. *Woman and the Demon: The Life of a Victorian Myth.* Cambridge, Mass: Harvard University Press, 1982.
Babbage, Charles. *The Exposition of 1851; or Views of the Industry, The Science, and The Government of England.* London: John Murray, 1851.
Bailey, Peter. *Leisure and Class in Victorian England.* London: Routledge and Kegan Paul, 1978.
Baldick, Chris. *In Frankenstein's Shadow: Myth, Monstrosity, and Nineteenth Century Writing.* Oxford: Clarendon Press, 1987.
Barbusse, Henri. *Under Fire* and *Light,* tr. W. Fitzwater Wray. London: J. M. Dent, 1929.
Beaver, Patrick. *The Crystal Palace: A Portrait of Victorian Enterprise.* London: Hugh Evelyn, 1970.
Bergonzi, Bernard. *Heroes Twilight: A Study of the Literature of the Great War.* London: Macmillan Press, 1980.
Bettelheim, Bruno. *The Uses of Enchantment: The Meaning and Importance of Fairy Tales.* New York: Vintage, 1976.
Birkhead, Edith. *The Tale of Terror: A Study of the Gothic Romance.* London: Constable & Co., 1921.
Blaikie, W. G. *Heads and Hands in the World of Labour.* London: Alexander Strahan, 1865.
Blakely, Dorothy. *The Minerva Press (1790–1820).* London: Oxford University Press, 1939.

Block, Ed, Jr. "James Sully, Evolutionist Psychology, and Late Victorian Fiction." *Victorian Studies* 25 (Summer 1982), 443–468.
Blunden, Edmund. *Undertones of War*. London: Penguin, 1982.
Bodichon, Barbara Leigh Smith. *Women and Work*. New York: C. S. Francis and Company, 1859.
Briggs, Asa. *Iron Bridge to Crystal Palace: Impact and Images of the Industrial Revolution*. London: Thames & Hudson, 1979.
———. *Victorian Cities*. New York: Harper and Row, 1982.
Briggs, Julia. *Night Visitors: The Rise and Fall of the Ghost Story*. London: Faber, 1977.
Brome, Vincent. *Havelock Ellis, Philosopher of Sex*. London: Routledge & Kegan Paul, 1979.
Brown, George. *The Book of Robert Louis Stevenson*. London: Methuen, 1919.
Brown, Malcolm. *Tommy Goes to War*. London: J. M. Dent, 1978.
Brumberg, Joan. *Fasting Girls: The Emergence of Anorexia Nervosa as a Modern Disease*. Cambridge, Mass.: Harvard University Press, 1988.
Buckley, Jerome. *The Victorian Temper: A Study in Literary Culture*. New York: Vintage Books, 1964.
Burke, Edmund. "A Philosophical Enquiry into the Origin of our Ideas of the Sublime and Beautiful." *Works*. London: C. and J. Rivington, 1826, vol. I, 81–322.
Burnett, John. *Destiny Obscure: Autobiographies of Childhood, Education and Family from the 1820s to the 1920s*. New York: Penguin, 1984.
———. *Useful Toil: Autobiographies of Working People from the 1820s to the 1920s*. New York: Penguin Books, 1984.
Burton, Elizabeth. *The Early Victorians at Home (1837–61)*. London: Longman Press, 1972.
Calder, Jenni. *RLS: A Life Study*. London: Hamish Hamilton, 1980.
———. *Women and Marriage in Victorian Fiction*. New York: Oxford University Press, 1976.
———, ed. *Stevenson and Victorian Scotland*. Edinburgh: University Press, 1981.
Campbell, P. J. *The Ebb and Flow of Battle*. Oxford: Oxford University Press, 1979.
Carpenter, Edward. *The Intermediate Sex: A Study of Some Transitional Types of Men and Women*. London: Swann, Sonnenschein, 1908.
Carr, William. *A Time to Leave the Ploughshares: A Gunner Remembers 1917–1918*. London: Robert Hale, 1985.
Chadwick, George. *The Works of Sir Joseph Paxton (1803–1865)*. London: The Architectural Press, 1961.
Chalders, Erskine. *The Riddle of the Sands: A Record of the Secret Service*. London: Smith, Elder & Co., 1903.
Chapman, Guy. *Vain Glory: A Miscellany of the Great War*. London: Cassell & Co., 1968.
Chesney, Kellow. *The Victorian Underworld*. London: Pelican Books, 1982.
Chester, Lewis, Leitch, David, and Simpson, Colin. *The Cleveland Street Affair*. London: Weidenfeld and Nicolson, 1977.
Chesterton, G. K. *The Man Who Was Thursday: A Nightmare*. London: Arrowsmith, 1944.
Clark, Alan. *The Donkeys*. London: Hutchinson, 1961.
Clarke, I. F. *Voices Prophesying War 1763–1984*. London: Panther Books, 1984.
Clausen, Christopher. "Sherlock Holmes, Order, and the Late Victorian Mind." *The Georgia Review* (1984): 104–123.

Collins, Willkie. *Heart and Science: A Story of the Present Time.* 3 vols. London: Chatto and Windus, 1883.

———. *The Woman in White,* ed. Julian Symons. Baltimore: Penguin Books, 1976.

Cominos, Peter T. "Late Victorian Sexual Respectability and the Social System." *International Review of Social History* 8 (1963): 18–49, 216–250.

Conan Doyle, Sir Arthur. "Danger! Being the Log of Captain John Sirius." *The Strand Magazine.* Vol. 48 (July 1914), 1–22.

Cooke, Arthur L. "Some Side Lights on the Theory of the Gothic Romance." *Modern Language Quarterly* 12 (1951): 429–36.

Crowe, Catherine S. *The Night Side of Nature.* London: George Routledge and Sons, 1882.

Cullen, Tom. *Autumn of Terror: Jack the Ripper, His Crimes and Times.* London: Bodley Head, 1965.

Cunningham, Gail. *The New Woman and the Victorian Novel.* London: Macmillan, 1978.

Daiches, David. *Robert Louis Stevenson: A Revaluation.* Glasgow: William Maclellan, 1977.

———. *Robert Louis Stevenson and His World.* London: Thames and Hudson, 1973.

Dallas, Gloden, and Gill, Douglas. *The Unknown Army: Mutinies in the British Army in World War I.* London: Verso Press, 1985.

Dalziel, Margaret. *Popular Fiction 100 Years Ago.* London: Cohen and West, 1957.

Darnton, Robert. *The Great Cat Massacre and Other Episodes in French Cultural History.* New York: Basic Books, 1984.

Darwin, Erasmus. *Zoonomia, or the Laws of Organic Life.* 2 vols. Philadelphia: Edward Earle, 1818.

Davies, Robertson. *The Mirror of Nature.* Toronto: University of Toronto Press, 1982.

Davis, Terence. *The Gothick Taste.* London: David & Charles, 1971.

Desmond, Adrian. *The Hot Blooded Dinosaurs.* New York: Warner Books, 1977.

Dickens, Charles. *Bleak House,* ed. Morton Zabel. Boston: Houghton Mifflin, 1956.

———. *Hard Times,* ed. George Ford and Sylvere Monod. New York: Norton & Co., 1966.

———. "On Duty with Inspector Field." *Household Words: A Weekly Journal* 14 June 1851: 268–273.

———. *The Uncommercial Traveller and Reprinted Pieces, etc.* London: Oxford University Press, 1958.

Dickens, M., and Hogarth, G., eds. *The Letters of Charles Dickens.* 2 vols. London: Chapman & Hall, 1880.

Dickenson, H. W. *A Short History of the Steam Engine.* Cambridge: University Press, 1939.

Dijkstra, Bram. *Idols of Perversity: Fantasies of Feminine Evil in Fin-de-Siècle Culture.* New York: Oxford University Press, 1986.

Dodds, John W. *The Age of Paradox: A Biography of England, 1841–1851.* New York: Rinehart and Company, 1952.

Douglas, Mary. *Natural Symbols: Explorations in Cosmology.* New York: Vintage Books, 1973.

Drinka, George Fredrick. *The Birth of Neurosis: Myth, Malady, and the Victorians.* New York: Simon & Schuster, 1984.

Drysdale, G. *The Elements of Social Science, or Physical, Sexual and Natural Religion.* 35th ed. London: Standring and Co, 1905.

Eigner, Edwin. *R.L.S. and the Romantic Tradition*. Princeton, N.J.: Princeton University Press, 1966.
Ellis, Havelock. *The Criminal*. London: Walter Scott, 1901.
Farson, Daniel. *Jack the Ripper*. London: Michael Smith, 1972
———. *The Man Who Wrote Dracula: A Biography of Bram Stoker*. New York: St. Martin's Press, 1976.
Fay, C. R. *Palace of Industry: A Study of the Great Exhibition and Its Fruits*. Cambridge, England: Cambridge University Press, 1951.
ffrench, Yvonne. *The Great Exhibition: 1851*. London: Harvill Press, 1953.
Figes, Eva. *Sex and Subterfuge: Woman Writers to 1850*. London: Macmillan, 1982.
Fix, John. *The Glass House*. Cambridge, Mass.: MIT Press, 1974.
Ford, Ford Madox. *Parades End* (in *The Bodley Head Ford Madox Ford*, vols. 3 and 4). London: Bodley Head, 1963.
Frayling, Christopher, ed. *The Vampyre: Lord Ruthven to Count Dracula*. London: Victor Gollancz, 1978.
Fry, Carrol L. "Fictional Conventions and Sexuality in *Dracula*." *Victorian Newsletter* 42 (Fall 1972): 20–22.
Fussell, Paul. *The Great War and Modern Memory*. London: Oxford University Press, 1975.
———. *Samuel M. Johnson and the Life of Writing*. New York: Harcourt Brace Jovanovich, 1971.
Gay, Peter. *The Bourgeois Experience: Victoria to Freud*. 2 vols. New York: Oxford University Press, 1984.
Geduld, Harry M. *The Definitive "Dr. Jekyll and Mr. Hyde" Companion*. London: Garland Pub, 1983.
Gibbs Smith, C. H. *The Great Exhibition of 1851: A Commemorative Album*. London: His Majesties' Stationary Office, 1950.
Gitter, Elisabeth G. "The Power of Women's Hair in the Victorian Imagination." *PMLA* 99 (October 1984), 936–54.
Gombrich, E. H. "Freud's Aesthetics." *Encounter* 26 (1966): 30–40.
Graves, Robert. *Goodbye to All That*. London: Cassell & Co, 1957.
Greenwall, Graham. *An Infant in Arms: War Letters of a Company Officer, 1914–1918*. London: Lovat, Dickson & Thompson, 1935.
Grinnell-Milne, Duncan. *Wind in the Wires*. London: Hurst and Glackett, 1933.
Grosskurth, Phyllis. *Havelock Ellis: A Biography*. London: Allen Lane, 1980.
Hadfield, J. A. *Dreams and Nightmares*. London: Penguin Books, 1973.
Haggerty, George. "Fact and Fancy in the Gothic Novel." *Nineteenth Century Fiction* 39 (March 1985): 379–391.
Haining, Peter. *The Legend and Bizarre Crimes of Spring Heel Jack*. London: Fredrick Miller, Ltd. 1977.
Hamlin, Christopher. "Providence and Putrefaction: Victorian Sanitarians and the Natural Theology of Health and Disease." *Victorian Studies* 28 (1985): 381–411.
Hammond, J. R. *A Robert Louis Stevenson Companion*. London: Macmillan, 1974.
Hansard, T. C., ed. *The Parliamentary Debates from the Year 1803 to the Present Time*. Vol XXI. London: Longman, etc., 1812.
Harrison, Fraser. *The Dark Angel: Aspects of Victorian Sexuality*. London: Sheldon Press, 1977.
Haste, Cate. *Keep the Home Fires Burning: Propaganda in the First World War*. London: Allen Lane, 1977.
Hayes, Michael, ed. *The Supernatural Short Stories of Charles Dickens*. London: John Calder, 1978.

Heller, Terry. *The Delights of Terror: An Aesthetics of the Tale of Terror*. Urbana: University of Illinois Press, 1987.
Hellman, George Sidney. *The True Stevenson: A Study in Clarification*. Boston: Little, Brown, 1925.
Hennessy, James Pope. *Robert Louis Stevenson*. London: Jonathan Cape, 1974.
Hibbert, Christopher. *Queen Victoria in Her Letters and Journals*. Hammondsworth, England: Penguin, 1985.
Hiley, Michael. *Frank Sutcliffe: Photographer of Whitby*. Boston: David Godine, 1974.
―――――. *Victorian Working Women: Portraits from Life*. Boston: David Godine, 1979.
Hobhouse, Christopher. *1851 and the Crystal Palace*. London: John Murray, 1950.
Houghton, Walter, E. *The Victorian Frame of Mind*. New Haven: Yale University Press, 1957.
Howarth, Patrick. *Play Up and Play the Game: Heroes of Popular Fiction*. London: Methuen, 1973.
Howells, Coral Ann. *Love, Mystery, & Misery: Feeling in Gothic Fiction*. London: Athlone Press, 1978.
Hughes, Winifred. *The Maniac in the Cellar: Sensation Novels of the 1860's*. Princeton, N.J.: Princeton University Press, 1980.
Humphreys, Anne. *Henry Mayhew*. Boston: Twayne, 1984.
Hunter, Jefferson. *Edwardian Fiction*. Cambridge, Mass.: Harvard University Press, 1982.
Jacks, Lawrence P. *Life and Letters of Stopford Brooke*. 2 vols. London: John Murray, 1917.
Jennings, Humphrey. *Pandaemonium 1160–1886, The Coming of the Machine as Seen by Contemporary Observers*, ed. Mary Lou Jennings and Charles Madge. London: Andre Deutsch, 1985.
John, Angela V. *By the Sweat of Their Brow: Women Workers in Victorian Coal Mines*. London: Croom Helm, 1980.
Jones, Ernest. *On the Nightmare*. New York: Liveright, 1951.
Jordan, R. Furneux. *A Concise History of Western Architecture*. London: Harcourt, Brace, 1969.
Kaufmann, Walter. *Nietzsche: Philosopher, Psychologist, Antichrist*. 4th ed. Princeton, N.J.: Princeton University Press, 1980.
Kellow, Chesney. *The Victorian Underworld*. London: Temple Smith, 1970.
Kiely, Robert. *Robert Louis Stevenson and the Fiction of Adventure*. Cambridge, Mass.: Harvard University Press, 1964.
Kingsley, Mary Henrietta. *Travels in West Africa*. London: Macmillan and Company, 1897.
Klaits, Joseph. *Servants of Satan: The Age of the Witch Hunts*. Bloomington: Indiana University, 1985.
Knight, Charles, ed. *London*. 6 vols. London: Charles Knight and Company, 1841.
Kohlmaier, Georg, and von Satory, Barna. *Houses of Glass: A Nineteeth Century Building Type*. Trans. John Harvey. Cambridge, Mass.: M. I. T. Press, 1981.
Korg, Jacob, ed. *Twentieth Century Interpretations of "Bleak House."* Englewood Cliffs, N.J.: Prentice Hall, 1968.
Krafft-Ebbing, Richard von. *Psychopathia Sexualis*, tr. Harry E. Wedeck. New York: Putnam, 1965.
Lacan, Jacques. *The Language of Self: The Function of Language in Psychoanalysis*. Trans. with notes and commentary by Anthony Wilden. Baltimore: Johns Hopkins Press, 1968.

La Capra, Dominick. *History and Criticism*. Ithaca, N.Y.: Cornell University Press, 1985.
Landes, David S. *The Unbound Prometheus: Technological Change, 1750 to the Present*. Cambridge, England: University Press, 1969.
Landsbury, Coral. "Gynaecology, Pornography, and the Antivivisection Movement." *Victorian Studies* 28 (Spring 1985): 413–439.
Leavis, F. R., and Leavis, Q. D. *Dickens the Novelist*. London: Chatto and Windus, 1970.
Leatherdale, Clive. *Dracula: The Novel and the Legend*. Wellborough, Northampshire: Aquarian Press, 1985.
Lemedorfer, Eugene. "The Manuscript of *Dr. Jekyll and Mr. Hyde*." *The Bookman* 12 (Sept. 1900–Feb. 1901): 52–58.
Le Queux, William. *The Invasion of 1910, with a Full Account of the Siege of London*. London: Eveleigh Nash, 1906.
Levine, George. *The Realistic Imagination: English Fiction from Frankenstein to Lady Chatterley*. Chicago: University of Chicago Press, 1981.
──── and Knoepflmacher, eds. *The Endurance of "Frankenstein": Essays on Mary Shelley's Novel*. Berkeley: University of California Press, 1982.
Lewis, Cecil. *Sagittarius Rising*. New York: Penguin Books, 1977.
Lewis, Matthew Gregory. *The Monk*. New York: Grove Press, 1959.
Linton, E. Lynn. *The Girl of the Period and Other Essays*. 2 vols. London: Richard Bentley & Son, 1883.
Lombrosio, Cesare. *Criminal Man*. London: Putnams, 1911.
London, Jack. *War of the Classes*. London: Macmillan and Co., 1905.
Longford, Elizabeth. "Mary Kingsley," *Eminent Victorian Women*. London: Weidenfeld and Nicolson, 1981.
Low, Donald A. *Thieves' Kitchen: The Regency Underworld*. London: J. M. Dent, 1982.
Lubbock, John. *Pre-Historic Times*. London: Williams and Norgate, 1865.
Ludlam, Harry. *A Biography of Dracula: The Life Story of Bram Stoker*. London: Foulsham, 1962.
Mackay, Charles. *Extraordinary Popular Delusions and the Madness of Crowds*. New York: Harmony Books, 1980.
MacKenzie, Norman, and MacKenzie, Jean. *Dickens: A Life*. Oxford: Oxford University Press, 1979.
McMillan, James. *The Way We Were, 1900–1914*. London: William Kimber, 1978.
McNally, Raymond, and Florescu, Radu. *The Essential Dracula*. New York: Mayflower Books, 1962.
Magee, Bryan. *The Philosophy of Schopenhauer*. Oxford: Oxford University Press, 1983.
Manvell, Roger. *Ellen Terry*. New York: Putnams, 1968.
Marcus, Steven. *The Other Victorians*. New York: Bantam, 1967.
Marwick, Arthur. *The Deluge: British Society and the First World War*. London: Macmillan, 1965.
Maturin, Charles Robert. *Melmoth the Wanderer*. 3 vols. London: Richard Bentley, 1892.
Maxiner, Paul. *Robert Louis Stevenson: The Critical Heritage*. London: Routledge and Kegan Paul, 1981.
Mayhew, Henry. *London Labour and the London Poor: A Cyclopedia of the Condition and Earnings of Those That Will Work, Those That Cannot Work, and Those That Will Not Work*. 3 vols. New York: Harper and Bros. 1851.

———. *Selections from "London Labour and the London Poor,"* ed. with an introd. by John L. Bradley. London: Oxford, 1965.
———. *Voices of the Poor: Selections from the Morning Chronicle (1849–50)*, ed. with an introd. by Anne Humphreys. New York: Frank Cass, 1971.
——— and Binney, John. *The Criminal Prison of London and Scenes of Prison Life.* London: Charles Griffin and Co., 1862.
Means, Andrew, and Preston, W. C. *The Bitter Cry of Outcast London.* London: James Clarke & Co., 1883.
Mellersh, H. E. L. *Schoolboy into War.* London: William Kimber, 1978.
Messent, Peter, ed. *Literature of the Occult: Modern Essays in Criticism.* Englewood Cliffs, N.J.: Prentice Hall, 1981.
Mill, John Stuart. *Three Essays: On Liberty, Representative Government, The Subjection of Women.* London: Oxford University Press, 1912.
Miller, Karl. *Doubles: Studies in Literary History.* Oxford: Oxford University Press, 1985.
Mixner, Paul. *Robert Louis Stevenson: The Critical Heritage.* London: Routledge and Kegan Paul, 1981.
Miyoshi, Masao. *The Divided Self: A Perspective on the Literature of the Victorians.* New York: New York University Press, 1969.
Monk, Samuel. *The Sublime: A Study of Critical Theories in XVIII Century England.* Ann Arbor: University of Michigan Press, 1980.
Montague, C. E. *Disenchantment.* Westport, Conn.: Greenwood Press, 1978.
Morris, Kevin. *The Image of the Middle Ages in Romantic and Victorian Literature.* London: Croom Helm, 1984.
Moynihan, Michael, ed. *God on Our Side: The British Padres in World War I.* London: Seckler & Warburg, 1983.
———. *Greater Love: Letters Home, 1914–1918.* London: W. H. Allen, 1980.
———. *People at War: 1914–1918.* Newton Abbot, England: David & Charles, 1972.
———. *A Place Called Armageddon: Letters from the Great War.* London: David & Charles, 1975.
Murray, Henry A. *Myths and Mythmaking.* New York: George Brazillier, 1960.
Muthesius, Stefan. *The High Victorian Movement in Architecture.* London: Routledge and Kegan Paul, 1972.
Nabokov, Vladimir. *Lectures on Literature*, ed. Fredson Bowers, with introd. by John Updike. London: Weidenfeld and Nicolson, 1980.
Nead, Lynda. *Myths of Sexuality: Representations of Women in Victorian Britain.* Oxford: Basil Blackwell, 1988.
Nettleton, John. *The Anger of the Guns: An Infantry Officer on the Western Front.* London: William Kimber, 1979.
Noble, Andrew, ed. *Robert Louis Stevenson.* London: Vision Press, 1983.
Ober, William, M. D. *Boswell's Clap and Other Essays: Medical Analysis of Literary Men's Afflictions.* Carbondale: Southern Illinois University Press, 1979.
*Official Catalogue of the Great Exhibition of the Works of Industry of All Nations: 1851.* London: W. Clowes & Sons, 1851.
Pearsall, Ronald. *Edwardian Life and Leisure.* Newton Abbot, England: David & Charles, 1973.
———. *Night's Black Angels: The Forms and Faces of Victorian Cruelty.* London: Hodder and Stoughton, 1975.
———. *Public Purity, Private Shame: Victorian Sexual Hypocrisy Exposed.* London: Weidenfeld and Nicolson, 1976.

―――――. *Tell Me Pretty Maiden: The Victorian and Edwardian Nude.* Exeter, England: Webb & Bower, 1981.
―――――. *The Worm in the Bud: The World of Victorian Sexuality.* London: Penguin, 1973.
Peck, Louis F. *A Life of Matthew G. Lewis.* Cambridge, Mass.: Harvard University Press, 1961.
*Penny Dreadfuls and Comics: English Periodicals for Children from Victorian Times to the Present Day.* London: Victoria and Albert Museum, 1983.
Praz, Mario. *The Romantic Agony.* London: Oxford University Press, 1970.
Prickett, Stephen. *Victorian Fantasy.* Bloomington: Indiana University Press, 1979.
Pugin, A. W. N. *Contrasts* (2nd edition, 1841), introd. H. R. Hitchcock. New York: Humanities Press, 1973.
Punter, David. *The Literature of Terror: A History of Gothic Fiction from 1765 to the Present Day.* London: Longmans, 1980.
Quennell, Peter, ed. *Mayhew's London.* London: Spring Books, n.d.
―――――. *Romantic England: Writing and Painting.* New York: Macmillan, 1970.
Radcliffe, Ann. *The Mysteries of Udolpho: A Romance,* ed. Bonamy Dombree. London: Oxford University Press, 1966.
―――――. "On the Supernatural in Poetry." *New Monthly Magazine* 7 (1826).
Ragland-Sullivan, Ellie. *Jacques Lacan and the Philosophy of Psychoanalysis.* Urbana: University of Illinois Press, 1986.
Raino, Eino. *The Haunted Castle: A Study of the Elements of English Romanticism.* New York: Humanities Press, 1964.
Ray, William. *Literary Meaning: From Phenomenology to Deconstruction.* Bath, England: Basil Blackwell, 1985.
Reader, W. J. *Life in Victorian England.* New York: Capricorn Books, 1967.
*Reports from Commissioners (1): Children's Employment (Mines).* Parliamentary Papers 13, 14 (1842). London: William Cowes & Sons, 1842.
*Reports from Commissioners (2): Children's Employment (Trades and Manufactures).* Parliamentary Papers 15, 16 (1843). London: William Cowes & Sons, 1843.
Richter, Donald. *Riotous Victorians.* Athens: Ohio University Press, 1981.
Rickman, Philip. "Horror Fiction." *Words* 1 (1986): 30–35.
Rolt, L.T. C. *Victorian Engineering.* London: Penguin 1970.
Rose, Phyllis. *Parallel Lives: Five Victorian Marriages.* New York: Knopf, 1984.
Roth, Phyllis A. *Bram Stoker.* Boston: Twayne, 1982.
Rubenstein, Richard L. *The Age of Triage.* Boston: Beacon Press, 1983.
Sassoon, Siegfried. *Memoirs of an Infantry Officer.* London: Faber & Faber, 1965.
*Second Report of the Commissioners for the Exhibition of 1851.* London: W. Clowes & Sons, 1852.
Schopenhauer, Arthur. *The World as Will and Idea (1883),* tr. R. B. Haldane and J. Kemp. London: Routledge & Kegan Paul, 1964.
Schreber, Daniel Paul. *Memoirs of My Nervous Illness.* trans. Ida Macalpine and Richard Hunter. London: M. Dawson and Sons, 1955.
Scott, Sir Walter. *On Novelists and Fiction,* ed. Ioan Williams. London: Routledge & Kegan Paul, 1968.
Shelley, Mary Wollstonecraft. *Frankenstein, or the Modern Prometheus,* ed. M. K. Joseph. London: Oxford Univeristy Press, 1969.
Shpayer-Makov, Haia. "Anarchism in British Public Opinion 1880–1914." *Victorian Studies* 31 (1988): 487–516.
Skarda, Patricia, and Jaffe, Norma C., eds. *The Evil Image: Two Centuries of Gothic Short Fiction and Poetry.* New York: New American Library, 1981.

Small, Christopher. *Ariel Like a Harpy: Shelley, Mary, and "Frankenstein."* London: Victor Gollancz, Ltd. 1972.
Stein, Richard. "Milk, Mud, and Mountain Cottages: Ruskin's Poetry of Architecture." *PMLA* 100 (1985): 328–341.
Stevenson, Catherine Barnes. *Victorian Women Travel Writers in Africa.* Boston: Twayne, 1982.
Stoker, Bram. *Dracula*, ed. A. N. Wilson. Oxford: Oxford University Press, 1983. (All references in text are to this edition.)
———. *Dracula*, annotated by Leonard Wolf. New York: Clarkson Potter, 1975.
———. *Personal Reminiscences of Henry Irving.* 2 vols. New York: Macmillan, 1906.
Stone, Harry. *Dickens and the Invisible World: Fairy Tales, Fantasy, and Novel Making.* London: Macmillan, 1979.
Strachey, Lytton. *Eminent Victorians.* New York: Penguin, 1980.
Sullivan, Jack. *Elegant Nightmares: The English Ghost Story from LeFanu to Blackwood.* Athens: Ohio University Press, 1980.
Summers, Montague. *A Gothic Bibliography.* New York: Russell & Russell, 1964.
Terry, Ellen. *The Story of My Life.* New York: Schocken, 1982.
Thomas, Ronald. "In the Company of Strangers: Absent Voices in Stevenson's *Dr. Jekyll and Mr. Hyde* and Beckett's *Company*." *Modern Fiction Studies* 32 (1986): 157–174.
Thomis, Malcolm I. *The Luddites: Machine Breaking in Regency England.* Newton Abbot: David Charles, 1970.
Toynbee, Paget. *Strawberry Hill Accounts.* Oxford: Clarendon Press, 1927.
Trench, Richard and Hillman, Ellis. *London under London: A Subterranean Guide.* London: John Murray, 1984.
Tropp, Martin. *Mary Shelley's Monster: The Story of "Frankenstein."* Boston: Houghton Mifflin, 1977.
Trudgill, Eric. *Madonnas and Magdalens: The Origins and Development of Victorian Sexual Attitudes.* London: Heinemann, 1976.
Tuchmann, Barbara. *The Proud Tower: A Portrait of the World Before the War, 1890–1914.* London: Macmillan Press, 1980.
Turner, James. *Reckoning with the Beast: Animals, Pain, and Humanity in the Victorian Mind.* Baltimore: Johns Hopkins, 1980.
van Keuren, David K. "Museums and Ideology: Augustus Pitt Rivers, Anthropological Museums, and Social Change in Later Victorian Britain." *Victorian Studies* 28 (1984): 171–85.
Vansittart, Peter. *Voices from the Great War.* London: Jonathan Cape, 1981.
Varma, Devendra. *The Gothic Flame* New York: Russell & Russell, 1957.
Vasbinder, Samuel H. *Scientific Attitudes in Mary Shelley's "Frankenstein."* Ann Arbor, Mich.: UMI Research Press, 1984.
Vaughan, Edwin Campion. *Some Desperate Glory: The Diary of a Young Officer, 1917.* London: Fredrick Warne, 1981.
Veeder, William, and Hirsh, Gordon, eds. *"Dr Jekyll and Mr. Hyde" After One Hundred Years.* Chicago: University of Chicago Press, 1988.
Walker, George A. *Internment and Disinternment.* London: Longman, 1843.
———. *First, Second, and Third Series of Lectures on the Actual Condition of the Metropolitan Grave-Yards.* London: Longman, 1846, 1847.
Walpole, Horace. *The Castle of Otranto: A Gothic Story*, ed. W. L. Lewis. Oxford: Oxford University Press, 1982.
Walvin, James. *Victorian Values.* Athens: University of Georgia Press, 1987.

Watt, William. *Shilling Shockers of the Gothic School: A Study of Chapbook Gothic Romances.* New York: Russell & Russell 1932.
Welsh, Alexander. *The City of Dickens.* Oxford: Clarendon Press, 1971.
Whitmore, Richard. *Victorian and Edwardian Crime and Punishment.* London: B. T. Batsford, Ltd. 1978.
Wilson, Colin. *Order of Assassins: The Psychology of Murder.* London: Rupert Hart Davis, 1972.
Winter, Denis. *The First of the Few: Fighter Pilots of the First World War.* London: Allen Lane 1982.
Wohl, Anthony, Ed. *The Victorian Family: Structure and Stresses.* London: Croom Helm, 1978.
Yglesias, J. R. C. *London Life and the Great Exhibition of 1851.* London: Longmans, Green and Co., 1964.
Young, G. M. *Portrait of an Age: Victorian England.* Oxford: Oxford University Press, 1983.

## *Periodicals and Newspapers Cited*

*Academy*
*Athenaeum*
*Bradford Daily Telegraph*
*Critical Review*
*Daily Telegraph*
*Daily News*
*East London Advertiser*
*East London Reporter*
*Evening News*
*Illustrated London News*
*John Bull*
*Morning Post*
*Punch*
*Strand Magazine*
*Times*
*Westminster Review*

# Index

Acton, Dr. William 136-37, 164
Aiken, John 20
Albert, Prince 45, 60, 69
Aldington, Richard 5
Aldini, Giovanni 31
Alison, Archibald 20, 183
Allen, Grant 150, 154
anarchism 173-74, 176
anti-vivisection 124-25, 172-73, 177, 200
architecture 2, 8, 18, 44-5, 48-57, 65-71, 81, 85-87, 91, 182-83; *see also* classicism, Gothicism
Arkwright, Richard 34
Asquith, Lord 206
asylums 85-86, 140
Atkins, Private Ernest 191
Austen, Jane 1, 3-4, 7, 12-27, 109, 141-44, 180, 189, 195, 199

Babbage, Charles 55, 62
Baldick, Chris 7, 30, 39
Balzac, Honeré de 153
Barbusse, Henri 201
Barry, Charles 49
Baudelaire, Charles 153
Beckford, William 19, 28, 50, 72, 81
Beerbohm, Max 177
Bell, John 60
Benedictsson, Victoria 166
Bentham, Jeremy 85
Bettelheim, Bruno 7
Blake, William 35
Blakely, Dorothy 15
*Bleak House* see Dickens, Charles
Block, Ed 121
Blunden, Edmund 183, 186, 189-90, 193, 200, 207, 210, 218

Bodichon, Barbara Leigh Smith 137, 168
Boswell, James 39
Bottomley, Horatio 206
Boulton, Matthew 33
Bouvier, Jean 195
Braddon, Mary 65
Brooke, Stopford 176
Brooks, Mary 79
Burke, Edmund 20, 184-85, 187
Burke and Hare 124
Burton, Decimus 51
Burton, Sir Richard 135
Byron, Lord (George Gordon) 28-9, 31, 36-7

Caird, Mona 150
Campbell, Major Robert 194
Carlyle, Thomas 51
Carpenter, Edward 166-67
Carr, William 196
Case, Robert 185
*Castle of Otranto* see Walpole, Horace
Cavell, Edith 206
Cavendish, Lord 112
Chalders, Erskine 177
Chapman, Anne 114
chartist movement 27, 63
Chesney, Sir George Dorking 174
Chesterton, G.K. 174
Churchill, Winston 192
the city 8, 31, 44, 50, 54, 68-9, 77, 79, 83, 86, 106, 175, 190, 205
Clairmont, Claire 28
Clarence, Duke of 115
classicism, movement in architecture 49-50, 85; *see also* architecture
Cockburn, Captain R.S. 182

231

Coleridge, Samuel Taylor 5–6, 29, 32, 35–6
Collins, Willkie 125
Colyer, W.T. 179
Cominos, Peter 146
Conan Doyle, Sir Arthur 73, 92, 95–9, 102, 104, 118, 135, 176
Conrad, Joseph 121
Cream, Neill 115
Crystal Palace 45, 47–62, 65–8, 77, 79, 86–87, 90–91; *see also* Great Exhibition of 1851
Cubitt 33

Darnton, Robert 69
Darwin, Charles 2, 8, 90, 95, 98, 121
Defoe, Daniel 13
Dickens, Charles 1, 8, 45, 64, 67–74, 76, 77, 79, 81, 83–84, 86, 91, 103, 108, 118, 188, 189, 192, 195, 197, 201–02, 211
*Dr. Jekyll and Mr. Hyde* see Stevenson, Robert Louis
Dore, Gustav 61
the double 205, 207, 210–211
Douglas, Mary 155
Doyle, Sir Arthur Conan see Conan Doyle
*Dracula* see Stoker, Bram
dreams 13, 18, 30, 44, 98, 107–08, 128, 141, 183, 194–97
Druitt, Montague John 132
Drysdale, George 137, 151, 157
Du Maurier, Guy 175

East, John M. 175
ecclesiastical movement 49–50
Eddowes, Catherine 113–14
Eliot, George 121
Ellis, Havelock 2, 122, 132
Engels, Friedrich 27, 75
Evangelical movement 50, 101
evolution 2, 91, 98, 120, 122, 124; *see also* Darwin, Charles
Eyries, J.B. 28

factory system 8, 30–9, 46, 48, 83; *see also* Industrial Revolution
fairy tales 7, 15
Farson, Daniel 136

Fiedler, Leslie 1
Field, Inspector 74
Fielding, Henry 13
film 4, 5, 7, 40–1, 100, 138
Firth, W.P. 19
Fonthill Abbey 19, 50; *see also* Beckford, William
Ford, Ford Madox 182
Fowles, John 105
*Frankenstein* see Shelley, Mary
French, R.D. 125
French Revolution 3, 26–9, 172
Freud, Sigmund 4, 27, 117, 121–22, 166, 205
Fussell, Paul 179, 207

Gay, Peter 116
ghosts 13, 15, 30, 40, 70, 76, 81–2, 118, 175, 187, 194–197; *see also* supernatural and Gothic fiction
Godwin, William 29
Gombrich, E.H. 4
Gothic movement in literature 7, 13, 18, 28–43, 48, 61, 65–7, 69–87 *passim*, 92, 96–100, 102, 104, 108–09, 113–20 *passim*, 136, 140–46, 154, 174–219 *passim*
Gothicism, in architecture 49, 50, 54, 85, 107
Grainger, R.D. 79
Graves, Robert 6, 179, 198
Great Exhibition of 1851 5, 8, 44–69, 73–77, 83–86; *see also* Crystal Palace
Greenwell, Graham 207
Grenfell, Captain Francis 182
Grey, Sir Edward 193
Grinnell-Milne, Duncan 185, 188, 210
Gull, Dr. William 115, 151

Hadfield, J.A. 7
Haig, Sir Douglas 178
Hardy, Thomas 121
Harrison, Fredric 205
Hartmann, Edouard Von 120
Hawkins, Benjamin Waterhouse 69, 90
Helvetius, Claude 31–2
Hinton, James 133
Hobhouse, Christopher 57
Hood, Thomas 161
Hooke, Robert 31

horror *see* Gothic movement in literature
Houghton, Walter 149
Hunt, Leigh 55
Huxley, Thomas Henry 90

Industrial Revolution 2, 8, 25, 30–42 *passim*, 82, 172; *see also* factory system, technology
Irving, Henry 134–5, 161, 166
Isherwood, Major Frank 188

Jack the Ripper 2, 8, 92, 110–18, 129–32, 133, 136, 153, 177, 188, 200, 202, 204, 206
Jacquet-Droz, Henri 31
Jerrold, Douglas 48
Jones, Ernest 146

Kay, James Phillips 32
Kelly, Mary 116, 132
Kilvert, Rev. Francis 61
King, Stephen 135
Kingsley, Charles 67, 165, 175
Kingsley, Mary Henrietta 164–5, 166
Kipling, Rudyard 206
Klait, Joseph 155
Klein, Emanuel 124
Knight, Charles 74, 76
Knox, Robert 124
Krafft-Ebbing, Richard von 129, 152

Lacan, Jacques 126
Landes, David 33
Landsbury, Carol 125
Lane, William 15
Le Fanu, Sheridan 134
Leighton, Fredric 61
Le Queux, William 175–6
Levi-Strauss, Claude 7
Lewes, George Henry 72
Lewis, Cecil 194, 210
Lewis, Matthew Gregory 17, 72, 134, 141, 193, 218
Linton, Mrs. E. Lynn 151
Lloyd, George David 192

Lombrosio, Cesare 90–1, 95, 97–8, 122, 132, 174
London, Jack 173
Low, W.H. 100
Lubbock, John 90
Luddite movement 36, 63
Lusk, George 113

MacGregor, Private Peter 193
Machen, Arthur 196
Mackay, Charles 65
McLennan, John 90
Mann, Thomas 122
Mann, Tom 85
Manning, Frederick 64–5
Mansfield, Richard 110
Marx, Karl 27, 75
Mason, Private C.W. 182
Maturin, Charles 172, 179, 201
Mayhew, Henry 45, 77–86, 113, 115, 151, 180, 184, 189, 197, 202, 217
Medawar, Peter 1, 2, 179
Mill, John Stuart 62
Miller, Florence Fenwick 130
Miller, Karl 205
Miller, Sanderson 19
Milton, John 29
Minerva Press 15, 29
Mitchell, Dr. Weir 146
*The Monk* see Lewis, Matthew Gregory
Montague, C.E. 203
Monti, R. 60–1
Moore, Thomas 37
Morris, William 51
Mumford, Lewis 44
Munby, Arthur 162
Murray, Henry A. 136
Myers, F.W.H. 153
*Mysteries of Udolpho* see Radcliffe, Mrs. Ann
myth 7, 29, 30, 31, 81, 109, 114, 136, 164, 168, 181, 203

Nabokov, Vladimir 101
Nasmyth, John 83
Nichols, Dr. T.L. 137
Nightingale, G. 188
nightmare 4, 5, 6, 9, 100, 138, 174, 183, 194; *see also* dreams
Noble, James Ashcroft 100

*Northanger Abbey* see Austen, Jane
Northcliffe, Lord 206

Osbourne, Fanny 129
O'Sullivan, Second Lieutenant Blake 192
Owen, Richard 68-9, 90
Owen, Robert 32
Owen, Wilfred 184, 219-9

Pankhurst, Mrs. Emmeline 173
Pater, Walter 110
Patmore, Coventry 149
Paxton, Joseph 46, 48, 51-68 *passim*, 79, 83, 85, 87; *see also* Crystal Palace
Peacock, Thomas Love 12
Peake, Richard Brinsley 39
Pemberton, Max 174
Peterloo massacre 37
Pitt-Rivers, Augustus 91, 95, 97
Poe, Edgar Allan 99
Polidori, Dr. John 28, 134
pornography 17, 84, 125, 138, 141-2, 145, 162, 200
Power, Hiram 60
Poynter, Edward 61
Pressey, William 178
Prest, Thomas P. 134-5, 139, 202
prisons 33, 37, 68, 70, 81-2, 85-6, 128
prostitution 62, 64, 77, 97, 106, 112, 115, 118, 124, 133, 136, 138, 150, 153, 162, 173, 205
Pugin, Augustus Welby 49-50, 51, 54, 182

Quetelet, Adolphe 55

Radcliffe, Mrs. Ann 14, 30-31, 71, 78, 102-103, 179, 187-89, 197-200 *passim*
railroads 40, 44, 48, 54, 57, 143, 181; *see also* technology
Reynolds, G.W.M. 76, 113
Rolt, Edward 56
Roqueplan, Camille 60
Rossetti, Dante Gabriel 135
Ruskin, John 51, 67

St. Leger, Lieutenant William 198
Sala, G.A. 202
Salt, Titus 85
Sand, George 153
Sanger, Margaret 173
Sassoon, Siegfried 6, 183, 187, 193-4, 196, 198, 204, 209
Schopenhauer, Arthur 120-1, 122, 127, 128, 131
Schreber, Daniel Paul 167
Scott, Sir Walter 152
sculpture 55, 60, 61, 79, 84
Shelley, Mary 1, 6-8, 28-42, 72, 78, 82, 92, 95, 118, 134-5, 180, 184, 189, 196-7, 200, 210-1
Shelley, Percy 29, 31, 37, 40
Sherlock Holmes see Conan Doyle, Sir Arthur
Showalter, Elaine 151, 190
Sitwell, Mrs. Albert 121
Smirke, Sir Robert 49
Smith, Major Henry 111
Smollett, Tobias 4, 13
Southey, Robert 32, 36
Speer, Albert 46
Spiegel, Freiherr von 178
Spring Heel Jack 114
Stanley, Henry M. 62
Stead, W.T. 115, 133
Stephen, James K. 101, 115
Stephenson, George 40
Stephenson, Robert 48
Stevenson, Catherine 165
Stevenson, John Allen 153
Stevenson, Robert Louis 1, 92, 95, 96, 99-109, 110-2, 115, 117, 118-24, 126-9, 131, 133-5, 138, 155, 174, 176, 181, 195, 197, 202, 204-5, 211
Stoker, Bram 1, 6-8, 92, 95-96, 102, 104, 130, 133-69, 174-6, 181-4, 200, 202, 204, 211
Stoker, Charlotte 161
Stopes, Marie 173
Strawberry Hill 19, 50; *see also* Walpole, Horace
the sublime 20, 83, 180-7, 191, 194, 215
Sully, James 121
Summers, Montague 15
the supernatural 2, 3, 15, 30, 71-2, 102, 109, 117-9, 154, 188, 194, 196; *see also* ghosts, Gothic
Surfleet, Private Archie 200, 207
Sweeney, Private Daniel J. 210-11
Swinburne, Algernon Charles 142

technology 8, 29–39, 44, 57, 176; see also Industrial Revolution, factory system, railroads
Tennyson, Alfred, Lord 90, 135, 157
Terry, Ellen 135, 161
Thackeray, William 56, 75, 77, 82
Thevithick, Richard 40
Thompson, James 108
Tolstoy, Leo 121
Turgenev, Ivan 121
Turner, Richard 51
Twain, Mark 135
Tyson, Edward 90

Ure, Andrew 32

*Vathek* see Beckford, William
Vaughan, Edwin Campion 7, 178, 182–3, 186, 197–9, 204, 211, 217
Victoria, Queen of England 55–7, 112, 125, 172, 175

Walker, George A. 76–7, 86, 197, 200, 202
Walpole, Horace 13, 50, 69, 72, 81, 91, 118, 120, 134, 140, 144, 179, 180, 187–9, 197–8, 211
Ward-Jackson, Major Charles Lionel Atkins 186
Warren, Sir Charles 131
Watkins, Edward 114
Watt, James 34
Wellington, Arthur, Duke of 55, 63
Wells, H.G. 173, 176
Wharton, Edith 144
Whistler, James 135
White, Hayden 6
Whitman, Walt 135
Wilde, Oscar 167
Wilhelm, Kaiser of Germany 175
Wills, William Henry 67
Wilson, Colin 125
Wilson, Edmund 27
Wilson, Lavina 67
Wolf, Leonard 153
Wollstonecraft, Mary 29
Woolson, Abba Gould 155
Wordsworth, Dorothy 35
Wordsworth, William 28, 33, 35, 36
workhouses 81–2, 85–6
World War I 2, 5–9, 49, 132, 173, 178–219
world's fairs 54; see also Great Exhibition, Crystal Palace

Young, Edward 218

Zola, Emile 121, 153